THE

GIRLS' EMPIRE.

An Annual Volume for

ENGLISH-SPEAKING GIRLS ALL OVER THE WORLD.

PUBLISHED BY

SHORT BOOKS, 3A EXMOUTH HOUSE, PINE STREET,
LONDON, EC1R 0JH

This edition first published in 2007 by
Short Books
3A Exmouth House, Pine Street
London EC1R 0JH

10 9 8 7 6 5 4 3 2 1

A CIP catalogue record for this book
is available from the British Library.

ISBN 978-1-906021-17-7

Printed in Great Britain by Clays Ltd, Suffolk

Every effort has been made to obtain permission
for the material reproduced in the book. If any
errors have unwittingly occurred, we will be
happy to correct them in future editions.

INDEX.

(*)

POETRY

How to be Strong.

SPECIAL EXERCISES
WITH THE SANDOW GRIP DUMB-BELL.

PART I.

AMONG the many marvellous changes that have taken place during the last ten years, none can claim to be of more importance than the transformed ideas in regard to the position which women occupy in the affairs and welfare of the nation; and consequent upon this, a large amount of attention is being paid to physical development.

The old-fashioned fallacies regarding health, diet, exercise, dress, &c., have nearly all been exploded, and to-day women are dis-carding the old ideas and methods, and entering into the new *régime* with a zest and vigour which bodes well for the future.

Without further remarks, therefore we will proceed to the first of the series of exercises, which, if carefully and continuously performed,

EXERCISE 1.

will prove very beneficial, and tend to improve bodily health, muscular develop-ment, and uprightness and grace of carriage, that shall be the highest form of beauty.

At this juncture, however, a few words as to the most suitable form of dress, &c., is very necessary.

First and foremost, it is necessary to point out that these exercises can only be of fullest benefit when each muscle is exercised to its fullest extent, and the body should therefore be perfectly free and supple, be entirely uncramped and unrestrained. The ordinary stiff corset must be removed; it has no place in our *régime*. We would, indeed, go so far as to say that, if a corset is felt to be absolutely necessary, instead of the steel and bone contrivances now so much in vogue, a plain corset made out of strong linen canvas, cut to shape, and about eight to ten inches deep, should be worn, it being made adjustable. As will be seen in the illustration, the skirt (of blue serge) should be short, reaching to about three to four inches below the knee, and be cut sufficiently full to allow for a stretching or striding exercise in any direction. The bodice should not be of the tight-fitting variety, as you will be wanting to bring the lungs and chest into fullest play. The most suitable pattern of bodice is the sailor-blouse shape, with open neck. The under-vest should also be loose fitting. One last word as to shoes. Shun as a poison, the French high-heel shoe! Nothing is more injurious to the feet, and more productive of deformed instep and undignified "strut" in walking, rather than a graceful step. Half an inch is quite high enough for a shoe or boot heel for walking.

Now as to the exercises. Take a pair of light dumb-bells (about 1lb.) and, standing in an upright position, with toes slightly turned out, and a dumb-bell firmly grasped in each hand, perform the exercise in the following manner: — The arms should be bent, the elbows being pressed quite close to the body, and slightly forward, thus bringing the forearms perpendicular. The dumb-bells should then be level with the shoulders. Holding the head well back, shoot the right arm upwards, keeping the body erect the whole time. Draw back the arm to your side sharply, at the same time extending the left arm above the head in a similar manner. With each change of motion, the head should be turned in the corresponding direction. By this exercise, the muscles of the arms, shoulders, neck, and sides are brought into play. This exercise should be repeated morning and evening, commencing with fifteen to twenty times, and gradually increasing to thirty-five to forty.

Cosy Corner Chats.

I. – FRIENDSHIPS FOR WOMEN

MY DEAR HELEN: A week from to-day you will be having your first experience of a boarding-school. Here is my little preparatory sermon. Your teachers, both in the high school and in the school to which you are going, will hammer away on the importance of your getting good training and good equipment. Let me tell you that there is still a third object which you must not ignore. You must learn in a new and deeper sense the joys, privileges, duties, even the sorrows of friendship. Whatever other mistake you may make in a choice of a friend, at least do not let it be a hasty one. I know it is a hard saying, but again and again a girl at school picks out her particular friend within two hours after she sees her, and in two weeks they have sworn each other allegiance. Fortunately, this does not always work so badly as one would expect, but often it does come out unfortunately for one or both of the young women; and, it seems to me, one can never have the highest satisfaction in a friendship so made. One is ashamed of being cheated in a gown because one chose it too hastily or in a poor light. Why not ashamed still more of being cheated in a friend?

Another word about the beginning of friendship. Friendship differs from what we call "love" in its character, its variety, and its greater freedom from jealousy. Society is organised on the scheme that each woman shall have one lover, but may have many friends. I think, myself, too few friends almost as undesirable as too many, and too many

as too few. The many-sided girl needs a larger circle of friends than the girl of extremely simple nature. Not too many to know well, and not too few, lest one becomes exacting!

If there is any one test sufficient to determine whether a given relation is to ripen into a friendship, it is perhaps this: does there exist an entire confidencebetween the two, together with that indefinable drawing to each other's society for which we have no name— Either of these without the other is a poor makeshift for the real thing. Without a more substantial foundation it is sure soon to wear out. The memory of such a failure is likely to be a sore one for a lifetime. In other words, there must be a real congeniality, as well as a certain fascination, when friendship is to be great and lasting. This congeniality must not be founded on a similarity of weakness if it is to be a healthy friendship, but on a similarity of aspirations.

I remember one particularly ill-advised association between two girls, which ended disastrously. I asked one of them why she had

picked out the other as a friend, since she seemed particularly unsuitable, and she replied, "Oh, well, we were each of us always ready for anything." You could scarcely find a flimsier reason for a friendship. The girl that is always ready to help on her friend in mischief is a poor friend. I do not say that I want you to select a prig as your chosen ally for the first year of your school life. I insist only that the correspondence of the two natures shall be of the higher and not of the lower qualities. Again, friendship must not be so absorbing as to destroy your sense of the proportion of things. You must see more than one girl in your horizon: you must see something besides the delights of conversation and of intimacy, in the seven days of the week. A good test of the healthfulness of a friendship may be found in the question as to whether the two friends waste each other's time. Of course, I do not mean that you are never to have the pleasure of leisure together. Years hence you will recall not only the pleasant rivalries of the classroom or the athletics contests, but the long twilight talks in a window-seat, in which life grew and thrived; but that this should be the only business in which one feels a real interest is absurd. A friendship which wastes time presently begins to waste itself; and, before you know it, all its charm will have vanished.

Again, a real friendship must be truth-telling; it must hate the sweet flattery which is so easy to give and so tempting to take. Do not consider yourself called upon to tell your friend all the disagreeable truths that may come to your mind. Sometimes friendship seems to imply a certain brutality degrading to both friends. Delicacy and sensitiveness should be the very structure of the girlish mind: they must not be broken. To tell lies to one's friend for the sake of being pleasant is wrong. On the other hand, friendship has its own fine reticence, and does not talk too much about its ardours or its pains.

In our modern life I think it is pretty well settled that a genuine relation between women must be active, not passive, on the part of both friends. The French have a proverb, long passing for truth, that in love one always offers the embrace, while the other presents the cheek. I think it a cynical and hateful belief, and I am sure it is not founded on fact. The most substantial relations I have ever known between women have been by no means those of the oak and ivy description. There has been a reciprocity, a partnership, a give and take, which have justified themselves in the eyes of the world. It is not self-respecting to be always sitting on a foot-stool at the feet of one's friend. If there is a girl who wants you always there, let her get on without you; and, on the other hand, do not accept a doglike devotion from any-one, least of all from a girl younger than yourself.

My ideal friendship must be impregnably on the side of right, against whatever temptation of impulse. That I am permitted to be a friend of a fine woman is a kind of pledge of loyalty to the highest. In a partnership one partner may well be held to a stern virtue by the thought that any lapse from it will involve the name and honour of the firm. So in all human relations. Friendship is a series of concessions in respect to unimportant questions, but it must never concede when it comes to the weightier matters of life. My friend may be a refuge and a protection in temptation, but she must not be an apologist for me if I have fallen.

So much for the tests to be applied to friendship. About its joys it is not so necessary to speak. I like to believe that you will find them all out for yourself. Unlike most pleasures it is heightened by the passing of the years, and rightly so. It reveals to us as nothing else can the nobility of human nature. Of course it will have its stress and struggles; but they will pass. From its road, as from a mountain path, one catches the closest vision permitted to mortals of the divine nature which resides in the breast of every man and woman. In its noblest form it is the constant pledge and reflection of that Divine Friendship which alone saves and glorifies our human life.

HELOISE EDWINA HERSEY.

Athletics for Girls.

HOCKEY. – I.

BY E. M. ROBSON, HON. SEC. ALL ENGLAND WOMEN'S HOCKEY ASSOCIATION

PERHAPS no game has ever been taken up with such keenness by girls as hockey. The reason for this growing popularity of the game is not far to seek. It provides plenty of amusement and excitement, and is in addition a splendid form of exercise.

A girl, accustomed in the summer months to outdoor exercise, and by nature, if one may be pardoned for using a slang term, a "sportsman," is naturally anxious that she should be able to indulge in some form of really active exercise in the winter. Her thoughts turn to hockey, and when once initiated into the mysteries of the game, she cannot for the life of her understand how she has existed so long without it.

The girl who has made up her mind to start, naturally first considers the most important implement required – a stick. Where shall I get it? What shape shall it be? Sticks vary very considerably in their shape. One

PLAY! THE BULLY OFF.

manufacturer may make a shape with a long hook, and another one with a short and squarer bend. It is difficult to recommend any special shape as being most suitable, and it had far better be left to the player's own fancy. This much may be said, however: to one playing "forward," a short curve will be found most suitable, whilst to a "half" or "back," one provided with a longer curve; and for this reason, that players in the back division are required to cover more ground.

With regard to its weight, do not let it be too heavy. For a forward, nineteen to twenty-one ounces is quite sufficient, whilst for a half or back one weighing one to two ounces more will be found quite heavy enough. On no account let it be too long. The longer the stick the clumsier will be your play. Let it be one that can be handled easily and freely, and can be used, when occasion demands, with one hand. Too long a stick is a disadvantage, as there are occasions (as, for instance, when one is hemmed in by an opponent) when a stick of too great a length is absolutely useless. In the case of a forward, the stick should be lighter than that of one in the back division, and must also be shorter. A back or half-back has to hit the ball harder and farther, and, as has been previously said, has to cover more ground, and, therefore, requires a longer reach. For a longer reach, a longer stick is naturally needed.

Only a few years back sticks were made in one piece. At the present time they are very different articles. Cane-spliced handles, and handles bound like a cricket-bat, are now alone used. As in wet weather the string becomes slippery and greasy, consequently causing the stick to slip in one's hand, enclose the handle either in a rubber or leather cover. You will then find you have a much firmer hold of your stick, and need have no fear of its slipping from your grasp.

A thick rubber ring placed at about the com-

PASSING TO THE RIGHT.

mencement of the splice is also a great protection, preventing as it does, time and again, an opponent's stick sliding up your own and giving you a nasty blow on the hand,

Now, as to one's personal attire. Boots or shoes? Which are most suited for the game? Without a doubt one has no hesitation in saying – boots. And boots with low heels, too. Boots are but a trifle heavier than shoes, and whilst the latter may perhaps be slightly easier to move in, they do not afford the protection to one's ankles. Boots, however thin the sides may be, offer a certain amount of resistance to the force of a blow on the ankles, and, at any rate, lessen the force of it. Boots, in addition to protecting the ankles, also support them, and the strongest of ankles may be liable to get twisted on turning suddenly. Let the soles be either "studded" or "barred." Without "studs" or "bars" it is impossible to obtain a firm foothold on a wet ground. One stud of about half an inch long on the heel, and three of the same length on the sole, will be quite sufficient. Shin guards should always be worn. At first they may feel a trifle clumsy and uncomfortable, but one soon gets accustomed to them, and finds they in no way hamper one's movements.

Gloves should also be

worn. Many prefer cricket batting gloves with rubber backs, others wear thin kid ones. The latter perhaps are more generally used, because the hand and fingers are freer, and in addition are not so heavy. Of course, the rubber glove saves many a nasty blow which a kid glove can only do in a lesser degree. As a general rule, one advises forwards to wear thin kid, halves and backs rubber-back gloves. Each, however, to her own taste, but at any rate, protect your hands.

The skirt is an impediment to free movement, and should not be worn too long. At the very least it should be six inches off the ground. Of course, it is impossible to drive a ball through a skirt trailing on the ground, but in the long run one would find a shorter skirt far more advantageous, and, at any rate, you would be compelled to play a more scientific game, for you would have to stop the ball either with your stick, hand, or foot, and not rely upon the length of your skirt to do the work for you.

If you do not like to play without a hat — and by the rules of the All England Women's Hockey Association, straw hats, or hats with hard brims are strictly forbidden — wear a cloth cap or Tam-o'Shanter. You would feel far freer if you eschewed a hat of any kind. Projecting hat-pins are also strictly forbidden, and very rightly too. They are most dangerous, and

A TRICKY PASS BY CENTRE TO THE RIGHT WING.

might be the cause of many accidents.

With this brief outline of the necessary outfit required, we will now turn to the game itself and give a few hints as to the way it should be played. A team is made up of eleven players, each one having a special place appointed for her. The eleven places are: "centre" forward; "outside" and "inside right" forward; "outside" and "inside left" forward; right half-back, centre half-back, and left half-back; right back and left back, and goal-keeper. The latter is often dispensed with, and plays as centre-back instead. Goal-keeping at the best of times is not an enviable post. To stand shivering, as a goal-keeper often has to do, with your side attacking and playing a winning game, is but a poor form of enjoyment. With but little to do except freeze, can one wonder that the post is not popular?

The backs, two or three in number as the case may be, must be strong hitters and good tacklers. With their side attacking they must also to a certain extent attack themselves, gradually moving nearer towards their opponents' goal. A back's position should be from twenty-five to thirty yards behind the half-back line. As the half-back line moves forward, so should the backs; on the half-back line retiring, so should the back line.

Whilst actually on the defensive, the best plan to adopt is to get the ball away into "touch," and avoid as much as possible hitting in front of goal. Many a goal has been scored by the reckless play of a back in hitting the ball across her own goal, when it should have been driven into "touch."

Upon the halves may be truly said to fall the hardest work. With their forwards attacking, they must follow them closely up to within a distance of five to six yards, so that should their forwards lose the ball they can at once return it. Then, again, they must be back in a moment to help the backs in defence. It is a hard place to fill, and one which requires stamina of no slight degree. The object of a half-back is to let her line of forwards have the ball as soon as possible, and also break up the attack of the opposing forwards. Reckless hitting is useless. Pass the ball to whichever forward you consider is in the most advantageous position, and do not pass wildly. Perhaps this would now be a fitting place to discuss the question of "combination and passing."

(To be continued.)

How to Make Home-Made Sweets.

WHAT girl is there who has not made toffee and, alas! how few are there who haven't burnt it? We all remember that toffee that set so nicely, and was so crisp and looked such a rich brown colour, but when we tasted it what a shock we had! We pretended to crunch it gleefully, but inwardly we loathed its pungent flavour, then when no one was looking we threw the rest away.

Or, worse still — we just left the toffee to cook itself for a minute, and the minute was rather long, and soon we noticed an aroma of something burning. We rushed to our toffee to find a black mass bubbling over an utterly ruined saucepan, and our expensive cooking ran into shillings instead of pence.

But with a very little care it is quite easy to make

delicious toffee in a very few minutes, provided that we do not run away for that fatal moment. Here is a simple recipe for EVERTON TOFFEE. – Get a thick enamel-lined saucepan, and place it near, not on, a slow fire. Put quickly into it 3ozs. of butter, let this melt, then pour in three table-spoonfuls of golden syrup. Stir these together, then add 8ozs. (or heaped up tablespoonfuls) of white granulated sugar, and one teaspoonful of water. Stir occasionally until the mixture boils, then stir oftener, but do not let it boil too quickly. When it looks done, drop a little on to a plate; if it hardens quickly it is cooked enough. Pour out on to a flat tin, which must be slightly buttered. With a moderate fire this toffee will take about half an hour to make.

BUTTER SCOTCH can be made in the same way as the toffee, only that the ingredients are different, being simply butter and Demerara or any other brown sugar. Take twice the quantity of sugar and add to the butter, and thus any quantity, large or small, can be made by remember-ing this simple rule. As before, if the toffee only boils gently it is not neces-sary to stir constantly, which is a great consideration; one's arm soon aches with a very little stirring. When the right colour test as before, and if crisp pour on to a buttered tin. When cold it will be very brittle and easily snap into pieces, and is very good indeed.

My third sweet is RUSSIAN TOFFEE, and is a little more difficult to make successfully, as it requires more care, but it is well worth the trouble and is always liked by everyone. As with butter scotch take a thick enamel-lined saucepan and have ready a slow fire. Melt $^1/4$lb. butter, then add $^1/2$lb. brown sugar; stir these together, then add one tin of condensed milk (the Milkmaid Brand is good). Stir continually until boiling. Then keep the mixture boiling slowly for a quarter of an hour, never ceasing to stir it, as it burns so very easily, and this is the difficulty in making it.

If it has boiled steadily the toffee is now done; but before taking it off the fire add either one or two tea-spoonfuls of vanilla, and stir in well. Pour the mixture on to a buttered tin, and leave until cold. When cold, Russian Toffee should be soft, not crisp, and not sticky; cut it into strips with a knife, and then across again to form squares the size of caramels. It is a most delicious confection, its only fault being that it dis-appears too quickly.

An easy sweet to make is COCOANUT ICE, as there is almost no cooking to be done, and desiccated cocoanut at sixpence per lb. can be bought at any grocer's. Dissolve 1lb. cas-tor sugar in half a gill of water (half a teacupful), and boil together for four min-utes after dissolving. Then take off the fire, and add quickly 3ozs. cocoanut (or a larger quantity if liked better), one teaspoonful of lemon-juice, with half a teaspoonful of cream of tartar. Mix thoroughly. Then pour out half the quantity on to a flat tin lined with a sheet of white paper (saturated in cold water beforehand). Spread it evenly. Colour the remainder pink with a few drops of cochineal, and spread at once over the white ice. After five minutes cut the ice into blocks.

CHOCOLATE TOFFEE is very inexpensive and simple. Grate 2 ozs. chocolate, and melt $^1/2$lb. sugar with the chocolate in half a gill water, add two teaspoonfuls vinegar, and boil until the toffee snaps when dropped into cold water. Pour into a buttered tin, and make into squares when cool, break when quite hard.

The delicious sweet introduced I believe from Germany, and known as "MARZIPAN," is easy to make, but is not so quickly made as some other sweets. Blanch $^1/2$lb. of cooking almonds by putting them into boiling water until the skins loosen, then immediately plunging them into cold water — the skins will then come off quite easily. Add four bitter almonds, then pound all together in a mortar very finely, and moisten with a little rose-water. Put the pounded almonds next into a saucepan with $^1/2$lb. of castor sugar, and stir over the fire till a paste is obtained which does not stick to the fingers when touched. Then turn the mixture out on to a pastry-board, previously sprinkled with castor sugar freely, and roll out thinly. Then cut into squares, and bake on paper in a slow oven until the marzipan becomes pale yellow. It is then done.

If you do not mind the trouble of shaving a fresh cocoanut you can very easily make COCOANUT CHIPS, and very cheaply too. Carefully cut a cocoanut into shavings, then whisk the white of an egg in a basin, add about $^1/4$lb. castor sugar, throw the cocoanut into the mixture, and stir well together. The lay out thinly on a sheet of white paper, and bake in a very slow oven till hardened without spoiling the white colour. Half of the cocoanut may be made into pink chips by adding a few drops of cochineal to the white of egg and sugar.

ALMOND HARDBAKE is a nice change from the ordinary toffee, and is no harder to make, except for the trouble of blanching the almonds. Get them ready beforehand in the manner I have described before, only for hardbake they must be split and then dried. Take next $^1/2$lb. Demerara sugar, and add one gill of water, boil together until it hardens when dropped into cold water. Then add 1oz. of butter, and boil again until it hardens, when it is done. Pour out on to a buttered tin after adding as many almonds as you think sufficient. When cool, but not cold, mark into squares with a knife, and leave until it hardens, when it can easily be broken up.

The last recipes I am going to give are more experimental, as they are not so easy, although the ingredients are very cheap and simple. The first is the simplest and is LEMON CARAMEL. Boil 1lb. white sugar by itself, until it melts and snaps when poured into cold water, over a very slow fire; continue stirring until a very light brown, adding by degrees a little essence of lemon (any other flavour will do, or a little strong coffee), work well together, then pour out on to a slightly-oiled baking-sheet. Mark out with a knife in small squares, and separate them when cold.

Next is BARLEY SUGAR. As with the above recipe, boil 1lb. sugar to the snap, add a few drops of essence of lemon, and one teaspoonful of citric acid. Pour out on a slab, and work the mixture with two knives by lifting it into a heap. When cool enough to handle, pull out into six-inch lengths, twist like a cord, and leave to cool.

SATINETTES. — Mix together 1lb. white sugar, two-thirds teacupful cold water with a pinch of cream of tartar. Boil to 280 degrees (212 degrees is the boiling-point of water.) That is to go on boiling a little after it comes to the boil, then put in, well mixed $1/4$oz. tartaric acid, and $1/4$oz. carbonate of soda. Stir well, with a few drops each of cochineal, vanilla and almond flavourings. Pour on to a greased slab, and get a hook, greased also. When the candy is cool enough, pull it over the hook until it is like satin, then cut into cushions and leave to cool.

My last recipe is for AMERICAN PULLING CREAM CANDY, and is for a large quantity – of course, less in proportions could be taken. Put into a saucepan 5lbs. white granulated sugar, with just enough water to cover it, with two teaspoonfuls of vinegar, and three tea-spoonfuls of vanilla (just before it is done), and butter the size of an egg. Boil slowly, but do not stir, only skim round the edges. When brittle when dropped into water it is done. Then add the vanilla, and empty out on a greased marble slab, and pull until it is white.

I feel sure here are some recipes to please all my readers, and I hope that many of them will succeed in turning out sweets satisfactory to themselves and any on whom they bestow a taste of their home-made confections, and that there will be no waste of materials or spoilt saucepans by having too hot a fire or leaving the sweets to cook them-selves. If neither of these untoward events occur I can safely promise success to all who follow my directions.

The Slogger   Stumped   A Slight Misunderstanding

Girls' Pets and How to Manage Them.

THE FOX TERRIER.

FOR an indoor or out-door companion there is no better breed of dog than the fox terrier. He is intelligent, faithful, easily trained, and a good-looking dog besides. Even the poorest specimen with a very mixed descent retains some of the bright intelligence of the thoroughbred.

Our advice is to obtain a puppy from a litter of which you know the history. The extra few shillings spent in obtaining a well-bred dog at the start will be saved in the long run. One must pay for a good article.

There is a hazard, however, in buying a puppy even from a good stock, for you can never foresee how it will turn out when it grows up. Go, therefore, to a sales-man whom you can trust.

There are two breeds of fox terriers — the wire-haired and smooth-coated kinds. As fanciers cannot agree as to which is the better variety, we will not express any opinion. The former, however, is general-ly looked upon as the hardier of the two.

A fox terrier when fully grown should have "good legs and feet, the former straight, clean, muscular, and not too fleshy; the latter close, round, and well braced up. The chest should be deep and narrow; the shoulders should be thin, long, well laid back; the neck should be of moderate length and thickness, slight-ly arched, and sloping gracefully into the shoul-ders." As to colour, white should predominate, with black or tan, or black and tan, marking on the head. "A tan or lemon on each ear, and a patch over the eyes and at the root of the tail, is the best marking." A full-grown dog should weigh from 16lb. to 18lb.

Perhaps the best thing a girl can do is to visit some local dog show. She will then see for herself what a well-bred fox terrier is like. This will be far more satisfactory than the mere passing glance at one as he runs at the heels of his master in the street.

Let us imagine then, that you are starting with a puppy, and have got to rear him in the way he should go. Buy your dog at from six to eight weeks old, and commence by feeding him on coarse oatmeal porridge made with broth from scraps of meat left from the table. This should be given in five instalments each day at stated times. For a change use potatoes, pearl barley, or a little rice with the broth, and occasionally bread and milk for one meal a day. Continue to feed him thus until he is about eight months old, when you can begin to try his teeth by giving him less of sopped foods. But, while growing, give him boiled skim milk. Spratts' bone meal mixed with it will help to build up his frame.

Spratts', Old Calabar, or ship's biscuits may now be used, and it is as well to drop down to only three meals a day — morning, noon, and evening. Plain, wholesome food will suffice if you wish to preserve his health. Scraps from dishes, parts of cakes, sweetmeats, &c., which are sometimes thrown down to the dog will ultimately spoil him and render him liable to all sorts of diseases. Throw the food on the ground when feeding your grown-up dog; the earth that becomes attached to it does the dog a deal of good. Never give raw meat. Cold cooked meat, lean, or paunch well cleaned, occasionally, may be given, but this greatly depends upon the life your dog leads.

Now and again you can give, as part of a meal, some well-boiled green vegetables, which will go far towards keeping your dog healthy.

Take care that he does not get fish bones or small meat bones, which he can voraciously gulp down. A large bare bone may be thrown to him to gnaw at leisure, it will help to keep his teeth in good condition.

If your parents wish you to keep the dog out of doors and you cannot afford a big outlay, make him a kennel. If you cannot do this, obtain from the oilman a paraffin barrel, which must be "burnt out" before using, by means of a handful of lighted shavings or straw; care must be taken, however, not to char the inside. After this has been done, thoroughly scrub out with hot water and soft soap, and allow it to dry before using. Place the barrel under the shelter of a wall, or better still, in one of the outhouses, and put a wedge under each side to prevent it rolling. You will find it answer very well for a kennel, and is easily cleaned out.

In the management of dogs, patience, firmness, and good temper are

By kind permission of "The kennel News."

THE DUCHESS OF NEWCASTLE'S PRIZE TERRIER.

necessary. It is best to come to an understanding when the first act of disobedience is committed – that is, when your dog is old enough to know better. "One thorough good whipping does far more good than a series of minor corrections. The dog remembers it far longer, and in his heart he knows he deserved it for something or other; but if he is always being scolded and slightly punished, his master soon appears in the light of a persecutor, and the dog becomes either permanently cowed or of uncertain temper."

Well groom your dog with a hair glove before giving him a weekly bath. The water should be cold, not warm; nothing is so debilitating to him as a warm bath. After you have well lathered his coat with soap, and well rinsed it, let your dog have a good run in the open air; never allow him to lie before the fire shivering and whining until he is dry. In the summer time he can have a dip in the river, if you live near one.

A dog is reckoned to be full-grown when he is about eighteen months old, and by the time he reaches this age he should have formed good habits. You can then treat him as an adult dog, and should feed him regularly twice a day – one light meal in the morning before you have your breakfast, and a more substantial meal about tea time. One biscuit and a half daily is considered enough for a dog of the size of a fox terrier.

The most common disease a dog is liable to is constipation, and this can generally be relieved by giving him a piece of raw liver and daily exercise.

Plain, wholesome food, fresh water, a clean bed, and a wash once a week, combined with plenty of exercise, these are essential to the keeping of your dog strong and healthy.

In the Doctor's Sanctum.

HYGIENE OF THE EAR.

IT is our duty to keep the external ear in a clean condition, but Nature has provided her own cleaning apparatus of the ear passages. At the entrance of the auditory canal are numerous fine hairs which serve to keep out dirt and insects. The lining membrane of the canal contains small glands, which secrete a thick, yellowish, oily wax that is very bitter. Because of this bitterness, no insect will of itself invade this canal. What becomes of the wax? It dries up in the form of small whitish scales, which peel off from the surface, and, aided by the action of the jaw, drift out of the ear. This is Nature's way of keeping this passage clean.

In health the canal is never dirty, and becomes so

only by our frequent attempts to keep it clean. It is for this reason that some people who love cleanliness, and others who are more or less fastidious in their habits, often suffer most from ear troubles. Many well-meaning mothers do more harm than good by drying to clean the wax out of their children's ears by artificial means. The child invariably cries or makes some demonstration of pain when this is attempted. Twisting the corner of a towel or a handkerchief and turning it round in the ear is one of the worst methods of trying to remove the wax, and does a great deal of harm. Not only is the wax not removed, but the canal membrane is irritated by the friction and often becomes inflamed.

It is a dangerous practice to introduce ear spoons, ear sponges, pins, hairpins, toothpicks, &c., into the ear to remove the wax. There is as much wisdom as humour in the old adage, "Put nothing into your ear smaller than your elbow."

If an insect gets into the auditory canal, drop in a little sweet oil, which will either drown it or cause it to crawl out. The ear should never be probed to remove a foreign body. Do not be afraid that it will get into the brain or even into the middle ear.

Washing the auditory canal with soap and water is also injurious, as it moistens the wax, thus increasing its quantity, and forming a better surface for the collection of dust and dirt. Washing should extend no farther than the finger can reach.

No cold water or any other cold liquid should be put into the ear. Bathing or swimming, when the ears are submerged, is no doubt one of the causes of ear trouble. It is a well-known fact that dogs that are in the water a great deal become deaf. Cotton should be put in the ears if one intends to dive while swimming. If out in a cold, piercing wind or in a driving snowstorm, the ears should be protected. It is best, if possible, to face the wind. If cotton is placed in the ear at such a time, it should be removed as soon as possible.

When there is an unhealthy condition of the auditory canal, as a result of measles or scarlet fever, the accumulation of wax can easily be removed by dropping a very little warm sweet oil into the ear, letting it remain until the wax is softened, and then douching out the ear with, preferably, a fountain syringe, using from half a pint to a quart of water, at a temperature of about 105 deg., or not warmer than 110 deg. F.

Avoid violent blowing of the nose in an acute cold, for this may cause the inflammation to extend into the Eustachian tube, impairing the hearing, and perhaps resulting in deafness.

Never box the ears. Such a practice is both wicked and cruel, in that it drives the air with such force against the drum-head as often to rupture it, resulting in defective hearing.

Supposed inattention in children is often the result, not of a lack of attention, but of a lack of hearing. When such a person expects to be spoken to, he may hear distinctly; whereas, if unexpectedly addressed, he may seem very dull. This indicates that there is some fault in the hearing.

Leading from the middle

ear to the throat is a small tube, a little more than one inch long, called the Eustachian tube. Every time we swallow, this tube is slightly opened, and the air enters it, thus equalising the air pressure on both sides of the ear-drum. The air within the tube is quickly absorbed, and the increased pressure from without presses in the ear-drum, locking the little bones of the middle ear, and preventing their moving freely; if the tube leading into the throat is permanently closed, and air prevented from entering, deafness is the result. Catarrh of the throat causes about ninety-five per cent. of all cases of deafness. The mucous membrane about the opening of the Eustachian tube, as well as the lining of the tube itself, becomes thickened, and this closes it, preventing the entrance of air. Normally, the tube is not always open, but only while swallowing, which is due to the action of a little muscle attached to it just as it enters the throat. In a severe cold, when the nose is blown, there is a sensation of fullness in the ears, which is relieved only by swallowing, it being necessary to swallow several times before the air is drawn out. It is a bad practice to blow the nose violently at any time, and especially during a cold, for infecting mucus is thereby forced in the middle ear, producing earache, suppuration, and even deafness.

How to be Strong.

PART II.

ONE of the most useful adjuncts to these exercises is the use of the cold bath. It seems to put a life and vigour into our bodies, and we are enabled to go about our daily occupation feeling full of "go" and ready for whatever may happen. It should always be taken in the morning, immediately after the exercises are finished, and whilst the pores of the skin remain opened by the exercise.

As you are doubtless aware, there is a large amount of poisonous gases contained in the body, and these, having been brought to the skin's surface by the exercise, are given off by the pores. All persons are not constituted alike, and, although the bath need only occupy a half-minute, yet the shock to the system would be too great for some who are naturally weak, and we, therefore, want to point out that the place of the bath can be taken by a sponging of the body with cold water, and then, as after the bath, rubbing the skin vigorously with a rough towel. By this means the blood is put in circulation, and the whole body speedily feels all aglow. One word of warning is necessary, and that is — when you have finished your bath or sponging proceed to dress immediately, whilst the skin is still warm. Do not "poke about" and waste time; it is then that colds are taken, and the results of the same wrongly

set down to the cold bath when it is entirely erroneous. There is little chance of your coming to any harm if the foregoing instructions are adhered to.

The exercise for this month (No. 2) will doubtless

EXERCISE 2.

prove one of the severest tests as to how far you have? profited by the previous exercises and instructions. By means of this exercise the muscles of the back, arms, wrist, chest, and neck are brought into play. The following method should be followed: — First of all, lie out flat on the carpet, face downward, with the hands underneath. Proceed to raise the body upward by straightening the arms until they are rigid from the wrist to the

shoulder. The knees should remain stiff, and the legs entirely rigid, so that only the flat hand, and the toes touch the ground. When the body has been raised as far as it will go, lower yourself again to the original position and repeat the exercise as before. A steady and gradual rise should be cultivated, all jerking being avoided. The bicep muscles at the back of the arm will be brought into use in this exercise; and as this is one of the muscles that are more infrequently used than others, you will doubtless notice a considerable stiffness the first time this exercise is performed. This, however, will speedily disappear.

(To be continued.)

Florence Nightingale.

By Eliza F. Pollard.

FLORENCE, the "City of Flowers," and named Florence after that lovely city on the banks of the Arno, was the birth-place of Florence Nightingale.

Those who bent lovingly over her cradle little imagined that the name they gave the child would grow to be famous in the annals of her country; that it would become a household word, honoured and loved by a grateful nation.

Florence Nightingale was the second daughter of Mr. William Shore Nightingale, of Lea Hurst, in Derbyshire, and here she spent the greater part of her early youth. A happy, healthy childhood, full of those daily innocent joys which leave sweet memories for ever in the heart. To and fro she went, when still but a child, amongst the poor, in and out of cottages, bringing sunshine with her, "A ministering angel," learning even at that tender age what sorrow and suffering meant.

From the first the hand of God led her in the way He would have her go, though she knew it not. She only knew that pain and suffering appealed to her, whether in human beings or in dumb animals her hand was ever outstretched to give relief. As she grew in years she realised that to be of any real use in the world she must acquire knowledge. The touch, the tenderness, the love, were hers, but precious as these gifts are, to attain their full growth and power, they must be brought into subjection, they must be trained. In the cottages of the poor, in their sicknesses, she saw how utterly ignorant they were of the primary laws of cleanliness and health. It pained her. How could she help them? And the answer came to her by putting her own hand to the plough.

She never hesitated, she recognised her vocation. Young, with all that the world has to offer of delights and pleasures at her command, she just showed herself for one brief season in society, and then turned away. She did not find there what she required, that world did not satisfy her soul! For ever and ever above the din of music she heard the cry of suffering humanity ascending

FLORENCE NIGHTINGALE.

to Heaven, from loathsome alleys, from overcrowded hospitals and prison houses. "Is there none to help us?" they cried, and she answered as Elizabeth Fry and John Howard had answered, "Lord I am ready." Ready to give up the joys to which

most women aspire, ready to bear the idle jeer, the mocking laugh of those who could not understand her motives.

In those days, a woman who worked or desired to work beyond the pale of her own house was looked down upon, she lost caste. It was for Florence Nightingale to pave the way for women workers; she was the pioneer who has taught the world what women can do,

and dare, and be!

The place she was intended to fill was vacant, and quietly as if she foresaw the future she prepared herself for it. She recognised that ignorance was the great bane which lay at the root of so much evil, and before attempting to undertake any work or to preach to others, she applied herself to master the cause of disease and suffering, and how they could be alleviated.

Miss Nightingale spent several months visiting the London hospitals, then she went to Dublin and Edinburgh for the same purpose, examining the minutest details of hospital life. Afterwards she went abroad to France, Germany, and Italy, and in the hospitals of these foreign cities her eyes were opened to the great mistake in the organisation of English hospitals. Whilst we employed only paid nurses, many of them untrained, and totally unfit for their work, the Sisters of St. Vincent de Paul devoted their lives to nursing the sick and visiting the poor. They had no other thought, no other interests. Their lives were mapped out for them, and they were entirely devoted to the accomplishment of their duties. In Protestant Germany there were the Deaconesses, and so strongly was Miss Nightingale impressed with the necessity that a body of women should be set apart for nursing the sick, that she went, at two different periods of her life, to Kaiserwerth, the institution created by Pastor Fliedner, where nurses were especially trained, and sent forth far and wide to do their work amongst the sick. So this great and good woman travelled from city to city, from town to village; storing up knowledge, learning wisdom. She never asked herself when or how she should make use of it — that was in God's hands, believing that as she sowed so would she reap, in His good time.

In 1849 she enrolled herself as a voluntary nurse, first in the Kaiserwerth Institution, and afterwards in Paris with the Sisters of St. Vincent de Paul. Thus she realised to the full the intelligent working of both establishments, and she became convinced that the keynote to all such work is system. The Deaconesses of Kaiserwerth, the Sisters of St. Vincent de Paul were women set apart, there was no question of doctrine, they were simply labourers in Christ's vineyard, and their motive power was love. They lived in the world and for the world, striving to make it purer and better. Wherever there was sin, sorrow, or suffering, these women were to be found, treading softly with knowledge and experience at their command.

Sadly Florence acknowledged that in this respect England was behind her neighbours. Would it ever be otherwise? she asked herself. Would anything happen to break down the barrier of insular pride, and make English men and women understand that wherever there is suffering there must needs be work, and that neither birth nor education can or ought to exempt woman from this field of labour, for which she is so eminently fitted?

After her experience in Paris Miss Nightingale returned for rest to her own beautiful home at Lea Hurst.

Before He took up His three years' ministry, Christ went alone into the desert, and communed with God; even so should we follow in the footsteps of our great example. No great work ought to be lightly entered upon, it were well to retire from the world, to fast and pray before we put our hands to the plough.

Florence Nightingale had no idea what lay before her, she was waiting in perfect faith and patience for the call to arise and go "about her Father's business."

Not even when war was declared did she know it was her "call." Not until the shout of victory had gone up, when Alma had been fought and won, did the bitter cry come floating across the waters.

"Where are our women? Will not they help us, as only women can, with their tender touch and their gentle presence? Surely they will not leave us to die like dogs; they will come to us."

The great "Times" war correspondent wrote passionately:—

"Are there no devoted women amongst us, able

and willing to go forth to minister to the sick and suffering soldiers of the East in the hospitals of Scutari? Are none of the daughters of England at this extreme hour of need ready for such a work of mercy? France has sent forth her Sisters of Mercy unsparingly. Must we fall so far below the French in self-sacrifice and devotedness, in a work which Christ so signally blest as done unto Himself? 'I was sick and ye visited Me.'

Other appeals followed, but they were not needed. Florence Nightingale understood that this was the end of all those long years of training and of patient waiting. She knew what was needed, and she knew that she was capable of answering that cry for help. Without hesitation she sat down and wrote to the Minister of War offering her services as nurse to the army in the East. How thankfully the offer was accepted! What a relief it was to those in office to have such a woman to deal with, one who was so thoroughly acquainted with all the details of organisation and nursing!

In three weeks from the time the appeal was made she had assembled her band of nurses, and was ready to start for the East. She set sail with her thirty-eight nurses on the 22nd October, quietly under cover of night to avoid public observation, but at Boulogne a rumour got abroad among the fisher-women that English nurses were on their way to the Crimea, and when they appeared, a quiet band in their black cloaks, they were surrounded, their bags, wraps, and trunks conveyed to the train for them, and all these rough fisherwomen asked in return was to shakes hands with *"les soeurs,"* and wish them "God speed," and the train steamed out of the station to the cry of *"Vive les soeurs."*

On the 5th November Miss Nightingale landed at Scutari. The same day the Battle of Inkerman was fought and six hundred wounded were sent down to Scutari. From that time forth the work accomplished by this handful of brave women excited the astonishment and admiration of the whole world. Florence Nightingale's power of organisation, her quiet systematic way of going to work, inspired surgeons and clergy with a feeling of security. She and her nurses had been received by the medical staff with a certain degree of prejudice, but in a few weeks this feeling vanished, and everyone felt that Miss Nightingale was the right woman in the right place.

It is impossible to tell in this short sketch the tithe of the work she accomplished. We are told that from early morning till late at night Florence Nightingale moved hither and thither. More than once after a great battle, she was twenty-four hours on her feet without thinking of rest. She attempted, and in a measure succeeded in cleansing the hospitals where she worked. So terrible was their condition that they might veritably be compared to the Augean stables. The water was putrid, rats and vermin attacked the limbs of those who were too weak to defend themselves. The death rate was higher than in London during the cholera. And through the midst of all this mortality and suffering, the quiet figure of this brave woman went and came; when others slept, she watched. In the still hours of the night, when men were racked with fever, and worn out with pain, a soft woman's hand would be laid on the aching head, a straightening of the sheet, a few gentle words would bring at least momentary comfort, and then, holding her lamp on high, the figure would pass on. Was it a woman or an angel? Dying men watched for her coming and kissed her shadow as she passed by. Was there ever before such a glorious testimony to a woman's power? Love, divine love, had guided her to this work, and in return for her obedience she has received the overflowing love and gratitude of thousands, and an immortal name written:—

"On England's annals through the long
  Hereafter of her speech and song,
  A light its rays shall cast,
  From portals of the past."

"A lady with a lamp shall stand
  In the great history of the land
  A noble type of good
  Heroic womanhood."

This was Florence Nightingale's actual work, which she carried on for two long years, and which all men saw and appreciated. But the effect of her work, the aftermath, so to speak, is the real test of its greatness. She broke down barriers which have never been built up again. She opened out to her fellow women a field in which they need fear no rivalry. Never again will that helpless wail of misery reach our ears, for where our soldiers go to fight battles, Englishwomen, trained in all necessary knowledge, go also to tend and care for them.

It is given to few to see the fruit of their labours as completely as Miss Nightingale from her retreat has done. We were behindhand with the nations when the Crimean War broke out, but in the fifty years which have elapsed since then we have sur-

passed them. We have but just passed through the throes of another war, with thankful hearts we have celebrated a great peace, which is to unite aliens to our Empire. It has been a terrible war, but we are told by one of our legislators that it has been waged, on England's side at least, with as much mercy and loving kindness as possible. Everywhere on the battlefield and in the besieged cities English nurses were seen, well trained, intelligent women, who knew their work, and did it in a spirit of self-devotion. There was no waiting, no calling for them; they were there on the spot as a matter of course. What in Florence Nightingale's time created astonishment, is now an accepted fact. It is for this she laboured. She stands forth, and ever shall stand, a shining star, to guide women onwards and upwards, to teach them that "England expects every woman to do her duty."

Cosy Corner Chats.

II. – THE CHOICE OF A CAREER.

By Lady Henry Somerset.

M Y DEAR R. – The position of a young girl endowed with a strong individuality must have been pathetic beyond our power to imagine in the days when woman had but one vocation, and no avocation outside the four walls of home. Doubtless, many a dream of what she might do, and do well, floated before her eyes. Perhaps she had strong powers of reasoning, a sunlit imagination, a deft and cunning hand. When she saw her brother developing his powers of thought at school and college, or when, if he had talent as a draughtsman, a painter, or sculptor, it was encouraged and cultivated, she must have thought – though, doubtless, she seldom dared to say – "I feel that I might do what he does; and where is the justice of the world that not only does not encourage but positively forbids me from following out my strongest impulses as to what I would do that I may gain an individual expression of my powers, and may support myself honourably?"

The loss to the world that has hedged women away from doing all that they could has been incalculable, and the mutual companionship and good understanding between brothers and sisters of the same household, and the men and women of the larger household that we call the world, have been grievously interfered with.

If I were a girl once more, I would do what, as a girl, I strongly desired to undertake – I would be a painter. Probably this overmastering tendency was inherited from my father; but, although I was permitted to learn to draw, I was forbidden to go on with my studies on the ground that it was not for me!

The points I have here made sufficiently indicate the advice I would give to a young girl about choosing a career. First of all I would lift up my heart to God, and consecrate to Him whatever talents I possessed; and most earnestly of all I would make over to Him my best gift of all, whether of heart, or brain, or hand. This done, I would proceed to cultivate that gift to the best of my ability; nor do I think that this would interfere with a true marriage, which is, after all, the most desirable goal of a woman's life, and, for that matter, of a man's! For the most complete development of a woman's strongest tendency toward good work would but make her more of a woman, a better companion for her husband, a greater force for good in her home and in the circle of society.

If, as is the case with American, Daniel Webster, said to a young lawyer who complained that there were too many in the legal profession, "Remember, the national societies that send them forth enough new workers, membership fees and subscriptions, to make it for the interest of those societies to furnish them a field. There are many who are willing to do this work on a salary; only the most gifted could afford to do it on a percentage, but they could, and there is ample room here.

Naturally enough, I am writing of those lines of work about which I am informed and that is probably what the editor desires, but it is my observation that young women who join the ranks of altruistic workers expect to go forward with leaps and bounds, and to find a salary forthcoming on short notice. This, however, is not the method that ensures the best growth in character or work. If the young women who wish to develop along the lines I have indicated were willing to join a local auxiliary in their own neighbourhood, and put in enough strokes of work there to prove that they are capable of a larger field, they would find that field opening before them. They must be

LADY HENRY SOMERSET.

some, there were several directions in which one felt equally drawn, I would let circumstances determine, and as a rule would choose to go forward along the line of least resistance, letting circumstances help me all that they would. It would also be well — other things equal — to choose an occupation that was not over-crowded. That great young man, that there is always plenty of room higher up." For instance, the most difficult thing in literature is the short story, and there are not too many who write it well. Capable organisers of local societies, women's clubs, and women's philanthropic and reform associations of every kind — remember, I say, capable — would be able to bring into content to creep before they walk, and to walk before they run. It is by this slow, steady, reasonable process that all those have obtained, who deserved it, the success that so many desire without having either the ability or the disposition to pay the price.

What I have written is the result of years of personal observation and frequent counsel with other workers in the white fields of God. We regard every young woman who comes to us with a balanced character and trained ability as being priceless beyond words; but

I am sorry to say that the mass of those who come do not answer this description. But to the girls of true spirit and power may it be said, as Milton said of our first parents when they went forth from Eden, "The world is all before them where to choose."

The Game of Golf:
Its Pleasures and Pains.

BY BERTHA WOON.

GOLF is, perhaps, the one game in which women are most capable of competing with men. For indeed, it is a science more than a game. Accuracy of aim and the power of judging distance, combined with a fair amount of muscular strength, being of more value than mere "brute force." Seeing, then, that golf or gowff, as some people prefer to call it, is a pastime eminently suitable for girls, and that not to golf is to lose one of the pleasures of life, let us study the best way to become an efficient player.

The game consists of hitting a small white ball from a given spot into a hole some distance away by means of a club. The ball must not be touched by hand or foot, or in any way moved from the position in which it has fallen, except by means of a club – all of which sounds very simple, but is in reality most difficult to accomplish. If anyone doubts this, let her try how many strokes it takes her before she accomplishes the apparently simple task of holing her first ball.

A match is played by two or more people, each playing his or her own ball. After the first stroke has been played, the ball then lying farthest from the hole must be played first, and the player who holes out in the fewest number of strokes wins the hole, the score being counted by means of the terms – odd the like, one more, two more, one off two, and so on.

Now that golf is so universally popular, it will not be a very difficult matter to find some experienced player who will explain to you the meaning of the various terms used, and perhaps give you a lead round the links. But, as in all other games, practice is necessary, as measuring distances with the eye, and the amount of force required to cover a given distance, can only be gained by experience. There is a capital story told of a certain professor who was being taught golf by his caddie. He was wondering at his want of success and his inability to learn an art which seemed so very simple. On asking his caddie for an explanation, he was somewhat surprised to receive the following reply, "Oh, sir, ye see, oney body can teach thae laddies (meaning students at the university) Latin and Greek, but golf, ye see, sir, golf requires a heid!"

In starting for a round of golf, see that you are suitably dressed, namely in a skirt short enough to walk in easily, and a blouse, or coat loose enough to allow free play to the arms. To complete your costume, wear a plain sailor hat or tam-o'-shanter cap.

The next thing to consider is the choice of clubs, of which the full outfit is thirteen – the driver, the bulger driver, the long spoon, the mid spoon, the short spoon, the brassey, the cleek, the niblick, the mashie, the driving iron, the lofting iron, the putting cleek, and the putter. You will find four – the driver, the cleek, the lofting iron and the putter – quite enough to begin with.

Having reached the first "teeing ground," as the starting point is called, place your ball on a small mound of sand, which is called a "tee." Then stand as naturally as you can in front of your ball, with the driver firmly grasped in both hands, your left heel almost in a line with the ball, and your left shoulder in the direction of the hole to which you are driving. Keep your eye firmly fixed on the ball, and, after taking careful aim, swing your club over the right shoulder until the arms are extended to their fullest length; then bring smartly back, hitting the ball, and carrying your club right through towards the left shoulder, which will not only give the greatest amount of force to the stroke, but will also help to keep the right direction.

Let us suppose that fortune will favour you, and that you will now find your ball in a fairly good "lie" – say, some 160 yards from the hole. Take your lofting iron, and, standing with your feet well apart, and the ball lying about half way between them, swing your club in the same way as in driving, but hitting the ball well underneath, in order to "loft" it over any obstacles that may be in the way of it.

If, on the other hand, your ball should have taken a bad "lie" on mud or sand, play very calmly and deliberately, and take care not to press, or you will most probably only succeed in getting deeper and deeper into the pit which you will have digged for yourself; but take careful aim, and get your lofting iron well under the ball. If your ball is entirely hidden by whin or rushes you may move them aside, so that you can see the ball, but on no account must you touch the ball itself, or the loss of the hole will be the penalty. Two good lofting strokes should bring your ball to about fifty yards

The Game of Golf.

from the hole. Now comes the most scientific, and to some people the most interesting, part of the game, as accuracy in these "approach shots" and successful "putting on the green" itself may often remedy a bad drive, and win the match. What you must try to do now is to loft the ball as near as pos-sible to the hole, making full allowance for the roll of the ball on the green.

Your left shoulder being, as always, kept in the direction of the hole, stand with your knees slightly bent, and with your right arm kept well in against the right side, and your left elbow raised; shorten your club, and, after carrying your eye backwards and forwards from the ball to the hole, take a sharp stroke from the wrists, hitting well underneath the ball, and shifting the weight of the body from the right foot to the left as your club follows the ball through towards the hole. Now you will have arrived well on the "putting green."

See that your caddie removes the flag from the hole; then, taking your putter, measure mentally the distance to be covered, keeping your eye steadily on the ball; place your putter behind it, and strike smoothly, without any jerk, and with more or less force, as the distance to be traversed may require. If your ball is some distance from the hole, or if the green is undulated and uneven, be content to take two strokes with your putter to be sure of "holing out," rather than risk putting past the hole.

See that your caddie replaces the flag with the number facing the previous "teeing ground," there to begin your journey over again, up hill and down dale, over walls, burns, and sand-pits to the next hole, and so on, to the end of the course. A full course consists of eighteen holes, but many golfing courses for ladies consist of nine holes. After a while with your gradually decreasing score, you will begin to look quite calmly on those bunkers which at first you trembled before, to discuss the clubs and their uses, to criticise your fellow-players, and to talk technically how you were "bunkered," and, in spite of taking a bad "lie," and missing your "putt" you "holed"

out in five.

There are various little points of etiquette of golf which players must learn and practise. Before driving from any "tee," be sure that the players in front are well out of the reach of your ball, the general rule being that you must not drive off until the players in front have played their second stroke. Be very sure to see that any turf you may have cut up from behind your ball is at once carefully replaced.

After having holed out, move at once off the green, for the convenience of players coming up behind. Of course, the general rules of golf must be learnt, also the local rules of the links on which you may be playing. Your place is behind, and well to the left of the player, so that he may not catch sight of you or your clothes in aiming, and so get put off his stroke.

Golf is a very serious game, and a silent watcher will be much more appreciated than a chattering one. We have to thank our neighbours over the Border for passing on to us this fascinating pastime of this "royal and ancient game."

Typewriting as a Profession for Girls.

YOUR editor has asked me to talk to you about typewriting as a profession. In these days the choice of a profession has become as serious a matter to girls as to their brothers, because, from choice or from necessity, so many of them are going out into the world of business to carve a career for themselves; and, believing as I do, that typewriting is a splendid profession for any girl, I am glad to say a few words to you on the subject.

Suppose we look, first of all, at the necessary qualifications for a successful typist. There is no need to talk about patience, perseverance, and the like, because success in any profession presupposes these qualifications. First of all, you must have a sound education. If it includes one or more of the languages most frequently used in the commercial world, so much the better for your prospects, but a practical acquaintance with the mother tongue is sufficient to secure the majority of appointments. Technical terms with which you are unfamiliar may probably arise in the early days of business life, but such small difficulties are soon overcome. On the other hand, do not let your employer have to discover that your vocabulary is very limited, or your orthography shaky. It will not tend to inspire him with confidence in your ability.

Typewriting is not at all difficult to learn. Girls who have conquered Pitman, with more or less difficulty, who have wrestled with the curves, the circles, and hooks triumphantly, need not flinch from the additional task. A few days – indeed, almost a few hours – are mostly sufficient for familiarising oneself with the keyboard. To obtain rapidity and freedom of movement is a longer matter, but patient and careful practice will soon make any girl of average intelligence an efficient typist. Meanwhile, learn as much as possible of the smaller details of mechanism. If some little thing gets out of gear, your knowledge may save a troublesome delay.

Tuition is easily and fairly cheaply obtained. There are plenty of ways in which you can get trained at a minimum outlay, viz., at polytechnics, institutes, technical instruction classes, and the like. Others may prefer to take the course at commercial colleges, or at the large typewriting schools. Some, if not all, of the leading typewriter companies, have their schools, where instruction may be obtained on mutual terms, *i.e.*, the students giving two or three months' service in their office in return for training. The students are expected to know, or to be learning, shorthand. As these offices usually combine a labour bureau, the students find the difficulty of getting situations, without experience, somewhat obviated, and many girls have made a good start in this way.

It is needless and practically useless, too, to attempt to advise you which machine to learn. Diversity of opinion as to their relative merits is almost as general among typists as among makers. One pins her faith to the double keyboard, another to the single, one to the ribbon, and another to the pad, while a good many more declare preference to be only a matter of use. Get acquainted thoroughly with one of the leading makes. Know it perfectly, and then do not be alarmed by the number of different machines. When once you have grown familiar with a standard keyboard, you will find transition from single to double, or vice versa, is not a troublesome matter and you can soon grow accustomed to the change.

One word about this terrible bugbear of inexperience. It is really the worst difficulty to be overcome. The depressing effect on the girl who has worked hard, and knows that she has fitted herself to take a position, when she is confronted day after day in the columns of newspaper advertisements by those two ominous words, "experience necessary" can only be fully understood by those who have "faced the music." Sometimes she is tempted to wonder if there is any room in the world for inexperienced folk. And to be told on applying for an appointment that the advertiser intended giving ten shillings weekly remuneration, but could not offer *so much* to an inexperienced applicant, is the reverse of encouraging when it follows months of preparation.

Fortunately, though not extinct yet, such employers are rare, and the experience of such interviews is not such a frequent one. As a rule, an efficient typist will secure a living wage to start with, and can soon make for herself a position which many of her sisters, whose work is more arduous and less interesting, may well envy. For, take my word for it, girls, there is a real fascination in turning out careful work from those dainty little machines, with the dancing keys and swift, flashing type, and a girl must be hard to please who does not grow really attached to her profession, other things, of course, being equal.

Occasionally, the innocent typewriter is accused of being a severe tax on nerves, and of rendering the operators nervous. Certainly, this is a highly-strung age, but I do not think there is much foundation in this charge against the typewriter. From observation, and from a fairly long personal experience as typist as well, I believe it is one of the least trying occupations for girls. The work is not hard, the hours are mostly lighter than in employment exclusively characterised as feminine. Surely, the typist's lot is a good deal easier than that of many other girls, and no girl with average health need fear taking it up.

In conclusion, I recommend the profession warmly to any girl who is on the outlook for interesting work, who is prepared to give steady and reliable service, whose education is sound, and who is not afraid of a few initial difficulties. Master shorthand, then go and learn one of the best machines, and resolve to make "efficiency" your motto. In typewriting, as in every other profession, the lower part of the ladder is crowded with the inefficient and the half-hearted. Away at the top there is plenty of room, and the girl who is mistress of her profession will mostly find employment. There is sometimes an outcry against girls because they are accused of lacking thoroughness, of taking business engagements merely as a stop-gap, and, in consequence, only giving half-hearted attention. If you take up work in this spirit, girls, do not be surprised if the good things in this, or any other profession, never fall to your share. If you enter business life you must give the same conscientious work which your brothers are expected to give. Try to make yourselves necessary to your employer. Do not ask or expect concessions on the ground of your sex. Having taken your place in the business world, be content to stand on the same footing, and do not look for special privileges. Give of your best, and, unless you are singularly unfortunate, you will find that business life will pay you back in your own coin.

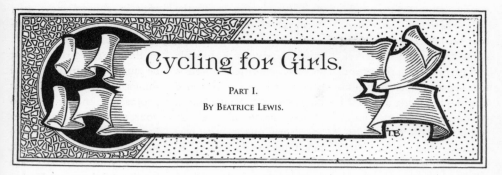

Cycling for Girls.

PART I.

BY BEATRICE LEWIS.

I SUPPOSE we all want to have tall, straight figures, and to hold ourselves well, and to look our best on our bicycles. Now, to make a point of this is no matter to be ashamed of on the score of vanity, though I should like to think that the idea goes deeper that just care for appearances. I wonder how many of us look upon cycling, or upon any of our other favourite sports and pastimes in the light of an aid to health and sturdy growth as well as pleasure? If we did we should hear less of delicate girls overdoing themselves and being forbidden to cycle altogether, and should certainly see less of bent backs and stooping shoulders amongst growing maidens.

There is no more beneficial exercise than cycling for girls of all ages, and in many cases delicacy and actual ill-health have been completely cured by means of cycling exercise. But we must use our own common sense with regard to moderation, and avoid all temptation to excess.

DISMOUNTING.

It is useless to attempt laying down any law as to the distance to be ridden or the number of hours to be spent in the saddle by growing girls. It is a matter in which they should learn to exercise their own judgement, for no one else can possibly tell so well as themselves, though the effects of over-exhaustion will soon be patent to all beholders.

One infallible sign of distress is loss of appetite after riding. If your limbs ache, and you feel too limp and fatigued to enjoy a good meal, or even to sleep peacefully when you get to bed, you may be sure there is something wrong.

For both pleasure and advantage it is desirable to

choose companions of one's own riding calibre. There is no possible fun to be got out of panting and struggling in the effort to keep pace with stronger riders, or to scale hills that you know to be beyond your legitimate powers. And here I would say a word to the young Amazons who seem capable of every effort. If you find yourselves in the company of younger or weaker riders, don't give way to the temptation of "showing off." If you see that a hill, which you could climb with a song on your lips is proving a severe strain on the more limited resources of your companions, it would be pretty and considerate on your part to be the first to jump off and suggest walking it.

The saddle should be fixed sufficiently forward to place the rider well over her work, and just high enough to permit her to reach the pedals with perfect ease and with no strain, when at their lowest point. Although the figure should be slightly thrown forward from the waist, great care should be taken to avoid a humpy back and rounded shoulders. Keep the hips level and steady, the knees as motionless as possible, and let the feet and ankles move with freedom, following the pedals round and clawing them up when at the lowest point.

Every girl should learn to adjust her own saddle, and to perform simple alterations in the general adjustment of her own mount. The day is happily past when a foolish helplessness was deemed attractive, and a girl who bothers someone else to do everything for her would soon be voted a great bore.

While insisting that suitable dress is by no means the only factor towards helping us to present a good appearance awheel, I am far from denying that it is a very important one. The first essentials of a cycling suit are that it should be plain, neat, and well cut. Anything trimmed, showy, or conspicuous on a bicycle looks not only unladylike but also unworkmanlike. The skirt is, of course, the important garment. If you can't afford to go to a good tailor for it, it is quite possible to make a nice one at home, provided you get a good pattern. Also, you must have someone to help you arrange it on the bicycle, which should be firmly fixed to the stand, with its back to a long mirror. You then mount it, and get your skirt, which is only tacked together, pulled down and arranged evenly on either side of the back wheel. If the folds fall straight and meet together while you are still, well and good, but that is by no means all! The great test comes when you commence to pedal, which you must manage to do, exercising great care in the management of your stationary mount. You should be able to move the knees forward without disturbing the set of back pleats.

If you are tall, don't cut your riding skirt short, as that has a very awkward effect. But in either case, whether long or short, I should advise you to wear elastic straps on each side to fix it down to your legs. Even if you are quite young, and a very small girl, you don't want to present the unseemly spectacle of wind-blown frock and uncovered legs that one often beholds in the streets. If your skirt is short, you had best fasten it to the knees; if long, round the foot under the instep. You can make these straps for yourself better than

anything bought. Get wide, black elastic, or, if you wear tan shoes, brown elastic. Make a loop to fit over your instep, or round your leg, as preferred, which you sew on to the skirt about four inches above the bottom edge.

It is important to have shoes of a comfortable fit, though not too large, and firm-soled without being heavy. The feet and ankles should be as free and supple as possible to do their rightful work, otherwise they throw the labour on to other limbs and muscles, causing unnecessary fatigue.

Girls' Pets and How to Manage Them.

A GOLDFISH AQUARIUM.

A LARGE glass globe, or an inverted propagating glass used by florists, will do for an aquarium. Either can be purchased at any china and glass dealer's, but the knob end must be fitted into a wooden stand. A square or oblong tank, however, is to be preferred.

It may not be within the

scope of every girl's ability or financial resources to buy the necessary materials and make an aquarium; but if she wants to try her hand, the following directions by a practical man may prove useful.

HOW TO MAKE ONE.

The size should be not less than 24in. long, 10in. wide and 12in. high. As a foundation or base get a piece of one-inch board; on this lay a sheet of 14 gauge VM zinc, and fix by means of long copper nails, one driven in at each corner. The heads of the nails must afterwards be soldered over to prevent leakage.

For the four uprights or pillars purchase four zinc double angles, and solder on to the bottom plate; then run your zinc grooves along the sides and ends, and it will be all ready for the reception of the glass.

For a top rail over the edges of the glass 5/8 split bell piping will do, properly mitred at the corners, and soldered. This not only gives a finish to the aquarium, but helps to strengthen the whole of the framework, and binds it together.

We will presume, by the above directions, you now know how to make the skeleton ready to receive the glass. Of course, the top rail of bell piping must not be fixed until the glazing has been completed. The most important part is to have the glass cut to the exact size; a tiny notch on any one of the edges will throw out the square, besides causing much bother. Plate glass is the best, but nothing less than a 32oz. make should be used, as it will have to stand a heavy pressure of water behind it. Obtain a clear glass, not one with a greenish hue.

You will require a special composition for glazing, consisting of red lead, litharge, and gold size, mixed up to a stiff paste. Place some of this evenly into the grooves; then slide in your glasses, after which trim away the surplus composition, and finish off in the same manner as a glazier would do when fixing in a new window-pane.

When the composition has dried you can then adjust the top rail, previously mentioned, and nail along the bottom board some three-inch picture frame beading, or three-inch ogee zinc guttering, top part downwards; this will form an ornamental stand. A frieze around the top will be pleasing to the eye, but it is not necessary. The main work will now be completed, and the rest, such as painting and general ornamentation, will only be a light pastime.

Bear in mind that the inside must not on any account be painted, or your fish will soon be poisoned, and come up to the top of the water at their last gasp.

Bronze-green paint (two coats) is a good colour to use for the outside work; and you can, if you wish, for the top rail, frieze, and the spandrels, if they are made of zinc, use some of Judson's gold paint.

A sheet of perforated zinc is required to place over the top of the aquarium to keep out the dust, and also to prevent the inmates from getting out. It will also keep the cat from going a-fishing on her own account, for the bright yellow or golden orange colours of the fish as they swim about have a great attraction for puss. Some aquariums have an ornamental movable top; this is supported by a narrow ledge at each corner. The design of this, however, can be left to your own fancy.

THE FISH.

Goldfish are to be found nowadays in most of the civilised countries of the world, though originally they came from China. They were first introduced into England in the year 1691, but we do not hear very much about them until 1728, when they were imported to this country in large numbers from Holland, where they had already become domesticated.

WATER PLANTS.

Have your aquarium thoroughly washed out inside before using, allowing the water to stand in it for a day or two, and clean the glass sides with a small piece of sponge tied to the end of a stick. When you are well satisfied that all the joints are watertight, and also that any poisonous properties the composition may have contained have been removed, you may then empty out the water and prepare the bed of the aquarium for the reception of the aquatic plants, for you cannot possibly keep your fish alive without them, supplying, as they do, the oxygen necessary for your fish to breathe, and consuming besides the carbonic gas given off by them.

The bed should be prepared after this manner. Lay down, to the depth of one inch, some well-washed shingle; over this you may place a few pieces of charcoal, and as a final covering some small stones. A tiny rock-work arch may be put in, but not sprays of coral and shells, which always look out of place in a freshwater aquarium.

Now introduce your plants. Crowfoot, milfoil (spiked), and duckweed are to be recommended; also the *Anacharis alsinastrum,* or Canadian water-weed or water-thyme, as it is sometimes called, besides numerous other plants, which we have not room to mention. Some of these can be obtained at a dealer's, if you are not botanist enough to get suitable plants for yourself in one of your Saturday afternoon rambles.

After you have set your plants fill in with either river water or pump water. On no account must boiled or "tap" water be used. Fill to within three inches of the top, and allow the plants to take root before you place in the fish. Stand the aquarium in a full light, but never where the sunshine plays upon it.

Three or four pond snails make capital scavengers, eating off the green slime which becomes attached to the glass sides, and also any pieces of decaying vegetable matter, which would cause disease among the fish. By keeping these, and having the proper plants in your aquarium, the necessity for frequently changing the water will be avoided; but it is as well to take out a little now and again by means of a siphon, say every three or four weeks and replace with fresh river water. Pour this in, holding your can a little above the top, as this helps to aerate the water. A small wateringcan with a fine rose is best for the purpose.

Feed the fish with ants' eggs, semolina, tiny blood worms, or a little piece of raw lean beef or mutton shredded, tied to a piece of string, and suspended in the water, they will enjoy nibbling at; this, however, should never be left in more than a couple of days at a time. Bread crumbs are decidedly injurious, as, if left uneaten, they become stale and sour.

The fish may be taken out of the water with a small landing net when necessary; but the aquarium should never be moved about nor shaken, as it will greatly retard the growth of the plants, and perhaps cause your fish to die, for they are easily frightened.

Cosy Corner Chats.

III. – THE VIRTUE OF RETICENCE.

MY DEAR HELEN: The publication of the letters of many distinguished folk has gone to a great length lately. It has come about that within two years we have had even the love letters of no less than three sets of lovers – the Brownings, Victor Hugo, and his future wife, and Bismarck and his future wife. We certainly are losing our sense of reserve. Much as these letters may tell us of the personality of their writers, I think every right-minded woman feels after reading them as if she were in the position of a person at a keyhole – a position not very dignified for the reader. Years ago Mr. Edward Rowland Sill wrote to me: "What a staggering lot of books the publishers turn out on a weary world! What gabblers we are! Gabblers that write and gobblers that read, for no doubt it is the demand that creates the supply." If that was measurably true a dozen years ago, it is twice true now. Every sort of personal influence which the author can make, he makes to the willing public.

Letters, autobiographies, interviews, the poems which set forth the discords of domestic life – all these are poured forth in an increasing flood.

Now this phenomenon in the literary world is indicative of what is taking place in the world of men and women about us. Reticence is out of fashion. Ready expression and quick sympathy have taken its place. They are not its equal in the art of building vigorous character.

We talk, talk, talk about ourselves. Many women

and many girls seem never to let a drop of sap get above a certain spigot – the lips; and consequently they never put forth a new leaf toward heaven. The chatterer is never a woman of thought. Deep purposes, keen insights, do not thrive on much talk. The needs of conversation are great, but the world waits for other service than that done by the pleasant talker. If you suggest that I am contradicting myself in what I have said to you about the large, free use of words, I shall reply, "No." The ability to talk, and to talk well, is a different thing from the habit of talking from morning to night.

Matters have not much changed since I was a girl, and in those days girls greatly enjoyed making confidences to each other. There was a thrilling excitement about it. Friendship often seemed to be cemented by such outpourings. One felt a certain virtue in them, as if they cleared the record of sins or faults and enabled one to begin again. Now I suspect that all this is really poor discipline for a growing spirit. There are

certain kinds of confidences which seem to me especially vicious. Let me tell you what some of them are. First, there are the confidences between girl friends which are brought forth at the midnight hour, often as the result of that moral relaxation which comes with physical weariness. They are exciting, egotistic, dramatic. They are likely to be out of keeping with the prosaic life of the next forenoon. They may be tales of personal experience made up of half-truths and of the results of a vagrant imagination. The mere putting of them into words is bad educationally, since it confuses truth and falsehood in the mind of both teller and hearer. I do not mean to imply that these confidences contain anything base or actually wicked, but that they are so foolish and inaccurate as to be weakening to the structure of character. They would not bear the sun, but they masquerade impressively under the cloak of night. It is a good rule never to tell anybody anything which you could not tell in broad daylight, with the

width of the room between you and your confidant.

In the second place, there are confidences regarding past faults and sins, made often for the sake of becoming interesting to your listener. It is possible for these to be carried to an unfortunate extent. I remember years ago, when a wave of temperance reform swept over the country, and many clubs were formed in small towns for the reclamation of the drunkard, that the weekly meetings of many of those clubs became positively disgusting on account of the revelations which the men seemed to enjoy making, of the depths to which they had fallen. This morbid appetite for notoriety grew; and it was difficult to believe that the men were really much better when intoxicated by their own confessions than they had been in the previous state which they so vividly pictured. Of course, nothing so gross as this would come into the experience of an ordinary girl; but I cite it as an illustration of an excess to which the impulse might easily go.

Again, I fear that there is

some truth in the common sneer that a woman loves to tell a secret. The forbidden confidence has charms for her. Even the most cautious and responsible woman can scarcely look back over her girlhood without blushing at the memory of some moment when she said to some other girl: "Will you promise never to tell? I ought not to tell you, for I promised not to; but, if you will never, never tell!" It may well take years of painstaking guard over the tongue to obliterate the shame of such a recollection.

If the tale of these deliberate confidences is a long one, that of the more impulsive, less open disclosures is longer yet. It is not simply that once and again a woman tells all that she has a right to tell of herself or of others. She goes farther. The glance, the shrug, the whisper, the rapid by-play, all have their parts in that conversation which might better not be. Shakespeare, the master of the human heart, knew well of what he wrote when he put into Hamlet's mouth the adjuration to Horatio and Marcellus. (We may get such comfort as we can from the reflection that he, at least, was speaking to men.)

"That you, at such time seeing me, never shall
With arms encumber'd thus, or this head-shake
Or by pronouncing of some doubtful phrase
As, 'Well, well, we know,' or 'We could, an' if we would,'
Or, 'If we list to speak,' or 'There be, an' if they might,'
Or such ambiguous giving out, to note
That you know aught of me: this not to do,
So grace and mercy at your most need help you,
Swear.'

It would be as useless as it is impossible to name all the temptations to speech when silence would serve better. I shall have my wish if these few instances may induce you to interpose one instant of reflection between the thought and the word. On that stern habit the spirit thrives. Reserve fosters strength, and strength in its turn transforms reserve from pain to pleasure. Two thousand years ago a wise old Roman said, "I have often regretted my speech, never my silence." Yet the years have not sufficed to teach us the wisdom of his confession.

HELOISE EDWINA HERSEY.

Cakes for Afternoon Tea.

IN this article I am going to give full directions for some very simple buns and cakes that any girl can easily make herself, unaided, with very little care. Every girl should be able to provide tempting little cakes in an emergency by making them herself. I will confine my recipes to simple ones, as I have said. It is best not to try elaborate ones until you are a practised hand at ordinary everyday cakes. Of course, this applies to all other branches of cookery.

The easiest buns of all to make are ROCK CAKES. Take $1/4$lb. of butter, dripping, or lard (butter, of course, is best), and rub it with the tips of your fingers (after beating it to a cream with a knife) into $1/2$lb. of flour; when thoroughly rubbed in, add two teaspoonfuls of baking powder, $1/4$lb.. of sugar, a good pinch of salt, $1/4$lb. of currants (previously well washed and dried), 2ozs. candied peel. Mix thoroughly together with a well-beaten egg, to which a little milk has been added. Beat well into a stiff dough with a fork, then place in little rough heaps on a floured baking tin, and bake at once in a quick oven. They should keep their rocky appearance; if they are too moist or the oven is too cool they will run out flat.

QUEEN CAKES – Cream together $1/4$lb. of butter and $1/4$lb. castor sugar. Then well beat two eggs and add gradually to the butter and sugar, alternately with 8ozs. flour, into which has been mixed half-teaspoonful of baking powder and a pinch of salt. Then add 3ozs. glacé cherries cut into halves, or sultanas, or cur-rants; also 2ozs. chopped citron or peel, and the grated rind of a lemon. Mix well together to a soft paste; if not moist enough, add a little milk. Put quickly into well-buttered bun tins or fancy tins, half fill them, and bake at once for about 20 minutes. N.B. – All little cakes should be made moist enough to run flat in the oven and then rise in the centre, when they look very tempting. The right consistency is soon acquired.

DOUGH NUTS: A Dainty Recipe: – Ingredients: $3/4$lb. flour, half teaspoonful of salt, $1^1/2$ teaspoonful of baking powder, 3ozs. butter, two eggs, three tablespoonfuls milk, 4ozs. castor sugar, grated rind of lemon. Make the above into a paste, as in other cakes, touching with the fingers as little as possible always, and roll on a floured board to a sheet $1/2$in. thick. Cut into rings with a pastry-cutter, and the middle of the ring can be cut out with an egg cup. Have ready a frying pan of heated lard. When it just begins to smoke it is boiling. Then at once put in the rings, a few at a time, as they must not touch each other. They will rise and become brown. When brown on one side turn over carefully with a skewer. When done take out and sprinkle with castor sugar. Quickly first, however, put more rings into the fat, and so on until they are all done. They look very pretty indeed, and are delicious. Keep them in a tin to preserve their crispness.

CHOCOLATE CAKE – Cream $1/4$lb. butter with 6ozs. sugar, add three eggs well-beaten, then 6ozs. grated chocolate melted in $3/4$-teacupful warm milk, then add $1/2$lb. flour, with one teaspoonful of baking powder, with a little cinnamon and essence to flavour if liked. Beat well, and put into a tin lined with buttered paper.

LUNCH CAKE – Beat $1/2$lb. butter with $1/2$lb. of castor sugar, add four well-beaten eggs, then $3/4$-cupful of milk, then 1lb. flour in which one teaspoonful of baking powder has been mixed well by degrees. Add $1/4$lb. each of sultanas and currants carefully prepared, and 2ozs. citron, also some flavouring or grated lemon peel. Beat well, and pour into lined tins, and bake carefully in a moderate oven.

HARD ICING: When cold the cake can be iced with the following:– Mix $1/2$lb. icing sugar smoothly with the white of an egg (not beaten), and spread with a knife; put in a cool oven a few minutes to harden, not colour. Bake carefully in a moderate oven.

This is a delicious cake also made without the fruit.

My last recipe is the simplest of all, and yet very dainty. COCOANUT PYRAMIDS. – To $1/4$lb. desiccated cocoanut and $1/4$lb. castor sugar add a small egg, mix together, and with the fingers pinch a small quantity into a cone-shaped heap. Make each little heap the same size, and bake them quickly on a tin in a moderate oven. They ought not to alter in shape in the baking.

I hope that many of the readers of the "Girls' Empire" will provide dainty cakes for many afternoon teas, and that the pleasure of eating them will be areward for the trouble of making them.

How to be Strong.

SPECIAL EXERCISES
WITH THE SANDOW GRIP DUMB-BELL.

PART III.

BEFORE proceeding to describe the exercise (No. 3) which forms this month's work, I find that it is necessary to call your attention to two or three simple rules in what is called hygiene. The first is this. Don't worry! Worry has killed more women than hard work ever will. It is true that there is a natural tendency in the majority of women to worry, and often over trifling things; still, this must be overcome or you will find your health is greatly upset, and the good

resulting from these exercises almost nullified. Take the famous advice of "Punch" to heart – DON'T. The second is this. Take a proportionate physical exercise, according to the amount of mental strain or brain work

EXERCISE 3.

you have to undergo. At night, when you take your exercise, prior to going to bed, never make the excuse that you have had a very fagging day and your brain feels done up. Then is just the time when you need vigorous physical exercise to counterbalance mental strain. On the other hand, I

raise a word of warning against "overdoing it" in any way. Whilst the dumb-bells usually have a reviving effect, it would be ridiculous to attempt to go through the full course of exercises when you are feeling utterly

exhausted. Better far do the exercise half a dozen times than half a score under these conditions. The third rule I want to point out is – always have plenty of fresh air in your bedroom! Many a girl rises from bed in the morning feeling heavy and depressed who would be one of the brightest and merriest of girls if she sleep only with her bedroom window partly open so that the foul air could escape and fresh air take its place. Another hint in this conjunction is – don't have too much drapery hanging about in your room and don't have too much clothes heaped up on the bed. Let the bedclothes be warm but light, and let the sun have free access into your room during the day. By a careful attention to these very simple rules you will find that very beneficial results will be obtained. With these few remarks, let us turn to the exercise (No. 3), which is specially designed to strengthen and develop the muscles of the stomach, &c., as well as the shoulders and back. Lie flat on your back on the carpet, with your hands extended above your head, the dumb-bells firmly grasped in each hand. Raise the body slowly, keeping the arms rigid, and continue the movement of the half-circle until the dumb-bells touch the toes. Return slowly to the original position, and repeat the usual number of times. On the forward motion (toward the feet), exhale the breath, on the return to the floor, inhale the breath. A great point with this and the preceding exercise, is that they should be done slowly, so that the full effect may be attained, and also that the head, neck, shoulders, and arms should all be kept rigid, as if they were all one solid piece.

A Queer Pet.

COSTING nothing to get, nothing to keep, and yet affording endless amusement and interest – "causing," as the street hawkers say, "great fun and roars of laughter" – surely our friend the toad is an ideal pet!

First catch your toad – in which case he will not only cost nothing, but will have all the more value in your eyes. If you cannot do that, fourpence will buy you a beauty – fat, gnarled, bloated, and pobby. But no purchased toad will ever shine in his owner's affections as one that has been pursued and captured in his native fastnesses. Not that he has any fastnesses to speak of, or will afford a very exciting chase to his captor.

Having caught your toad, then — no, don't cook him; cage him. There is no need to go to any expense over this. If you possess a window fernery, put him there, and he will think he has died and gone to Paradise. Otherwise, procure a fair-sized wooden box. If you are handy with tools, fix up a tray to cover the bottom, which can be slid in and out. This will facilitate the occasional cleaning and changing of earth which the cage will require. If you cannot manage the tray, never mind; its absence will only entail a little more labour in the periodical overhauling. Cover the bottom of the box with a fairly thick layer of fresh mould; if you can sow a little birdseed and raise a small green crop to act as carpet, so much the better. Keep the soil and the atmosphere slightly damp, and place an earthenware saucer in one corner, embedding it in the earth and filling it with water, so that Mr. Toad can have a bath when he feels dry or dirty. In another corner place a small flower-pot on its side, also embedded, whither the gentleman can retire into seclusion when modesty or fatigue prompts him. Cut a fair-sized hole in one side of the box, and cover it with perforated zinc, and let the lid of the box be formed by a sliding pane of common-window glass. The box, saucer, pot, and earth you can get for nothing; the perforated zinc will cost you about threepence or fourpence, and the glass about sixpence. So your toad will not ruin you.

Your cage complete, put your toad into his new home, and make friends with him. You will find him an excellent pal; and if you have patience (plenty of it), and tend him carefully, you will find that in time he will get to know you! We speak seriously.

There is a most delightful serio-comic air about a toad which makes him a most fascinating companion at any time — even when he is doing nothing but sit and stare. (Incidentally, you will discover that your new pet does his staring with an eye which is one of the most beautiful things upon God's earth.) But when meal-time comes! His food need cause you no trouble and not a tittle of expense. Flies and beetles of all sorts, cockroaches, small worms, caterpillars, woodlice, butterflies and moths — all come welcome alike to his capacious belly. And you will discover that a toad can eat! Perhaps he is not greedy — but he does like a lot! There can be no difference of opinion about that. He can also fast, can this obliging pet, for weeks on end, if necessary (but don't make it so). In giving him his food, drop the creatures into his cage alive, and watch the result. Clip one wing of any insect which can fly, so as to compel it to walk.

We will suppose our toad to be squatting in one corner (his favourite site), and to be staring hard (his favourite occupation), while his grey-speckled throat bobbles in and out in its customary absurd fashion. Enter a caterpillar from above, apparently out of the sky. It falls with a gentle plop in one corner, where the toad cannot see it. Caterpillar shakes itself together, and starts to walk. Presently walks within view of toad. A sudden jerk of the head shows that toad has seen it, and he stares more vigorously than ever. Caterpillar walks on serenely. Toad raises a thick foreleg, and starts in pursuit — silently, stealthily. Caterpillar continues with a bland smile. Toad creeps up behind; his eyes seem ready to drop out as he edges closer and closer — click! Where is the caterpillar?

The toad's manner of securing his food is well worthy of notice. His tongue is fastened in front, not at the back like ours; and the tip — which lies thus at the back, as it were, of his mouth — is sticky. The toad stalks his prey, as we have described, until within striking distance. Then the ribbon of tongue is thrown out and forward; the sticky tip alights upon, and adheres to, the luckless insect's back, and the latter is flicked back into the toad's mouth, and sent upon a tour of exploration into the latter's unknown interior.

Cosy Corner Chats.

IV. – READING.

By Annie E. Holdsworth.

MY DEAR R. – You need not make any apology for your letter, with its request for advice in regard to your reading.

We must think in order to read, if we are able to read in order to think. And in these days, when of "making many books there is no end," it becomes more than ever necessary to know how and what we are to read. Enterprising publishers have given us libraries of the best hundred books; and, neatly labelled and bound, the masterpieces of the world's literature look at us from their shelves. We, for the most part, look at them on their shelves, and leave them to fame, and, it may be, to posterity.

This is no doubt due to the contradictoriness of human nature, always ready to pass by the good that is near, in order to reach the advantage that is distant. But this paper is not intended for contradictory human nature, neither for those girls who have no thought beyond the correspondence column of the newspaper, nor for those whose reading is limited to the novelette or the society journal.

It is intended, first and solely, for the girl who because she thinks wants to think more.

The awakening of thought should be the chief end of our reading, though other points will come into view in our cruise round the topic.

It may be true that in thought, as in all else, there is nothing new under the sun, but need that affect the minds to whom the great old world unfolds itself as a strange unexpected wonder? Only that man need weep

for a new world who has grasped and made his own all that the old contains.

Just so is it in literature. Even if there is no original thought, if the new philosophy is only the old filtering through the strata of a mod-

ANNIE E. HOLDSWORTH.

ern mind, it should not prevent our reading the ancient truths. These appear and reappear through the ages just because they are truth and must live.

The girl who knows nothing of the thought of

the past will be very poorly equipped for meeting and fighting the problems of the present. Therefore I would say,

READ THE OLD AUTHORS.

Of these a few stand out as high peaks in the mountain range of literature — the writers of the Bible, Plutarch, Homer, Shakespeare, Thomas à Kempis. The girl who knows these with her brain, and with the understanding also, has received a liberal education, though she read no other printed work to the end of her days. She cannot understand the writings of the Bible, Homer and Shakespeare without having a wide knowledge of the literature and history of the past. It may happen, however, that these books, as literature, do not attract a girl. She sees no beauty in the poetry of Job and Isaiah; her imagination cannot people the past. Homer is a dead letter to her, Plutarch's lives are foolish fables. The Shakespearean drama is without form and void.

Be honest in your likings, and be sure that you understand what you like. Literary growth begins in sincerity; and the honest appreciation of a writer, though he be only a third-rate novelist, may be the first awakening of the critical faculty.

But, whatever you read, let the book be only the nucleus of spreading knowledge. Plutarch's Lives read intelligently, with reference to history, contain a whole library of information; Homer awakes a dead nation; Shakespeare is his own reward. And, when reading, do not forget your author; learn what you can of the man; study his times; find out what influences have gone to the shaping of his book. In this way you will do more than familiarise your mind with great thoughts; you will widen your outlook on men and things.

Yes, even at the risk of being misunderstood, I say, read what attracts you most. But I would have you remember that we find in a book what we bring to it; and the person who can find

pleasure in worthless novels, condemns herself as empty and thoughtless.

Here let me whisper a secret to the girl who is wholly and utterly absorbed in the romance of some fictitious heroine. Give up the study of the unreal and study yourself and the life round you.

The most absorbing and beautiful stories are being lived under your eyes, and if you teach yourself to read them you will gain a faculty that will open a world of interest to you.

Do not think I condemn novel reading. See, I put it first under my next head —

READ IN ORDER TO ENJOY LEISURE.

Here the novel is in its right place, and for pure enjoyment nothing is better than a good novel. But it must be good, and not a false picture of life written in bad English and worse taste. The novels of Thackeray, Sir Walter Scott, George Eliot, and Jane Austen can only delight and inform; while among the moderns we have a trio of Scotsmen who have given us the romance of human nature in its most attractive

shape — Robert Louis Stevenson takes us adventuring in many seas; J. M. Barrie and Ian Maclaren show us the pathos and beauty of Scottish village life.

And while you read for enjoyment you will not neglect the poets. Poetry alone may not appeal to all, but poetry in which we find such stories as Tennyson gives us in his "Idylls of the King" and "The Princess," and Longfellow in his "Evangeline" and "The Courtship of Miles Standish," must have a charm for every girl who cares to read. Cowper, as a poet, is, perhaps, out of date, but Cowper, as a writer, has left a volume of letters which for grace and naturalness are unequalled in our literature. One great element in enjoyment is acquisition, the enriching of ourselves; and to secure this you must choose those books that contain stores of knowledge. I wonder if you have read Sir John Lubbock and Darwin; their fairy stories of ants and bees, plants and earthworms. In these books we conquer new worlds; for, while in old authors we find new thoughts — while fiction gives us new friends and travel new countries — science opens out to us a new kingdom. For lighter moods it will be well to take up the great books of the recent past — the "Pilgrim's Progress," Boswell's "Life of Johnson," "Pepys' Diary," Montaigne's "Essays," Goldsmith's "Vicar of Wakefield" — and to live again in the times that have made history for us. In this way we make the past our own, for the literature of any age is the social history of that age, containing the bulk of the thought and feeling and life of the minds that governed it. To know an author is to be conversant with the sympathies and ideals of his times. It is those most strongly affected by the age in which they live who hand on its literature to the world.

The knowledge gained by reading leads me to another point —

READ IN ORDER TO APPRECIATE.

If you read only the empty fiction of the day, how shall you learn the wisdom and thought growing around you? How shall you discriminate between the true and the false? Only the cultured mind is capable of seeing culture. Only the thinker can recognise the thought of the thinker.

We have considered a few of the reasons why we should read, and have thought of some of the best books. Still is left the question of "When is the best time for reading?" To this there is only one answer — Now!

The days will come when your life will be too busy for books, when literature will become an ornamental fringe of leisure, no longer part of the fabric of your everyday life. And even should leisure be extended, as you grow older the keen zest of youth passes, until of books, as of all that is earthly, the soul says, "I have no pleasure in them."

To the girl standing on the threshold of literature, wistfully peering forward, I would give the advice which sums up this article — Read the best books! Read them intelligently! Read them now!

Athletics for Girls.

LAWN TENNIS. – I.

By H. M. Pillans.

 NEVER can the popularity of lawn-tennis, as a game, be disputed. It has remained in favour now for many years, and still holds its own against golf, cycling, and many other forms of amusement, which fashion decrees, from time to time, must be indulged in by all those who wish to be considered up-to-date.

It is true that among the many enthusiasts of the game there are few who obtain any real degree of proficiency, most girls reaching only a moderate standard, beyond which they find it impossible to advance.

Few games, however, can surpass it, providing as it does the combined advantages of healthy exercise for both body and mind, at the same time being an interesting game to watch, and affording much pleasant social intercourse.

The question has often been asked in the tennis world, "Why is the standard of the average girl's play so far below a man's?" Not implying, of course, that one ever expects to see "equality of the sexes" in this respect; but in the case of a game requiring skill rather than brute force, the weaker sex should certainly be able to show to better advantage than at present.

The answers to this problem are many and various. I will first enumerate some of the reasons usually given, afterwards adding my personal opinion as a player of more than ten years'

standing. The chief reasons usually adduced are –

1.   That a girl is not physically strong enough to make a powerful player.

2.   That the sex are naturally unoriginal and incapable of working out the theory of the game for themselves.

3.   That a woman's dress greatly impedes her movements, and handicaps her in more ways than one.

4.   It is also said that a girl cannot run, and on a tennis-court often stands upon her heels, thus rendering it an impossibility to move quickly.

The latter is surely more their misfortune than their fault. A woman has always been accustomed from her childhood to wear more or less high-heeled shoes. In tennis the rules of the games deny her this support, at the same time telling her to stand upon her toes. Observation shows, however, that she usually stands upon her heels, or strains the muscles at the back of her foot, which are unaccustomed to being stretched in this way. Doubtless this is one of the many reasons why a girl are as follows:—

1. I agree that although the average girl is very persevering, she will not apply any theory to the game. She simply clings to the idea that "practice makes perfect"; this I can tell her, from bitter experience, is a fallacy. Unless she is going the right way to work, she may play girl's natural way of playing lawn-tennis is usually the wrong way.

2. Sporting-women are practically a new creation. Until recent years it was never considered necessary for them to use either their brains or their muscles, which consequently have remained undeveloped for

A LAWN TENNIS TOURNAMENT.

tires so easily, because this strain must act indirectly upon the spine, and soon gives a feeling of exhaustion.

My personal opinions for half a century with practically no result. There is always a right and a wrong way to do everything; and unfortunately the generations. Therefore, it is not to be wondered at that the girl of the present day labours under many disadvantages.

3. They are too often handicapped by the problem of £ s. d. Girls and boys should be treated alike in this respect; with the former, however, it usually means an appeal to a parent or guardian, who is often willing to lavish money upon the boys, but grudges every sovereign asked for by a girl. This takes the spirit out of her at the very commencement, for to become a first-class player cannot be considered a cheap amusement.

4. On the vexed subject of dress there is a great deal of nonsense talked. A girl with any common sense never wears a long or heavy skirt for tennis, or, in fact, any garment in which she does not feel perfectly free and comfortable. Although I am an advocate for reform in many ways, I do not like to see dress made a handle for excuses. The faults much more often lie in the girl herself than in her dress. This does not take into account the frivolous individual with an eighteen-inch waist and a large hat who poses upon a tennis-court. Doubtless

her dress considerably impedes her movements; but happily this type of player is now almost as extinct as the dodo. In the matter of shoes, if a girl feels the want of support previously alluded to, and is included to stand upon her heels, it is a good plan to

FIG. 1. -THE OLD-FASHIONED STYLE.

have the shoes made with a half-inch cork elevator fastened inside. The upper leather of the shoes, of course, must be cut proportionately higher to allow for this heel.

Lessons. – On the subject of lessons in lawn-tennis there is much to be said. Not only is it beneficial for a beginner to receive tuition from a competent teacher, but undoubtedly it is an absolute necessity for all those who desire to become good players. Almost without exception instruction is needed before proficiency can be acquired in any accomplishment or sport. Therefore why not in lawn-tennis, which is acknowledged to be one of the most difficult of ball games? True, there are few professionals who teach the art, those at Queen's Club, West Kensington, FitzWilliam Club, Dublin, and at the covered court, Llandudno, being the only ones of any note, but if the demand for their services became greater, it would doubtless create a supply.

In these days when one hears so much about distressed ladies, I feel confident that if a few would turn their attention to "training the young idea," they would find it a remunerative and healthy employment. I seriously recommend it to their notice.

Verbal instructions, with practical demonstrations, are always much easier to grasp than book theories. Many girls, also, are too bashful to have tennis lessons from a man.

A book, recently published, entitled "Lessons in Lawn-Tennis," by Eustace M. Miles, however, gives a great deal of useful information, with diagrams of good positions and angles, and would be a great help to many. But it must not be supposed that people can be made good players all at once. The process requires great patience and perseverance, the would-be reformer remembering that it is much harder to unlearn a bad habit than to learn a good one. This recalls the incident of an impetuous young Irishman taking lessons from a professional. On being asked how he was progressing, he replied —

"I seem to have unlearnt all the strokes I used to score by, and still find myself unable to hit the ball as I am told. Therefore my last state is considerably worse than my first."

Like many other deluded mortals, he thought the strokes looked easy, and imagined he would be able to put the whole system into practice in two days.

This same professional mortally wounded the feelings of a poor damsel by telling her she did not possess a back-hand stroke. Poor girl! To be told this after many years of patient but blind practice was indeed mortifying. I notice, however, that this same lady is since considered to have improved her games more than fifteen, and she now plays in the matches for her county, besides blossoming as a first-class player in the open tournaments.

Positions. — The following remarks, let it be clearly understood, are in no way original, but simply a repetition of "counsel's opinion."

In recent years it will be seen that the general style of play has been altered considerably. Fig. 1 shows an example of the old-fashioned laborious style. This meant hitting the ball when quite near the ground, the striker standing directly facing the net. Needless to say, this was a lifting and most tiring stroke. Note the grip of the racket, with the wrist facing outwards, the position of the body, the right foot being foremost; also note where the ball touches the racket. The striker is evidently looking towards the spot where the ball is intended to go. Now look at Fig. 2; imagine this player standing in exactly the same place; compare the grip and position of the racket, the angle of the body, which is turned nearly sideways to the net, left foot foremost, the eyes being fixed on the ball, which is almost at the top of the bounce. Fig. 3 (p. 217) shows the position of the racket as it should appear at the finish of the stroke. The ball is now travelling across the net, into the far corner of the opposite court.

Advice to Beginners. — Stand in front of a cheval-glass, holding the illustration in your left hand, so that you see the reflection of it in the glass. (This enables you to see the figure facing the same way as yourself.) First put yourself into the position of Fig. 1, afterwards into the position of Fig 2, and remember that the one is up-to-date, and the other is out of date.

The Fore-hand Stroke. – Again take up your position in front of a long glass, standing in the attitude of Fig. 2. Describe a semicircle (slightly behind) with the racket, so as to get a swing, at the same time bringing the weight of the body on to the front foot at the moment the racket touches the (imaginary) ball, bending the front knee a little, and carrying on the racket now until it is in the position of Fig. 3 (p. 217).

After the stroke is finished, bring the feet back level with each other, and stand straight facing the net, weight equally divided upon both feet, the body leaning slightly forward, the racket horizontal, supported near the head with the left hand.

The Back-hand Stroke. – Fig. 4 (p. 218) shows the old style of a back-hand stroke. Notice the ball has already passed the striker,

consequently all power over it has been lost. The head of the racket is very much below the level of the wrist, the left (instead of the right) foot being in front.

It will be found that this stroke requires a superhuman amount of strength, and even then seldom reaches the top of the net. Fig. 5 (p. 218) shows the correct back-hand stroke – the weight of the body well on the front foot; right foot foremost, knee slightly bent, the head of the racket slightly above the level of the wrist, which is rigid as soon as it comes in contact with the ball.

The Volley. – This is a most difficult stroke for the average girl-player. The chief features to remember are, to always strike the ball when it is in front of you, and in the case of an overhead volley, reach well up to the ball (as if you were anxious to hit it as soon as possible). Turn a little to the side when the ball is coming, whether right or left. The pace depends much on the swing of the body. Point the toes of the front foot, and bend the knee slightly, bringing the

weight of the body from the back foot on to the front, as the racket meets the ball.

It is curious to note how many men break down at an over-head volley if they have to step back for it. It is so much easier to move forward a step than to move back one. Anyone who can carry out all these instructions has become a good player. It is easier said than done, and, as previously stated, it is much simpler to have the positions shown you than to acquire them from printed instructions.

General Instructions. –

1. Every ball must be hit when in front of the striker.

2. Always rest on your toes, and stand where you think the ball would fall at the second bounce.

3. Every stroke should be deliberate. The racket should meet the ball (never jerk it). The pace is regulated by the correct bodyswing in conjunction with the arms.

4. Keep your eyes always fixed on the ball.

5. The racket (when not in action) should be held in a horizontal position,

supported by the left hand; never head downwards.

6. Cultivate independence, always remembering your own handicap; score in games and points. Umpires are not immaculate!

The Service. – It is important to cultivate a good service. Whether it is an over-hand or an under-hand stroke, the chief object in view should be to impart the maximum of strength, expending only the minimum of force.

The over-hand service is undoubtedly the best style, and all should try to acquire it, but it is well also to cultivate an under-hand stroke, as variation has many advantages. For instance, in a mixed double, the man is often puzzled by a cut, low-bouncing, under-hand service. On the other hand, the girl often fails to make a good return from an over-hand stroke. Therefore suit your service to your opponent, and try to place it as much as possible.

Many girls have no idea where to stand to receive a service. The rule, as previously stated, is quite simple.

Always stand where you think the ball would fall at the second bounce. Example. – When waiting to receive a man's really hard service, your position should be about three feet outside the back line; but if it should be a screwed or twisted service, it will

FIG. 2. THE NEW STYLE.

sometimes be necessary to stand almost parallel with the ball as it bounces, as if prepared to take it back-handed, but in reality it will bound right over to your fore-hand. It must be a very twisted service, however, that bounces at

right angles instead of straight ahead. If you carefully watch your opponent's racket, you can always see whether it will be a cut or straight service.

Cutting the Ball. – This is a very usual fault with girls, and is a most difficult habit to get out of. Some say it is incurable when every ball is cut. This, of course, is not the case, but considerable patience and perseverance will be required before the fault can be eradicated. It is caused by the wrist being turned back at the moment the ball is hit; this again turns the face of the racket slightly upwards, and the ball is sliced rather than hit. The great disadvantage of this stroke is that it takes the pace off the ball and allows your opponent plenty of time to get to it, however well placed. On occasions, of course, it is useful to be able to cut a ball "short" over the net, but as a rule the habit is to be discouraged.

Imitation is the Highest Form of Flattery. – The next suggestion for the struggling amateur is to go as a spectator to a large "Open Tournament." Select a court where a first-class player (with notably good style) is in action. Set yourself to watch, not the game, but his positions, attitudes, on what strokes he succeeds best, where he fails, and the reason why. I am assuming that a man is taken for the model, because a girl's dress and other loose draperies tend to distract the eye. Now keep your eyes fixed on the model, watch closely how high he throws the ball before serving, the swing of the racket preparatory to striking the ball; then again watch the fore-hand stroke off the ground, where the model stands, the position of the feet, the angle and swing of the body, the position of the racket when the stroke is finished, likewise the back-hand, the volley, and in fact all the different strokes. This will provide you a much more instructive afternoon than commenting on the personal attractions and beauty of the players, "Handsome is as handsome does!"

Having made mental notes of all these positions, retire to a private court, get some charitable friend to send you easy balls, and see how far you can carry out the lessons you have learnt.

Health and Training. — Health and strength are undoubtedly the backbone of all sport. Without it none can ever hope to succeed; therefore it is a most important item in the career of a tennis player. Those who already possess these necessary and excellent attributes are to be envied, but the usual cry is, "I am not strong enough." To which my reply is, "Then make yourself strong enough," which is quite possible, providing you have not a weak heart or infirmities of that nature.

(To be continued.)

The Biography of a Beaver.

A BROAD, flat tail came down on the water with a whack that sent the echoes flying back and forth across the pond, and its owner ducked his head, arched his back, and dived to the bottom. It was a very curious tail, for besides being so oddly paddle-shaped it was covered with what looked like scales, but were really sections and indentations of hard, horny, blackish-grey skin. Except its owner's relations, there was no one else in all the animal kingdom who had one like it. But the strangest thing about it was the many different ways in which he used it. Just now it was his rudder — and a very good rudder, too.

In a moment, his little brown head reappeared, and he and his brothers and sisters went chasing each other round and round the pond, ducking and diving and splashing, raising such a commotion that they sent the ripples washing all along the grassy shores, and having the jolliest kind of a time. It isn't the usual thing for young beavers to be out in broad daylight, but all this happened in the good old days before the railways came, when Northern Michigan was less infested with men than it is now.

When the youngsters wanted a change they climbed up on to a log, and nudged and hunched each other, poking their noses into one another's fat little sides, and each trying to shove his brother or sister back into the water. By and by they scrambled out on the bank, and then, when their fur had dripped a little, they set to work to comb it. Up they sat on their hind legs and tail — the tail was a stool now, you see — and scratched their heads and shoulders with the long brown claws of their small, black, hairy hands. Then the hind feet came up one at a time, and combed and stroked their sides till the moisture was gone and the fur was soft and smooth and glossy as velvet. After that they had to have another romp. They were not half as graceful on land as they had been in the water. In fact they were not graceful at all. And the way they stood around on their hind legs, and shuffled, and pranced, and wheeled like baby hippopotami, and slapped the ground with their tails, was one of the funniest sights in the heart of the woods. And the funniest and liveliest of them all was the one who owned that tail — the tail which, when I last saw it, was lying on the ground in front of Charlie Roop's shack. He was the one whom I shall call the Beaver — with a big B.

But even young beavers will sometimes grow tired of play, and at last they all lay down on the grass in the warm, quiet sunshine of the autumn afternoon. The wind had gone to sleep, the pond glittered like steel in its bed of grassy beaver-meadow, the friendly woods stood guard all around, the enemy was far away, and it was a very good time for five furry little babies to take a nap.

The city in which the tail first made its appearance was a very ancient one, and may have been the oldest town on the North American continent. Nobody knows when the first stick was laid in the dam that changed a small natural pond into a large artificial one, and thus opened the way for further municipal improvements; but it was probably centuries ago, and for all we can tell it may have been thousands of years back in the past. Generation after generation of beavers had worked on that dam, building it a little higher and a little higher, a little longer and a little longer, year after year; and raising their lodges as the pond rose around them. Theirs was a maritime city, for most of its streets were of water, like those of Venice; rich cargoes of food-stuffs came floating to its very doors, and they themselves were navigators from their earliest youth, and took to the water as naturally as ducks or Englishmen. They

were lumbermen too, and when the timber was all cut from along the shores of the pond they dug canals across the low, level, marshy ground, back to the higher land where the birch and the poplar still grew, and floated the branches and the smaller logs down the artificial waterways. And there were land roads, as well as canals, for here and there narrow trails crossed the swamp, showing where generations of busy workers had passed back and forth between the felled tree and the water's edge. Streets, canals, public works, dwellings, commerce, lumbering, rich stores laid up for the winter — what more do you want to constitute a city, even if the houses are few in number, and the population somewhat smaller than that of London or New York?

There was a time, not very long before the Beaver was born, when for a few years, the city was deserted. The trappers had swept through the country, and the citizens' skulls had been hung up on the bushes, while their skins went to the great London fur market. Few were left alive, and those few were driven from their homes and scattered through the woods. The trappers decided that the ground was worked out, and most of them pushed on to the north and west in search of regions not yet depopulated. Then, one by one, the beavers came back to their old haunts. The broken dam was repaired; new lodges were built, and new beavers born in them; and again the ancient town was alive with the play of the babies and the labours of the civil engineers. Not as populous, perhaps, as it had once been, but alive, and busy, and happy. And so it was when our Beaver came into the world.

The first year of his life was an easy one, especially the winter, when there was little for anyone to do except to eat, to sleep, and now and then to fish for the roots of the yellow water-lily in the soft mud at the bottom of the pond. During that season he probably accomplished more than his parents did, for if he could not toil he could at least grow. Of course they may have been growing, too, but it was less noticeable in them

than in him. Not only was he increasing in size and weight, but he was storing up strength and strenuousness for the work that lay before him. It would take much muscle to force those long yellow teeth of his through the hard, tough flesh of the maple or the birch or the poplar. It would take vigour and push and enterprise to roll the heavy billets of wood over the grass-tufts to the edge of the water. And, most of all, it would take strength and nerve and determination to tear himself away from a steel trap and leave a foot behind. So it was well for the youngster that for a time he had nothing to do but grow.

Spring came at last, and many of the male beavers prepared to leave home for a while. The ladies seemed to prefer not to be bothered by the presence of men-folk during the earliest infancy of the children; so the men, probably nothing loath, took advantage of the opportunity to see something of the world, wandering by night up and down the streams, and hiding by day in burrows under the

banks. For a time they enjoyed it, but as the summer dragged by, they came straggling home one after another. The new babies who had arrived in their absence had passed the most troublesome age, and it was time to begin work again. The dam and the lodges needed repairs, and there was much food to be gathered and laid up for the coming winter.

Now, on a dark autumn night, behold the young Beaver toiling with might and main. His parents have felled a tree, and it is his business to help them cut up the best portions and carry them home. He gnaws off a small branch, seizes the butt end between his teeth, swings it over his shoulder, and makes for the water, keeping his head twisted around to the right or left so that the end of the branch may trail on the ground behind him. Sometimes he even rises on his hind legs, and walks almost upright, with his broad, strong tail for a prop to keep him from tipping over backward if his load happens to catch on something. Arrived at the canal or at the edge of the pond, he jumps in and swims for town, still carrying the branch over his shoulder, and finally leaves it on the growing pile in front of his father's lodge. Or, perhaps the stick is too large and too heavy to be carried in such a way. In that case it must be cut into short billets and rolled, as a cant-hook man

And sometimes the billet rolls down into a hollow, and then it is very hard to get it out again. He works like a beaver, and pushes and shoves and toils with tremendous energy, but I am afraid that more than one choice stick never reaches the water.

These were his first

his jaws together with a savage nip that left a deep gash in the side of the tree. A second nip deepened the gash, and gave it more of a downward slant, and two or three more carried it still farther into the tough wood. Then he would choose a new spot a little farther down, and start a second

HE SEEMED TO THINK IT WAS OF IMMENSE IMPORTANCE TO GET THE
JOB DONE AS QUICKLY AS POSSIBLE.

rolls a log down on a skid-way. Only the Beaver has no cant-hook to help him, and no skidway, either. All he can do is to push with all his might, and there are so many, many grass-tufts and little hillocks in the way!

tasks. Later on he learned to fell trees himself. Standing up on his hind legs and tail, with his hands braced against the trunk, he would hold his head sidewise, open his mouth wide, set his teeth against the bark, and bring

gash, which was made to slant up towards the first. And when he thought that they were both deep enough he would set his teeth firmly in the wood between them, and pull and jerk and twist at it until he had wrenched out a chip — a chip perhaps two inches long, and from an eighth to a quarter of an inch thick. He would make bigger ones when he grew to be bigger himself, but you mustn't expect too much at first. Chip after chip was torn out in this way, and gradually he would work around the tree until he had completely encircled it. Then the groove was made deeper and deeper, and after a while it would have to be broadened so that he could get his head farther into it. He seemed to think it was of immense importance to get the job done as quickly as possible, for he worked away with tremendous energy and eagerness, as if felling that tree was the only thing in the world that was worth doing. Once in a while he would pause for a moment to feel it with his hands, and to glance up at the top to see whether it was getting ready to fall, and several times he stopped long enough to take a refreshing dip in the pond; but he always hurried back, and pitched in again harder than ever. In fact, he sometimes went at it so impetuously that he slipped and

rolled over on his back. Little by little he dug away the tree's flesh until there was nothing left but its heart, and at last it began to crack and rend. The Beaver jumped aside to get out of the way, and hundreds and hundreds of small, tender branches, and delicious little twigs and buds came crashing down where he could cut them off and eat them or carry them away at his leisure.

And so the citizens laboured, and their labour brought its rich reward, and everybody was busy and contented, and life was decidedly worth living.

But one black November night our hero's father, the wisest old beaver in all the town, went out to his work and never came home again. A trapper had found the rebuilt city — a scientific trapper who had studied his profession for years, and who knew just how to go to work. He kept away from the lodges as long as he could, so as not to frighten anyone; and before he set a single trap, he looked the ground over very carefully, located the different trails that ran back from the water's edge toward the tim-

ber, visited the stumps of the felled trees, and paid particular attention to the tooth-marks on the chips. No two beavers leave marks that are exactly alike. The teeth of one are flatter or rounder than those of another, while a third has large or small nicks in the edges of his yellow chisels; and each tooth leaves its own peculiar signature behind it. By noting all these things the trapper concluded that a particular runway in the wet, grassy margin of the pond was the one by which a certain old beaver always left the water in going to his night's labour. That beaver, he decided, would best be the first taken, for he was probably the head of a family, and an elderly person of much wisdom and experience; and if one of his children should be caught first he might become alarmed, and take the lead in a general exodus.

So the trapper set a heavy double-spring trap in the edge of the water at the foot of the runway, and covered it with a thin sheet of moss. And that night, as the old beaver came swimming up to the shore, he put his

foot down where he should-
n't, and two steel jaws flew
up and clasped him around
the thigh. He had felt that
grip before. Was not half of
his right hand gone, and
three toes from his left hind
foot? But this was a far more
serious matter than either of
those adventures. It was not
a hand that was caught this
time, nor yet a toe, or toes.
It was his right hind leg,
wellup towards his body,
and the strongest beaver
that ever lived could not
have pulled himself free.
Now, when a beaver is
frightened, he, of course,
makes for deep water.
There, he thinks, no enemy
can follow him; and what is
more, it is the highway to
his lodge, and to the burrow
that he has hollowed in the
bank for a refuge in case his
house should be attacked.
So this beaver turned and
jumped back into the water
the way he had come; but,
alas! he took his enemy with
him. The heavy trap
dragged him to the bottom
like a stone, and the short
chain fastened to a stake
kept him from going very
far towards home. For a few
minutes he struggled with
all his might, and the soft

black mud rose about him in
inky clouds. Then he quieted down and lay very, very
still; and the next day the
trapper came along and
pulled him out by the chain.

Something else happened
the same night. Another
wise old beaver, the head
man of another lodge, was
killed by a falling tree. He
ought to have known better
than to let such a thing happen. I really don't see how
he could have been so careless. But the best of us will
make mistakes at times, and
any pitcher may go once too
often to the well. I suppose
that he had felled hundreds
of trees and bushes, big and
little, in the course of his
life, and he had never yet
met with an accident; but
this time he thought he
would take one more bite
after the tree had really
begun to fall. So he thrust
his head again into the nar-
rowing notch, and the wood-
en jaws closed upon him
with a nip that was worse
than his own. He tried to
draw back, but it was too
late, his skull crashed in, and
his life went out like a candle.

And so, in a few hours,
the city lost two of its best
citizens — the very two

whom it could least afford to
lose. If they had been spared
they might perhaps have
known enough to scent the
coming danger, and to lead
their families and neigh-
bours away from the doomed
town, deeper into the heart
of the wilderness. As it was,
the trapper had things all his
own way, and by working
carefully and cautiously he
added skin after skin to his
store of beaver-pelts. I
haven't time to tell you of all
the different ways in which
he set his traps, nor can we
stop to talk of the various
baits that he used from cas-
toreum to fresh sticks of
birch or willow, or of those
other traps, still more artful-
ly arranged, which had no
bait at all, but were cunningly
hidden where the poor
beavers would be almost
certain to step into them
before they saw them. After
all, it was his awful success
that mattered, rather than
the way in which he
achieved it. Our friend's
mother was one of the next
to go, and the way his brothers and sisters disappeared
one after another was a
thing to break one's heart.

One night the Beaver
himself came swimming

down the pond, homeward bound, and as he dived and approached the submarine entrance of the lodge he noticed some stakes driven into the mud — stakes that had never been there before. They seemed to form two rows, one on each side of his course, but as there was room enough for him to pass between them he swam straight ahead without stopping. His hands had no webs between the fingers and were of little use in swimming, so he had folded them back against his body; but his big feet were working like the wheels of a twin-screw steamer, and he was forging along at a great rate. Suddenly halfway down the lines of stakes, his breast touched the pan of a steel trap, and the jaws flew up quick as a wink and strong as a vice. Fortunately, there was nothing that they could take hold of. They struck him so hard that they lifted him bodily upwards, but they caught only a few hairs.

A week later he was really caught by his right hand, and met with one of the most thrilling adventures of his life. Oh, but that was a glorious night!

Dark as a pocket, no wind, thick black clouds overhead, and the rain coming down in a steady, steady drizzle — just the kind of a night that the Beavers love. Often of late the Beaver had noticed an unpleasant odour along the shores, an odour that frightened him and made him very uneasy, but to-night the rain had washed it all away, and the woods smelled as sweet and clean as if God had just made them over new. And on this night, of all others, the Beaver put his hand squarely into a steel trap.

He was in a shallow portion of the pond, and the chain was too short for him to reach water deep enough to drown him; but now a new danger appeared, for there on the low, mossy bank was an otter, glaring at him through the darkness. Beaver-meat makes a very acceptable meal for an otter, and the Beaver knew it.

The full story of that night, with all its details of fear and suffering and pain will never be written; and probably it is as well that it should not be. But I can give you a few of the facts, if you care to hear them.

The Beaver soon found that he was out of the otter's reach, and with his fears relieved on that point he set to work to free himself from the trap. Round and round he twisted, till there came a little snap, and the bone of his arm broke short off in the steel jaws. Then for a long, long time he pulled and pulled with all his might, and at last the tough skin was rent apart, and the muscles and sinews were torn out by the roots. His right hand was gone, and he was so weak and faint that it seemed as if all the strength and life of his whole body had gone with it. No matter. He was free, and he swam away to the nearest burrow and lay down to rest. The otter tried to do the same, but he was caught by the thick of his thigh, and his case was a hopeless one. Next day, the trapper found him alive, but very meek and quiet, worn out with fear and useless struggles. In the other trap were a beaver's hand and some long threads of flesh and sinews that must once have reached well up into the shoulder.

(to be continued.)

Athletics for Girls.

FENCING. – I.

BY AGNES HOOD.

OF all the very many sports, pastimes, and physical exercises in which women are now taking their share, fencing is the one which is most excellently suited to them. It is the least elaborate of them all. It does not need a mile or two of common, as does golf, nor woods and fields, horse and hounds, as do shooting or hunting. It does not compel ungraceful attitudes as does tennis, nor lead to apathy and ill-temper, as does croquet. It is within the reach of a woman of small fortune; it is, indeed, the exercise most suited to anyone to whom economy is a necessity, for an ordinary, well-lighted room or a back garden will give space enough, and a small outlay will cover the cost of the outfit.

It is the surest road to grace and health. Sloth cannot exist near a foil, or, if it does, she who suffers from it had better throw her weapon away, for Providence has not intended her to be a fencer. True, ill-temper may arise from an unfair thrust or a hit that seems unjustly awarded; but the skilful fencer can guard against the first and revenge herself for the second, and when the bout is over shake hands with her adversary with an unclouded heart.

If women knew the beauties and subtleties of fencing, its excitement and delights, they would show more eagerness to cultivate it. Unfortunately, they allow themselves to be discouraged by the difficulties that must always surround all but the most elementary arts. Sometimes, too, a woman throws herself enthusiastically into the task of learning the use of the foil for a few months; then something else takes her fancy, the lessons are neglected, and a promising fencer is lost. Patience is wanted, for I admit there are difficulties to be overcome, and a determination to overcome them will be needed by the girl who resolves to become a fencer. But the necessity for the practice of these virtues should increase the value of the exercise, and give the student the satisfaction of feeling that, while she is developing her physical powers, her moral qualities are also profiting.

I do not insist on these moral advantages, however, for too steady a reflection on them might destroy the light-heartedness that should fill the fencer when her fingers close tightly round the grip. I merely mention them to satisfy those careful persons who consider that any but the simplest forms of exercise are waste of time. There are other reasons why fencing appeals especially to women. They naturally wish it to be understood that they can do everything just as well as men, if they choose to try. Men are curiously slow to believe this truth, and point to several sports in which women are toiling painfully behind them. In fencing alone does a women stand on a perfect equality with man, for there strength alone is a disadvantage; quickness and lightness are wanted, and of these women have an equal share.

All women have suffered at some time from a man's kind forbearance in a mutual pastime, and from the knowledge that he is allowing her to get the better of him as he would

a child. In fencing she need not suffer from so humiliating a thought. If she is generous she may give him quarter, but she is not forced to accept it. There are few women who would not appreciate such an opportunity.

Another quality may

THE SALUTE.

induce a few to study fencing who are inclined to shrink from its difficulties. It is picturesque; the dress may easily be made to add to the wearer's charms. There is also an air of romance which clings about it, and which, though

it is quite unjustified, adds to its fascinations.

But having noted a few of its attractions — there are many more which want of space alone prevents me from mentioning — it is only just to name one drawback.

Now, having shown the advantages and disadvantages of fencing, I will try to give a slight idea of what lies before the future mistress of fence, if she has made up her mind to seriously apply herself to it, and to persevere in spite of the fits of discouragement which will attack her during the first few months of her study.

Let her understand at once that no book can ever teach her fencing; she must have personal teaching.

There are two schools of fencing – the French and the violent exercise, for it calls for great agility; but it lacks the delicacy of the French school.

In the Italian the foil is held in a cramped position; the fingers have little play, the body is bent forward; and many Italian fencers sors, both male and female, they have seldom had the early training which a Frenchman has enjoyed, and they have not the instinct for the foil which seems to be hereditary in the French.

Now, having found your teacher, the next thing is

THE LUNGE.

Italian. An adaptation of the latter is taught in the British Army, and is possibly useful for fighting purposes, though French authorities deny it even that virtue, and prefer their own more scientific method. The Italian style is good if one wants have adopted tricks which are ingenious and surprising, but are not the highest form of the art. For women the French style is undoubtedly the better, and Frenchmen make the best fencers; for though there are first-class English profes- to get your outfit – the illustrations show the usual form of costume. The jacket may be made of cloth, leather, or canvas. It is padded, and more on the right side than the left, for the right is the one exposed to the opponent's foil. The sleeve may be padded too, if the material is rather thin. Great are should be taken that the chest and side are well protected, for very serious consequences may follow if the body is not thoroughly guarded against blows. The padded jacket is but it is really better to get used to it at once, and the most skilful master might lose control of his foil for an instant. A pad is sometimes worn over a blouse instead of a jacket, and it is quite as useful, but not, I think, so comfortable. It is possible white is compulsory, as black gives its wearer an unfair advantage. The skirt should not reach far below the knee, as the position of the feet and ankles is important, and must be visible to the master. The wire mask can be bought at any

RIPOSTE.

uncomfortable at first, but one soon gets used to it. A little temporary discomfort is better than a possible injury.

Some masters dispense with the jacket for the first few lessons, as they are careful not to touch their pupils; to make either at home, and an old coat is an excellent foundation for a fencing jacket, as it will only want padding and covering. In the illustrations the fencers are in black, but for loose play a white jacket should be worn, and in competitions gymnastic appliance shop; like the jacket, it is an acquired taste. Any heelless rubber shoes may be worn, but if you wish to be very correct there are shoes which may be bought of most French masters, of Paris make, with leather soles, and curiously shaped.

Gauntlets, too, are a matter of personal choice; some fencers wear them large and padded, others are content with a thick, ordinary dogskin glove. Finally, the foils must be acquired, the most important part of your outfit. They cost from half-a-guinea to a guinea the pair. No. 5 blades are generally used. The best blades are marked with the name of Coulaix, and should be able to be bent almost into a circle. A good foil will balance if you hold it just below the hilt; the grip (the part between the hilt and the pommel) should be long and thin, and the pommel not too large.

Now you are ready for your first lesson, and that will be one on position. It sounds simple, but several weeks will pass before it seems to you. The photographs of the preliminary position of the guard and of the lunge, show what you must strive for. In the first te knees are well braced, the feet are at right angles, the head and body are erect, the arms hold the foil easily above the head.

To come on guard form that first position the right foot is advanced twice its length, and kept on a line with the heel of the left, the knees are well bent and in a line with the ankles. The left arm is lowered until the elbow is level with the shoulder, and the hand is allowed to fall easily. The body is balanced easily on both legs, the shoulders are thrown back, and slightly turned to the right. The right hand holds the foil softly but firmly, the thumb lies along the upper side of the grip, scarcely touching the hilt, and each finger has its work in controlling the weapon, but gently and without any harshness or heaviness. There are several faults that may disfigure this position of guard. The toes and the knees may turn inwards, the weight of the body be thrown too much on one leg; the head may be thrust forward, or the hand may be convulsively clutching the foil. But the careful student will soon learn to avoid these snares, and be ready for the lunge.

To lunge, the left leg is straightened and the right advanced, the wrist being slightly raised the instant the point of the foil touches your adversary's breast. To lunge well you must use every inch of your limbs, the right arm and the left leg must be stretched to their utmost. The left foot must rest solidly on the ground, and resist the tendency it will feel to rise — either at the heel or at the side. A bad lunge is when these points are disregarded, or when the balance of the body is disturbed, or any part of it stiff and awkward. To recover guard, the left knee is bent, which brings the right foot back to its old place, and the right arm is drawn back until the elbow just brushes the hip; it must never be pressed against the body.

These movements are simpler than the description of them sounds, and after a little practice they will become mechanical, and arms and legs will move together naturally, without any necessity for their owner to trouble about them, though she should never grow careless and allow herself to fall back into a bad position.

(To be continued.)

Girls' Pets and How to Manage Them.

FOWLS.

COMPARATIVELY few girls have the advantage of a meadow adjoining their parents' house, so that their fowls can be "allowed out," and it is, therefore, to the less favoured ones that we shall give our advice as to the accommodation which must be made before stocking.

We will presume that the intending fowl-keeper lives in a city suburb or a large country town, where a small garden is usually attached to the house. If you have only a small back-yard, do not keep poultry; it would be cruelty to attempt it.

THE HOUSE AND RUN.

Fix upon a spot in the garden well sheltered from the north and east winds, while, at the same time, plenty of sunshine falls upon it. If there is a brick wall running along the garden at the required spot, so much the better. Timber is cheap enough, and can be bought at any builder's yard.

First erect the frame-work for the house in a substantial manner; for the accommodation of six to eight fowls this should be about five feet high, six feet wide and from eight to ten feet long. Next nail on your weather-boarding to the sides, ends, and roof, not forgetting, however, to leave a hole with a sliding cover for the fowls to get through into the run. A pane of glass also can be let into the front, so that the house may be well lighted. A hole can be made in the roof for ventilating purposes. Into this hole a piece of zinc piping can be inserted with a cowl at the top to prevent the rain dripping into the house; also a piece of perforated zinc should form part of the door. As a same time as you tar the weather-boarding of the house. A roof treated in this manner will keep thoroughly waterproof for a long time, though it is as well to give it a thin coating of tar and a sprinkling of or gravel, if the ground is dry; or better still, obtain some old brick rubbish, break it up, level and harden it, and cover it with not too moist Portland cement. It will be easier to sweep out, and, besides, very little

By kind permission of]   ASSEL COCKEREL AND PULLET.   ["The Stockkeeper."

waterproof covering to the roof, nothing can better the ordinary tarred felting. Lay this on evenly, and tack it to the boards. You can then place another coating of tar over it, and sprinkle the surface with fine sand at the sand every spring.

Well limewash the inside of the house to ensure health among your fowls; this should be done at least twice a year. The floor may be earth, well beaten down; over this place cinder ashes more expense.

The perches must be about three inches in width, with rounded edges, so that the birds can securely grip them when roosting. Do not place these too high up, or the fowls will receive injury when flying down from them.

The nests recommended by a poultry-keeper in a large way are the ordinary half-bushel baskets used by market-gardeners. He condemns the boxes placed all in a row on a shelf, as being liable to swarm with vermin. To prevent this, first place a good layer of cinder ashes in the bottom of the nests with some flowers of sulphur sprinkled over them; then lay down straw to the depth of several inches. Keep a china egg in each nest; these you can obtain for a penny apiece.

The next thing to consider is the run. This should be twice as long as the house; but the larger the space you give the fowls the better for them. Use wire netting for the front, fastened with small staples. The height should be quite five feet, so that it will prevent the fowls flying over into your own or your neighbours' gardens. Three-quarter-inch mesh is to be preferred if you cover in the top, as it will keep out the voracious sparrows, for they are nimble thieves.

In a list to hand from an ordinary retail dealer's, we note that the price quoted per yard for this sized mesh is 6^1/2d., the width being forty-eight inches. Some of this, and some measuring twelve inches wide at 2d. per yard, will give you the required height – five feet.

The run should be covered over at the top to afford a protection from the rain, and also to keep the ground from getting damp and sloppy, otherwise your stock will become afflicted with rheumatism.

To the girl whose father places plenty of pocket-money at her disposal, we recommend the purchase of one of Spratt's ready-made portable poultry-houses, with open run, diagrams of which we are enabled, by their courtesy, to give.

This house is marked No. 304 in their catalogue, and is described as being made of well-seasoned yellow deal, grooved and tongued, painted three coats outside, lime-whited inside, roof covered with galvanised corrugated iron lined with wood, door for cleansing, also door for collecting eggs, fitted with locks, raised floor for shelter, glazed ventilator, nest boxes, perches, &c., complete. The run is made of wrought iron, painted, and covered with one-inch mesh galvanised netting. This house is made in sections, and fitted together with bolts and nuts.

Place plenty of sharp grit and sand in the run to assist the fowls' digestive organs, with a large piece or two of lime or chalk, as this helps in the formation of the egg-shells.

You will require a large earthenware or tin vessel for the drinking water, which should be soft if you can obtain it; also a dust bath.

STOCK.

Half-a-dozen pullets are quite enough for a small run. A cock bird is not needed where you intend only to go in for producing eggs for consumption.

We recently asked a well-known poultry-keeper which kind of fowl he would recommend a girl to purchase above all others for laying purposes. He unhesitatingly replied that, in his opinion, Black Minorcas were the very best. You can take this advice, if you care to, and choose this variety for your stock. They never want to "sit," and the egg they lay is large.

The Hamburgh is also good, both the silver and gold spangled or pencilled, and the black; the latter is the largest of the three varieties. The eggs are large, the birds non-sitters. Favourite fowls, too, with small keepers are Leghorns, Langshans, and Andalusians. All three are prolific layers. Mr. Cook, the well-known fancier at Orpington, Kent, in giving advice about laying varieties of fowls, says: "Leghorns, Minorcas, Andalusians, Spanish, Hamburghs, and all non-sitting varieties, will often lay all through the summer without having a rest."

For a good sitting hen, in our opinion, nothing beats the Dorking. Of course, there are many other varieties of fowls you can choose from, but most of them require a free range, and do not thrive well when shut up.

Never keep your hens till they get old. They should be killed off at the end of the second laying season. They will then be an acceptable addition to the dinner table; older birds eat very tough, as, perhaps, you have experienced.

FOODS.

For hard foods give maize, oats, barley, wheat, buckwheat, together with a little rice. Now and again a little dari or hemp – just enough for one meal by way of a change, and to act as a stimulant. A very good poultry mixture can be purchased from some corn chandlers, while others sell a very indifferent article.

For soft foods give barley meal, pollard and bran, maize meal, or oatmeal. These must be mixed with scalding water, and made thick enough for a stick or spoon to stand upright in it. You can include any scraps from the table, and boiled potato parings, cabbage leaves, or greens – in fact, vegetable roots of all kinds will do. Well boil them, however, before stirring in with the food.

Spratt's Criussel is recommended where the fowls do not obtain any insect food, such as earth-worms, slugs, &c. This must be first soaked in hot water, then mixed with the meal.

In the winter time some keepers chop up boiled lights or liver, and place in the mashes a little pepper or a few chillies; these have a stimulating effect, but we cannot recommend the practice, as it is unnatural for the birds.

Fresh green stuff may be thrown down in the run for the fowls to pick over, such as chickweed, groundsel, grass, lettuce, cabbage leaves, &c.; but never leave it there to become stale and offensive. Remove it every morning and throw down a fresh supply.

Get up every day as early as you can, and attend to your fowls, for they are early risers. Mix the mash for the first meal, and scatter it about the run, seeing, however, that each fowl obtains an equal share as far as is possible. Give a few handfuls of grain at mid-day, and a more plentiful supply for the evening meal. Regulate the quantity by the appetites of the fowls, but take care not to over-feed them.

DISEASES.

Most complaints, as we have said before in our previous articles, are to be avoided by studying the laws of health. Insist on strict cleanliness, warm and comfortable quarters, regularity in feeding, and a plentiful supply of fresh water. But it is as well you should know what to do in the more simple cases of diseases.

Diarrhoea is the most common ailment, and should

Cod-liver oil and quinine capsules are recommended; but the pills sold in boxes by some dealers have proved efficacious in several cases which have come under our notice.

Gapes is a very distressing disease, caused through a parasite becoming attached to the wind-pipe. A cure is to be effected by

not natural to give anything to assist fowls through their moult; they are bound to get over that; it is the course of nature. Be that as it may, we should assist nature as much as possible. We do not expect birds to lay at all during the winter in the wild or natural state, but if they are fed and managed properly they will produce eggs all

POULTRY-HOUSE.

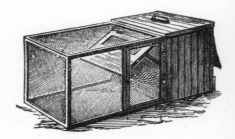

SITTING-BOX, WITH RUN.

be treated by administering a dose of warm castor oil, with three or four drops of laudanum in it. Also another cure is cold boiled milk, with a little raw flour placed in it after it has become cool. Feed on dry rice. This complaint is generally caused by allowing stale vegetable refuse to accumulate in the run.

Croup most affects fowls during the winter months.

submitting the affected fowl to the fumes of carbolic acid, which destroys the worm. But great care should be taken while treating in this way, or the fowl may be suffocated.

Moulting is quite a natural process, and occurs every autumn.

The editor of the "Poultry Journal," writing on the subject of moulting, says: "Some keepers say it is

through the cold weather. We have domesticated fowls for our own use, and we must treat them accordingly."

The same writer recommends that Cook's Poultry Powders should be given during this period, one teaspoonful four times a week will be sufficient for eight birds, and this should be mixed with the soft food. Bone meal also will be helpful, and should be mixed in the same way.

Rheumatism and cramp may be cured by rubbing the legs and feet with Elliman's Embrocation. As these complaints are traceable to the damp conditions of the house and run, remove the cause.

Before closing this article, there is one thing the fowl-keeper is often heard to ask, and that is, "How can I rear stock?" There is no reason, if you have plenty of room, why you should not raise at least one brood during the summer months.

First of all, you must make sure that the hen you propose to use is a good sitter. Test her qualities, say for twenty-four hours on the china eggs, previously preparing the nest by placing in it some damp garden soil well beaten down, or a fair-sized square of turf, greenside downwards. On the top of this sprinkle some flowers of sulphur, or a little insect powder, and then place in fresh hay. The eggs for sitting, say eleven or twelve in number, can be procured from some reliable source. These you should have at hand when you pay your visit to ascertain if the hen is sitting close. Remove the dummies if you are satisfied as to the hen's capabilities, and put the eggs underneath her, disturbing her as little as possible.

Look at the hen regularly once a day, and lift her off to feed. The food should consist of good maize or barley, with a little rice, and plenty of fresh drinking water; and do not forget to place a dust-bath within her reach, and give a piece or two of green stuff to regulate the bowels. She should never be off longer than fifteen minutes for the first twelve days, after that from twenty minutes to half an hour.

When twenty days have passed, you should look out for the chirrup of the chicks, but do not remove anything until the twenty-second day. Then you can lift the hen off, and find out how many chicks she has hatched. The chicks, too, will be strong, and will be able to peck about. For the first twenty-four hours they will not require food of any kind. After this time give them some hard-boiled eggs cut up small, and a few fine groats or some coarse oatmeal mixed to a paste, with milk for their drink.

If you can place your hen and her little family in a close wired-in coop, so that they can be kept well together. If you have a small grass lawn the chicks will thrive wonderfully well if you can place your coop there. In lieu of this a gravelly walk will do.

Beware of strange cats prowling about watching their opportunity to pounce upon any of your chicks when they stray beyond the mother's immediate protection. Rats also will cause your brood to decrease in numbers very rapidly if they can get to them.

HER TWENTY-FIRST BIRTHDAY.

By Olive Birrell.

"WHAT an extremely difficult position!" said an old lady dressed in deep mourning with a long pair of tortoiseshell eyeglasses. "I don't know what to do."

"We must find a situation for the girl without a week's delay, "said another much younger lady." That's the only thing we can do."

"Consider for five minutes," said the first speaker. "Let us look at the matter in all its bearings. Here is a girl nearly one-and-twenty, who has been educated for nothing in particular by no one in particular. She dresses well, dances well, plays the piano rather badly, and writes a good hand. This is the sum total of her attainments. Ever since she was seven years old her uncle and aunt have brought her up in habits of luxury. I always said that Gertrude was deeply to blame for doing so; but my advice is never followed. Then they are taken away, both Gertrude and her husband, and the unfortunate girl is cast on the world."

"Gertrude had nothing to leave," said the younger lady; "and, of course, Katie was her relation, her only sister's only child. I cannot blame my brother George. He was kind to the girl while she lived with him; a niece by marriage could not rank with his own nephews and nieces. It would be grotesquely unfair if she did. We must now break the news to Katie that no mention is made of her in the will. That is the first unpleasant duty we have to perform. And the next is even worse. We must advertise for a situation as nursery governess."

"I heard," said the old lady, in a very low voice, "that one of General Morton's sons had paid Katie marked attentions."

"He did; but he went to South Africa, and — well, one never knows. His family did not like the idea of such a connection at any time, and it would be utterly distasteful now. Katie's position has never been sufficiently defined."

The two ladies were sitting in a beautiful old library, with oak panels and many fine pictures. From the window a wide stretch of lawn could be seen, and, far off, the windings of a river. Lady Knight, the elder of the two, had sharp, handsome features; the younger one, Mrs. Johnson, was small, fair, and pale. They had been staying in the house ever since the death of its owner, ten days before, and longed to escape to more cheerful places. Legal business detained them, and the necessity of making some arrangement for Katie Berners, this superfluous girl whom the George Knights had adopted, and then forgotten to provide for.

While they were still discussing the dilemma, each anxious not to betray her whole thoughts, the door opened very gently, and a tall, slender girl came towards them. Her eyelids were red with much crying, and her colour lay in patches on a white face. A conviction that Gilbert Morton had only to see her at that moment to have his liking dispelled seized both ladies with appalling suddenness.

"I have brought you this advertisement to look at," she said. "It sounds as if it would just do for me. A nurse-companion to an old lady. I have been nurse-companion for the last two years, and I understand the duties perfectly. They are the only ones I do understand. All the people who want their children taught expect more than I could promise. Three languages, most of them, besides music and mathematics."

"Let me see," said Lady Knight. 'Well-educated young woman. Good references. Nurse-companion to an old lady; no menial duties. Salary £30.' It sounds good. Of course, you can have the highest references."

"I think you should accept at once," said Mrs. Johnson. "Could we not wire? But I forgot; this lady will want to see you."

"I ought to see her," suggested Katie timidly. "She may be a very terrible person."

"Oh, that is not likely!" cried both friends at once.

"Young people must put up with a good deal in their first situations," said Lady Knight.

"Go to town this afternoon and have a personal interview," added Mrs. Johnson. "Don't lose an hour. I shouldn't if I were you."

They displayed such feverish eagerness to settle the matter that Katie understood the tenour of their thoughts as well as if they had spoken openly. Outside the library she stood still, considering her next step. There was a train to London at 1.20. She must get that. No time for lunch. This elderly lady who wanted a companion lived near Victoria, and the journey was not difficult.

"If she is as stony as a Gorgon I must still accept her situation," thought the poor girl. "Lady Knight and Mrs. Johnson hate the sound of my footsteps.

Gilbert will soon come home; that's my only consolation. And when he does!"

"What are you thinking of, Katie?" asked a kind voice.

It was Denham Lee, the vicar's son, who had been Katie's friend and compan-

heard the story of the possible situation with deep interest.

"You must not go alone,"

a treasure she is going to secure."

"Suppose she is very formidable," said Katie.

THERE HE WAS, TALL AND PALE, HIS LEFT ARM IN A SLING, AND HIS YOUNGEST SISTER, MAUD WALKING BESIDE HIM.

ion ever since she ran about in pinafores. His good-natured face looked at her very tenderly now, and he

he said. "That's not to be thought of. I will come with you, and wait outside while the old lady discovers what

"Or suppose she has a horrid temper. I can't ask references for her character, though she can collect half a dozen about mine."

The old lady proved a great invalid. Katie must work for her from morning till night, but she would not sleep in her room. Someone else would do that. This point was greatly dwelt upon, also the fact that she might have every other Sunday evening to herself.

"Only for a few months," she said cheerily to Denham, when she met him again in the street. It will give me time to look round and search for something more suitable. Deep in her heart lay a conviction that Gilbert Morton would claim the fulfilment of her promise long before six months were ended. He had asked her to wait for him, and she had said she would, and they had exchanged many letters during the early part of his stay in Africa. Latterly the post had brought his less frequently, but this was a circumstance little to be marvelled at, since the fortunes of war had led him into very remote places. Poor Katie's heart sank when she thought of the risks her lover encountered. She worked very hard for her invalid mistress during those tedious months of waiting, wrote regularly to Gilbert, received only two postcards in reply, and grew each day thinner, paler and more weary. Denham was an immense support. He used to come every Sunday and take her out to taste such fresh air as London provides. Sometimes they went into Hyde Park, now and then he persuaded her to venture a little further afield. She confided the story of her engagement to him, explaining that Mrs. Morton, Gilbert's mother, knew, but no one else in the world. It was to be a secret from the whole family until the war was ended and Gilbert's desperate peril a tale of the past. Denham used to listen with patience, though his heart often burned as he did so. Katie was too preoccupied to notice that the answers she received were sometimes rather wide of the mark. She never dreamt of placing him on the same pedestal as Gilbert. His affection seemed a part of everyday life; just as certain and as natural as the rising of the sun.

"Do you remember the first birthday present you ever gave me?" she asked once. "I am sure you don't. It was a little doll in a red frock. I have that doll still. I shall always keep her."

"I think I had rather you tossed her away," said Denham.

"I was seven years old when you gave her to me," continued Katie, "and I shall be twenty-one to-morrow. What a long stretch of time! You have been wonderfully good to me all these years. When Gilbert comes back I mean to tell him about the Sunday evenings and your many kindnesses. He will be so grateful."

Denham winced at the mention of Gilbert's possible gratitude. He did not like to be the first to tell Katie that her lover's detachment of the Yeomanry had already come back. It seemed that the tidings had not reached her. Ill news flies fast. If Gilbert had been killed or left behind very dangerously wounded, she must have heard. But neither of these things had happened.

The next day Mrs. Evelyn, Katie's invalid

charge, sent her to New Bond-street on an errand. She felt rather dejected, having hoped for a letter which did not come. It was a good thing that incessant work kept her so busy she had no leisure to brood. From seven in the morning till ten at night her hands, feet, and head were expected to be always occupied. Everyone looked so smart in New Bond-Street that her old black frock seemed to put on an extra hue of brown by force of contrast. Her face looked shabby as well as the dress, or she thought it did, when a sudden turn brought her before a looking-glass hanging in a shop window.

"See, Gilbert, isn't it pretty?"

A girl's voice spoke, and Katie, flushing into sudden excitement because the familiar name sounded so sweet, glanced in that direction. There he was, tall and pale, his left arm in a sling, and his youngest sister, Maud, walking beside him. Katie's heart gave a wild leap.

"Why, Katie," cried Maud. "How very odd we should meet like this! Look, Gilbert, here is Katie Berners. Speak to mother, Katie."

Then Katie turned, and saw an open carriage in which Mrs. Morton was sitting with a very distinguished-looking girl at her side. How perfectly apparelled they all were, and what a miserable, second-rate creature she seemed, with her mended gloves and cheap sailor hat! Gilbert blushed crimson as he bowed, but said not a word. Maud sprang into the carriage, he followed, and away they drove, while Katie returned home, having blundered her commissions sadly. What could it all mean?

That afternoon Mrs. Morton called, and begged half-an-hour's respite from work for Katie.

"I have something to say, my dear child," she began.

"I know already," replied Katie. " At least, I think I do."

"Gilbert has come back severely wounded. He has been so ill until last week that he could not write letters nor be disturbed about business."

"Am I 'business'?" thought Katie.

"He is conscious of having behaved very foolishly," continued his mother. "I always considered you both very wilful. If you remember, I said so at the beginning. The truth is that he now feels he has made a great mistake — a very sad mistake, Katie. And the sooner we recognise it is a mistake, the less pain for every one of us. He has written, but I promised him I would bring the letter with my own hand and add my regrets to his own. I am sorry any son of mine should have laid himself open to blame in such a manner. You have both acted like a pair of inconsiderate children, but Gilbert is five years older than you, and the chief fault rests with him."

"Don't give me the letter," said Katie, turning very white. "I had rather not read it. I can imagine what is inside. I will go to Mrs. Evelyn now. That is her bell. Goodbye, and please burn that letter."

All the rest of the day she felt very sick and faint and miserable, but bedtime was the worst. Oh, how the poor child cried when she had a moment's leisure in which to realise her position! Two days after Denham called, and was greatly distressed to see her so changed.

"Don't ask me any questions," she said. "Some day I shall feel as I used to feel, but just now it is all blackness and confusion. Oh, there's the bell! Thank you, Denham, for coming. No one can help me."

The summer was very hot, and she grew each week more languid and spiritless. It seemed to her during those months that the whole world had been unkind. Uncle George had forgotten her future, though he always used to call her "the Busy Bee," because she darted about on his errands. Aunt Gertrude was not to blame. She would have felt very sorry had she foreseen this trouble. Katie knew she would. But Lady Knight and Mrs. Johnson were cruel, and Mrs. Morton was intensely selfish, thinking only of her own children. Poor Katie! Her mood became cynical, and her face began to wear a hard,

disappointed look. Denham saw it quite well, and manufactured five hundred excuses.

He was working hard at his profession as a lawyer, but never failed to come to Mrs. Evelyn's house to see Katie. One day she told him she had been dismissed.

"I am not strong enough," she said. "Mrs. Evelyn's doctor has warned the family I shall be ill on their hands unless they get rid of me. So I am going away. I don't know what I shall do. No other place will be much easier."

"I have brought a note for you from Aunt Jane," said Denham. "She has been in Italy all this time, and only heard where you were last week."

Aunt Jane was a relation of the Knights, whom most people dreaded, and some people liked. She had no connection with Denham, but he called her aunt because he happened to be one of those who liked her.

"She has asked me to stay in her house," said Katie, reading the letter. "Well, it is very kind, and I shall go, of course. She is certain to scold me, but I am

too tired to care if she does. I can rest in an armchair, and read some of the old story books again."

Aunt Jane did not scold Katie when she looked at her white cheeks. The next month seemed like a long, delicious Sunday to the poor, tired girl; and, whenever she spoke of going away, Jane told her in a very indignant voice to "stay where she was and be satisfied."

Katie confided some of her troubles at last — a sure sign that they were beginning to heal.

"I have left off caring about Gilbert," she said. "I think I never cared after that terrible birthday when I met him in the street. But I went on being unhappy. I wonder why I did."

"I wonder, too," said Aunt Jane grimly.

"It is dreadful to have to leave off believing in anyone," said Katie; "and I used to believe in him absolutely."

"Far more dreadful to go on believing until it is too late," cried Aunt Jane. "I have no patience with you, Katie. Instead of crying, you ought to have gone down on your knees in New Bond-street and given thanks for your deliverance. I would in your place."

"On your twenty-first birthday?" said Katie, doubtfully.

"Yes, on my twenty-first birthday!"

Aunt Jane snapped off a piece of cotton with her scissors very fiercely, as if she wished it had been Gilbert's head.

"When another man, worth a hundred Gilbert Mortons, has been working for you, and showing forbearance and sympathy you didn't deserve! I am ashamed of you, Katie; I am, indeed."

"Denham!" cried Katie. "Do you mean Denham? Of course, he is worth hundreds of others. But what has that to do with me?"

"Are you quite blind?" said Aunt Jane, laying down her work .

Kate blushed scarlet. "I have known for a long time past how foolish I used to be. Yes, Aunt Jane, I know it so well myself there's no need to tell me! But because I was so foolish once, I shall never be foolish in the same way again. As soon as I am able to find another situation I mean to work. If happiness comes I shall be very glad, but I never mean to sit down and wait for it!"

"That's the right spirit," cried Aunt Jane. "I won't argue any longer. But I think, and I always shall think, that your twenty-first birthday brought you extraordinary good fortune!"

The roses came back to Katie's cheeks, and she and Aunt Jane were so happy together they quite dreaded parting. One day Mrs. Johnson wrote to tell them she needed a nursery governess for her three youngest children at a salary of twenty-five pounds, and would be willing to try Katie.

"I won't interfere," said Aunt Jane. "I never do interfere or give my opinion without being asked. But I know those three children are imps of wickedness, and have worn out six governesses in three months and a half. Still, I say nothing. It is always my principle to avoid interfering."

Someone else, not Aunt Jane, heard of this situation in time, and did interfere to much purpose. When Katie saw her old friend, after he left her, she said — "You were right. My twenty-first birthday brought me extraordinarily good fortune, and I am the happiest girl in the world."

Cosy Corner Chats.

V. – THE OBSERVANCE OF SUNDAY.

MY DEAR MARGARET: I am not surprised that soon after your return to your home you are met by what we call "the Sunday problem." It is beginning to be a difficult one everywhere; and it appears to me that all educated women must address themselves to it, to find a working theory for its solution which shall be tenable in the face of all the varying practices that have place in city and country.

First, we must acknowledge that one of the steps which mark progress in civilisation is a recognition of the necessity that one day in seven shall be different in its relation to life from the other six days. This, of course, is entirely apart from the religious sanction for such difference. All human experience goes to show the importance of such a break. Even a railroad engine, I am told, lives longer by being allowed to rest on certain specified days. Surely it is true of a man or a woman. This being granted, it will be evident that the occupations and interests of Sunday should be, as far as possible, a distinct change from those of other days. All our methods of conducting business help to make this possible. The closing of the shops, the banks, the mills, and the great offices, determines a change in the current of thought for hundreds of thousands of people. Hence they must call upon either the lower or the higher part of their nature to take possession of the so-called "day of rest." That is, the occupations of Sunday, taken as a whole, must be either nobler than those of other days or less noble. The higher call is, I think, the one to which every sensitive spirit ought to answer heartily and cheerfully. Apart from any religious command, then, everybody ought to make of Sunday a better day, one richer in high experience, freer from trivial cares, less frivolous, less self-indulgent than the other days.

We must not stop here, however. We may say, in talking of Sunday, "I ought to do so and so, regardless of the religious requirement." In point of fact, however, one cannot be regardless of the religious requirement.

Strictly speaking, Sunday commemorates the day on which Christ rose from the dead. The early Church, to be sure, transferred to Sunday a large number of the observances of the Jewish Sabbath. This was done for convenience, and also because many of these observances were built upon a sound philosophy of life. Having a just conception, however, of what the Church ought to require in regard to the keeping of Sunday, we must remember to add to the Old Testament commandments, Christ's practices on the Jewish Sabbath, and then to add to those two elements the recollection that the day is primarily to the Christian Church the commemoration of the Resurrection – a weekly memorial of the great fact which Easter celebrates. Now, Christ's example and His few words about the Sabbath, you will remember. Most notable among them, perhaps, is the saying: "The Sabbath was made for man, and not man for the Sabbath." This goes to the root of the whole matter, and from it we come to the statement of the most fundamental thing we know about the ideal Sunday. Any plan for conduct on that day must be based on a habit of mind, and not on a code of action: it must be judged not by what we do, but by how we think and feel.

In determining my own conduct for that day, I have found that, in order that the observance of Sunday should show results in character, at least four elements should enter into it. The first is undoubtedly physical rest. That was the idea of the day laid down in Genesis, and it is the idea which should govern the whole world to-day. We need not cheapen the value of rest or apologise for it. The human spirit needs rest for the body, and the conduct on Sunday which excludes rest can never become fruitful of good results. It is right that the hard-working clerk and the equally hard-working merchant should have an hour or two of additional sleep and a sense of freedom from toil on Sunday.

To fill the day to the brim with various religious duties is to misconceive its initial purpose. We are bound to have some rest ourselves on Sunday, and we are still more bound to give it to any others whose lives we help to influence. There are at least two great classes of people who seem, by the demands of civilisation, to be cut off from the possibility of obtaining rest on Sunday. These are domestic servants and men employed by the great transportation companies. For each the day is often the hardest of the week. In many and many a household the Sunday dinner is the most elaborate of the week, and usually there are many guests. It appears to me that you and I, and people like us, ought to address ourselves, at least so far as our own personal example and influence can extend toward lightening the labours of these people. I am never happy unless my servants have an easier day on Sunday than on other days, and a certain number of hours of absolute freedom in which they may take advantage of the change in the current of thought and action which is so essential to me. The question of the transportation companies is more difficult, and all that I can do in the matter is not to join the crowd which doubles the labour of the motor-man and the car-conductor on Sunday.

The second element which I would bring into every Sunday is that there should be some act corresponding ever so faintly to what Christ did when on that day he healed the man with the withered hand. To do something for somebody in need is of all human acts the most gracious. To live for days without such an act means to grow harder and colder, less human. Of all the days in the week, Sunday should be the one full of compassion

The third element which I would put into my Sunday should be some period of solitude, to be spent in "just thinking." Out of all the busy whirl of life one hour should be caught somehow on Sunday which shall be given to reflection. The power of continuous reflection should be one of the marks of the educated woman. Without it, we are still children. We must not be content with single moments of insight which make motive and ideal clear,

as in a lightning flash. To have the ability to hold steadily and to study closely the motives of our conduct is to possess a strong safeguard against the assaults of sudden temptation. Such ability is to be acquired only by practice, and no circumstance is so favourable for it as the outward peace of the Lord's Day.

Finally, my last element of Sunday conduct shall be worship. For myself, this shall always be in church. I know many people claim to find God's own temple in the woods and fields; but I notice that people who do this seldom seem really to worship in that temple. The man who goes to worship on the links, armed with a bag of golf clubs, never especially impresses me with his sincerity. Just here I may say how I view the whole matter of Sunday golf. I am always pleading for the best for Sunday. Now, if the best of which any given man is capable is represented by a game, whether of skill or of chance, let him by all means play the game. Meanwhile we may be very sorry for the temperament that is so shallow. I can understand

how a man of few resources, of no taste for books, of little love for nature, of small experience in friendship, can find himself on Sunday drawn to the pleasant excitement of driving a small white ball over a field, and can really believe that he is a much-abused man if he is not allowed to do so. But how a man who has the freedom of the whole world of art, nature, humanity, and who once hears the call of Sunday for the best there is in him, can choose to give the day to golf, is to me a mystery. Personally, I find nothing so useful in solving the great problems of life as to lose myself in the crowd of men and women that are all trying to lift their hearts to god, whether in prayer or in music, or in the great sacraments of the Church. The whole spiritual history of the world clusters about public worship. I am not ready to ignore it or to abandon it for gatherings of a less serious nature.

So into my Sunday is to go some rest, some act of beneficence, some reflection, some worship. Dignified by these, the day cannot be wanting in result. With these as the foundation, many practical questions which arise in regard to the life of the home and of society will settle themselves. Shall I talk about some of them with you? In the first place, then, what shall be done about throwing open the doors of the home for a large number of guests on Sunday? I think the day a day for friendship and for the strengthening of the family tie. It is not the day for mere acquaintance, for idle gossip, or for uneasy chatter. The men and women that are asked to cross my threshold on that day shall be of the best. My little circle shall be drawn a bit closer than on other days. Everything that is flippant shall be excluded. This does not mean, of course, that the day is to be gloomy or lonely. It is not to be so, but rich in the noblest of human relations.

What shall we read on Sunday? First, the best of which we are capable; second, not the books which are concerned with our Monday morning task. For example, if I were to teach "Pilgrim's Progress" on Monday morning, I would not read it on Sunday afternoon, since my thoughts must inevitably be burdened with plans for Monday morning's classroom. I think the principle of change quite as important as that of selection.

Shall we have a different rule for Sunday for different classes of people? Surely. The best way of spending Sunday for the tired shop-girl that stands behind the counter all day long must be different from that of the young woman who has a ride every morning, a drive every afternoon and an abundance of fresh air and exercise the whole week through. The habit of mind, not the code of action, is to be our motto. A true philosophy of life does not ignore personal differences, but takes them into account completely and fundamentally.

Rightly used, Sunday ought to bring to us all a much-needed poise and calm, a clearer vision of the proportion of things. There will be in it nothing hard or cold or iron-bound, but everything will be spontaneous, happy, peaceful; and by such a method we ought to get out of it all the best that there was in the old Puritan Sunday and everything that is good in the greater modern freedom.

How to be Strong.

PART IV.

MEDICAL testimony proves the value of these health exercises, in the statement that "the woman who studies her body's welfare can get through twice the amount of work that can be accomplished by the woman of fashion, with unnatural compression of the body, distorting the figure, and giving rise to constant indigestion. Taking little or no exercise, her skin is unable to perform its work. Speedily her complexion becomes sallow, and loses all its freshness and vigour, whilst the woman who, recognising that good health and a sound, strong body are the best of God's gifts, seeks to use and develop her body to the best advantage, retains a freshness of bloom and beauty on her cheek that old age cannot steal."

One of the cardinal points which should not be forgotten is to always hold you head up when walking, and to breathe through the

EXERCISE 4.

nostrils, taking deep breaths. One of the saddest sights to be seen every day in the City of London is the hundreds of young girls and women with head bent, chest contracted, and shoulders bent and round, hurrying to and fro to their work, no doubt of such a kind that little or no exercise occurs during the rest of the day. It is quite safe to predict that in ten years' time more than one-half of these will be mere physical wrecks. As one writer has recently put it: "It is like the invigorating freshness of sea breezes after being pent up in a London fog to meet a woman with a pliable figure that is always charming to the eye with its beauty of line."

The exercise (No. 4) for this month is one of the most beneficial known. Its main feature is chest muscle development and lung expansion pure and simple, in addition to very materially assisting in producing an erect figure. If you have been in the habit of bending your head forward a good deal, it will make your neck ache at first, but who cares as long as the end in view is attained! The method of exercise is as follows:— stand erect, with your hands and arms stretched horizontally out in front of you, the muscles being tensioned by a firm grip of the dumb-bells. Your toes should be slightly turned out. Keeping the arms in an horizontal position, and holding the head back, bring the arms back straight out from and level with the shoulder, at the same time inhaling a deep breath and slightly raising yourself on your toes. When fully expanded, drop back on your heels, bringing your hands to your sides, and exhaling the air from your lungs. Continue this operation about 20 times. After the first month you will be simply astonished to find that you have increased your chest development nearly one inch, probably more, and that your muscles are no longer flabby but firm and hard, capable of three times the exertion as when you commenced these exercises, with much less fatigue.

A very useful way of performing this exercise is to count one (inhale), two (exhale), and so on throughout the whole.

Athletics for Girls.

HOCKEY. – II.

"PASSING" is not the mere hitting of the ball and getting rid of it as soon as possible without an object in view. Passing means "the transferring of the ball from one player to another on the same side when the person receiving the ball is in a more advantageous position than the striker." Before passing make certain to whom you intend sending it.

Do not hesitate, but make up your mind at once. The game is played so quickly that there is no time to wait and consider. "She who hesitates is lost."

A good individual player is, of course, useful, but if such a player plays for herself alone, and does not rely on the assistance of the other members of the team, she more often than not seriously jeopardises the success of the side, and the team would be more successful with a less selfish player. Selfish is perhaps a hard term to use, but one has no hesitation in saying that lack of combination is due to selfishness, and selfishness alone. After this somewhat lengthy, but at the same time important, digression, we will now pass on to the forwards.

By far the most difficult

and important post is held by the "centre." Upon her rests the whole combination of the front rank. She is in fact the pivot upon which the other forwards act. She must be quick on foot, quick with stick, and, above everything else, unselfish.

SO HIGH BUT YET NO HIGHER.

Centre forward (this also applies to the other four forwards) should never be out of her place; that is about midway between the two touch-lines. She must be a good and quick shot at goal, and able to give and take passes from either wing with equal certainty and precision. In passing to the wings, much judgment must be used. If passing to the outside player, the pass should be hard, and a yard or so in front of the player passed to. If passing to the inside wings, the pass would naturally not be so hard, owing to the closer proximity of the would-be receiver.

When approaching goal, "centre" should not pass too much to the outside wings, but rather to the inside players, and for this reason, that the insides are nearer to the shooting circle. Of course, there are occasions when a judicious pass to the outside is a good move. Take the following case. The centre and two inside forwards are close on to the circle, and are seriously hampered by the opposing halves. So hampered are they that they are unable to get a clear shot at goal. By sending the ball straight out to the wing, the defence is to a certain extent drawn away from the centre, and if the outside player returns the ball hard and without delay, the chances are very much in favour of either the centre or the insides being in a more favourable position, and not so closely marked as they were previous to the pass to the outside wing.

Outside right has per-

haps the easiest position of the whole five. In addition to the fact that all her strokes are made from right to left, she is often — more often than not — left quite unguarded, the opposing half being in nine cases out of ten engaged in watching the inside wing, and trying to intercept an intended pass. Let us assume that outside right has obtained possession of the ball and has got clear away. Whilst running, let her note the positions of the other forwards, and, having reached the "25 flag," she must at once drive the ball hard into the centre, and thus give the centre or inside wings an opportunity of

AN ILLEGAL STROKE! STICKS!

A FANCY SHOT—PASSING
BETWEEN THE FEET.

getting nearer the mystic circle.

Outside right must keep to her proper position, *i.e.*, on the touchline, or within a foot or so of it. Either with hand, stick, or foot she must at all costs prevent the ball from going into touch, and above everything else, must be ever on the alert and ready to run and take any passes that may come her way.

The latter remarks as to position, alertness, and saving, also refer to the outside on the left wing. Her position is not an easy one to fill. In order to pass the ball back into the centre, it is necessary either to stop the

ball dead before striking it (this, however, wastes time), or else she must learn to hit whilst running at full speed. To do this your left shoulder must be brought well forward and plenty of right wrist power brought into play.

To the two outside wings does not often fall the pleasure of scoring goals, but they must remember that it is often by their work on the wing and final pass to one of the inside forwards that the goal has been obtained.

As often as not, the actual goal-getter has done not a tithe of the work that has led up to a goal being scored. She certainly gets praise for her final shot, but spectators who under-

NO TIME WASTED.

stand the game know full well to whom praise should also be given.

Inside right and inside left have practically the same duties to perform. Each acts as a centre between the real centre of

REACHING OUT WITH ONE HAND.

the forward rank and the outside wing. Like all the other forwards, she must be quick both in giving and taking passes, and a clear and hard shot at goal.

Now as to a few general remarks that apply to all players, whether backs or forwards. Do not use your hand in fielding the ball more often than you can help. Time is only wasted, and if playing on a good level ground with a true surface, it is almost, if not quite, as easy to field the ball with your stick as with your hand. In hitting, be careful to avoid raising the stick about your shoulder.

You can hit quite as hard if you use your wrists. A quick turn of the wrist will send the ball as far as is needed, and there is no danger of your being penalised for raising the stick too high. A big and long hit is not made with one's body and by swinging your arms frantically over your head. As in tennis one uses one's wrists for hitting hard, so one must do the same when a hockey stick is the weapon, and not a racquet. As much as possible use both hands for holding your stick. You have thereby a much firmer hold, and are not as likely to have it knocked from your grasp as if you were using one hand only. There are occasions, however, when one-handed play is not only a necessity but also an advantage. This, however, should be done sparingly and with judgment. By reaching out with one hand you naturally have a longer reach, and may be able to get the ball away from an opponent who is too far off to reach with both hands. Again, should you stop the ball with your left hand while grasping your stick with your right, you can at once bring your stick into play without having to transfer your left hand again to the handle. As a general rule, however, use two hands.

In conclusion, remember, to be successful at the game you must be quick both in thought and action. Do not hesitate; make up your mind at once, and act upon it.

Daisy's Mistake.

By P. H. Hadfield.

NOW I am free — free to work or play, to do just as I like, just when I like, and just how I like," exclaimed Daisy Brown to her friend and companion Ruth Grant. "I have finished school at last. Once for all I have done with regular hours and constant work. Now I am free — free to work or play, to do just as I like, just when I like and how I like."

Ruth smiled to see her friend's eagerness to be free. She could not quite understand the feeling which prompted Daisy's outburst of joy. They had both been at school together and members of the same class. They had learned the same lessons and had been taught by the same teachers. Yet she had always felt perfectly free, while Daisy had regarded herself as entirely at the command of others.

"Then how do you mean to use your freedom?" asked Ruth. "Have you made any plans?"

"What a stupid you are, Ruth, to ask such a foolish question," cried Daisy. "People do not have plans when they are free to do as they like. I'm tired of working out plans. Do you think that I am going to be the slave of a bit of paper?"

"I do not see where the slavery comes in," said Ruth. "If you make a plan for yourself to do something you want to do, is not that all the freedom you want?"

"Of course not, if you have to carry out your plan. Oh, Ruth! You are such a goose to think it can be. Why I might make a plan to-day and think that it was just lovely, and to-morrow or the next day I might hate it. Plans are as bad as chains, they bind you down fast. You can't get away from them, even for a day. No, no, Ruth; no plans for me, if you please. Remember, I'm free now to do as I like, not once, but always."

So on the following day Daisy began to enjoy the

holiday, which she seemed to think was to last for ever. Like many boys and girls, she had never looked on work of some kind as necessary to happiness. She had made a great mistake in mixing up two things — work itself, and obeying the command of another person. At school she had to obey her teachers, who decided everything for her. They set the lessons, chose the subjects, said when she must do them, and so on. This was so irksome that Daisy thought the fault was in the work, when it was in herself. She did not exactly want to be idle, but she wanted to have her own way. To her the most glorious thing in the world was a day without a plan.

No one found fault with Daisy when she came downstairs at nine o'clock on the first morning. Breakfast was at eight, for her father had to be at business at nine, and the house had to be regulated to suit him. Her mother only laughed when her big girl, as she called Daisy, made her appearance so much behind the rest, and she at once waited on her and gave her a nice breakfast.

"What are you going to do now, Daisy?" asked her mother, when the girl had finished her morning meal.

"Oh, nothing," said Daisy, "just nothing at all. Now that I have done with all regular work I want to feel as free as the wind, which blows just where it likes, and you never know where it will blow next."

Mrs. Brown looked up with a comical smile on her face. She had once felt something like that, and she knew what I meant. So she simply replied, "Just as you like, my dear. Blow where you like, only don't forget to blow somewhere."

Getting up from the table, Daisy put on her hat and sauntered out into the garden, leaving her mother to cook the dinner and do the housework, assisted by an active maid of about Daisy's age.

Without a care for the present or a thought for the future, Daisy proceeded to "take it easy," and, having pulled a rose for her hair and picked a handful of ripe strawberries, she sat down on a garden seat to enjoy them.

"Oh, it is delightful to do nothing," she said to her mother, who had come into the garden to gather some fruit to make into a pie.

"I don't quite know how to do nothing," said her mother, "but I must say that I am glad when I have nothing to do. For then I know that everything is done and I can rest a bit. Tired people can enjoy a real rest, but idle people don't enjoy anything."

"That's just it, mother," said Daisy. "I am tired, as tired as I can be. I have been learning lessons so long, and doing constant work every day, that I shall never want to learn another lesson or do anything regularly again."

"No doubt you feel like that just now," said her mother, "but whether you wish it or not you have still another lesson to learn."

"Oh, mother," cried Daisy, "don't let me begin learning again — I'm sick of lessons. I feel as if I shall never again want to open a lesson book."

"That won't make any difference," said her mother. "The lesson you yet have to learn will teach itself without any books. You need not trouble yourself about it. Just go on doing nothing, my dear, I have no doubt that all will come right in the end."

Saying this, Mrs. Brown hurried away with her dish of fruit and left Daisy to wonder what the lesson could be.

When Mr. Brown came in to dinner, he said to Daisy:

"Well, my little woman, what have you been doing with yourself?"

"Nothing – just nothing, father," said Daisy, "and it is so nice."

"Is it?" replied her father. "You'll soon get tired of that."

"Tired of doing nothing?" exclaimed Daisy. "How can you be tired with nothing to tire you?"

"That is one of the queer things of life," said her father, "and one that you must discover for yourself."

On the following day Daisy was again late at breakfast, but her mother did not say a word about it. Then she sauntered out as she had done the day before, and idled about the garden, pulling a flower or picking fruit as she passed

from bed to bed.

She was half lying half sitting on the garden seat when a cheery voice crying out, "Good morning, Daisy," caused her to look up.

There was the minister coming up the garden walk, holding out his hand, and smiling to see his young friend at home.

"I hope you are not ill," he said; "I was afraid something was wrong when I saw you lying down at this hour in the morning."

Daisy flushed, and when she had found her tongue, explained that she was doing nothing.

"Doing nothing," said the minister, with a puzzled look. "I don't quite understand you. I suppose you mean that you have nothing to do."

"You see, I have left school," said Daisy. "Now I am going to stay at home and be quite free to do as I like. At present I like to do nothing."

"Now I understand what you mean, Daisy," he said with a smile. "I see exactly; but I'm afraid you will have hard work."

"What, to do nothing?"

asked Daisy. "Why, it's the easiest thing in the world!"

"I don't think so," he replied, as he passed on to the house to see Daisy's mother. When he returned to the garden a few minutes afterwards, he found Daisy still sitting where he had left her. As she returned his salutation he thought she did not look quite as satisfied as she tried to make believe she was.

One week of doing nothing that had the appearance of work convinced Daisy that she had made a mistake. The time passed slowly, and each day seemed to be duller than the last. She began to see the difference between doing nothing and having nothing to do. She even envied her mother, who never had a moment to spare from morning till night, and who was very happy though she had to do the same things every day.

One afternoon her friend Ruth Grant called, and the two girls went for a long walk in the woods and gathered some large bunches of ferns. Before starting for home, Ruth said:

"I hope you are having a good time now you do no

work and spend your time as you like."

"I had for a little while," replied Daisy, "but now I am utterly miserable. I seem to have no place anywhere. It does not matter to anyone where I am or what I am doing. No one pays me any attention. Even the dog and the cat get more notice than I do."

"And yet your mother told my mother that she was looking forward to the time when you would be at home altogether, and what a comfort it would be to have a big girl to lend a helping hand."

Daisy looked very serious when she heard these words, and the tell-tale blush on her cheek showed that she felt the rebuke they conveyed.

"I'm afraid I have started wrong," she said, "but I did so want to do as I liked and feel quite free. So far I have done nothing, and yet somehow I feel more tired than when I was always busy."

"Don't you see that you are just trying to kill time," said Ruth, "and that is the very hardest task anyone can have to do?"

"But I don't know where to begin to do better," said Daisy.

"Oh, that is easy enough. Get up early, do your share of the housework. Find out what your mother has to do, and do it for her. Wait on your father. Have one or two good books at hand to read when you are not otherwise busy. Take a class at the Sunday school, call on the children, go to the church sewing class, visit the sick and read to them and try to-"

"Stop, stop, Ruth, you don't mean one person to do all that. I should be worn to a skeleton in a few weeks."

"Do I look like a skeleton?" asked her friend, with a hearty laugh.

"But you don't work like that, I'm sure."

"Certainly, I do. Why I am going to pack mother off for a month to the seaside on Monday, and she says that I shall be putting her altogether on the retired list if I do not take things easier."

"Father is kind enough to say that I attend to him well. Then I have fourteen scholars in my class at Sunday school. I am secretary of the sewing class, and I visit one sick person everyday."

"How do you find time for so much work?" asked Daisy with a sigh.

"Oh, I just go right on and let the time take care of itself. I never have too much time, nor a minute I do not know how to spend. There is not a happier girl in the country nor one who more thoroughly enjoys both work and rest."

Daisy felt that her cheery, busy, hardworking friend was right, and when she got home she surprised her mother by walking straight into the kitchen and making tea. Then she helped to clear it away, and when her mother sat down to mend stockings, Daisy got a needle and joined in the work.

Mrs. Brown was a wise woman. She made no remarks, but kindly gave her daughter the place she was now willing to take. A few weeks afterwards she said, "I think you have learned that lesson I spoke of when you came home from school."

"I am sure I have," said Daisy, "and I would rather go back to school than be forced to have nothing to do."

The Biography of a Beaver.

PART II.

Y the time the Beaver's wound was healed — Nature was good to him, and the skin soon grew over the torn stump — the pond was covered with ice. The beavers, only half as numerous as they had been a few weeks before, kept close in their lodges and burrows, and for a time they lived in peace and quiet, and their numbers suffered no further diminution. Then the trapper took to setting his traps through the ice, and before long matters were worse than ever. By spring, the few beavers that remained were so thoroughly frightened that the

ancient town was again abandoned — this time for ever. The lodges fell to ruins, the burrows caved in, the dam gave way, the pond and canals were drained, and that was the end of the city.

Yet not quite the end after all. The beavers have vanished from their old habitation, but their work remains in the broad meadows cleared of timber by their teeth, and covered with rich black soil by the inundations from their dam. There is an Indian legend which says that after the Creator separated the land from the water, He employed gigantic beavers to smooth it down and prepare it for the abode of men. However that may be, the farmers of generations to come will have reason to

rise up and bless those busy little citizens — but I don't suppose they will ever do it. One city was gone, but there were two that could claim the honour of being our Beaver's home at different periods of his life. The first, as we have already seen, was ancient and historic. The second was brand-new. Let us see how it had its beginning. The Beaver got married about the time he left his old home; and this, by the way, is a very good thing to do when you want to start a new town. Except for his missing hand his wife was so like him that it would have puzzled you to tell which was which. I think it is very likely that she was his twin sister, but of course that's none of our business. Do you want to know what they looked like? They measured about three feet six inches from tip of nose to tip of tail, and they weighed perhaps thirty pounds apiece. Their bodies were heavy and clumsy and were covered with thick, soft, greyish under-fur, which in turn was overlaid with longer hairs of a glistening

answer for both of them.

They wandered about for some time, looking for a suitable location, and examining several spots along the beds of various little rivers, none of which seemed to be just right. But at last they found in the very heart of the wilderness, a place where a shallow stream ran

some distance back from the banks, so that the pond would have plenty of room to spread out. If they could have spoken they would probably have said that the place was a better site than any other they had seen.

Alder bushes laid lengthwise of the current were the first materials used, and for a time the water filtered through them with hardly a pause. Then the beavers began laying mud and stones and moss on this brush foundation, scooping them up with their hands, and holding them under their chins as they waddled or swam to the dam. The Beaver himself was not very good at this sort of work, for his right hand was gone, as we know, and it was not easy for him to carry things; but he did the best he could, and together they accomplished a great deal. The mud and the grass and such-like materials were deposited mainly on the upper face of the dam, where the pressure of the water only sufficed to drive them tighter in among the brush; and thus, little by little, a smooth bank of earth was presented to the

THE BEAVER DID NOT WANDER VERY FAR FROM HOME
THAT SPRING AND SUMMER.

chestnut-brown, making a coat that was thoroughly waterproof as well as very beautiful. Their heads were somewhat like those of gigantic rats, with small, light-brown eyes, little round ears covered with hair, and long orange-coloured incisors looking out from between parted lips. One portrait will

over a hard stony bottom, and here they set to work. It was a very desirable situation in every respect. At one side stood a large tree, so close that it could probably be used as a buttress for the dam when the latter was sufficiently lengthened to reach it; while above the shallow the ground was low and flat on both sides for current, backed up on the lower side by a tangle of sticks and poles. Its top was very level and straight, and along its whole length the water trickled over in a succession of tiny rills. This was important, for if all the overflow had been in one place the stream might have been so strong and rapid as to eat into the dam, and perhaps carry away the whole structure.

The first year the beavers did not try to raise the stream more than a foot above its original level. There was much other work to be done — a house to be built, and food to be laid in for the winter — and if they spent too much time on the dam they might freeze or starve before spring. A few rods upstream was a grassy point which the rising water had transformed into an island, and here they built their lodge, a hollow mound of sticks and mud, with a small, cave-like chamber in the centre, from which two tunnels led out under the pond — "angles," the trappers call them. The walls were masses of earth and wood and stones, so thick and solid that even a man

with an axe would have found it difficult to penetrate them. Only at the very apex of the mound there was no mud, nothing but tangled sticks through which a breath of fresh air found its way now and then. In spite of this feeble attempt at ventilation, I am obliged to admit that the

HE DECIDED TO GO OUT TO THE WOOD-PILE, AND GET SOMETHING TO EAT.

atmosphere of the lodge was often a good deal like that of the Black Hole of Calcutta, but beavers are so constituted that they do not need much oxygen, and they did not seem to mind it. In all other respects the house was neat and clean. The floor was only two or three inches above the level of the water in the angles, and

would naturally have been a bed of mud; but they mixed little twigs with it, and stamped and pounded it down till it was hard and smooth. I think it likely the Beaver's tail had something to do with this part of the work, as well as with finishing off the dam, for he was fond of slapping things with it, and it was just the right shape for such use. In fact, I fear that if it had not been for the tail, and for other tails like it, neither of the cities would ever have been as complete as they were. With the ends of projecting sticks cut off to leave the walls even and regular, and with long grass carried in to make the beds, the lodge was finished.

And now you might have seen the beavers coming home to rest after a night's labour at felling timber — swimming across the pond toward the island, with only the tops of their two little heads showing above the water. In front of the lodge each tail-rudder gives a slap and a twist, and they dive for the submarine door of one of the angles. In another second they are swimming along the dark, narrow tunnel, making the water surge around them. Suddenly the roof of the passage rises, and their heads pop up into the air. A yard or two farther, and they enter the chamber of the lodge, with its level floor and its low, arched roof. And there in the darkness they lie down on their grass beds and go to sleep. It is good to have a home of your own where you may take your ease when the night's work is done.

Near the upper end of the pond, where the bank was higher, they dug a long burrow, running back ten or fifteen feet into the ground. This was to be the last resort if, by any possibility, the lodge should ever be invaded. It was a weary task, digging that burrow, for its mouth was deep under the water, and every few minutes they had to stop work and come to the surface for breath. Night after night, they scooped and shovelled, rushing the job as fast as they knew how, but making pretty slow progress in spite of all their efforts. It was done at last, however, and they felt easier in their minds when they knew that it was ready for use in case of necessity. From its mouth in the depths of the pond it sloped gradually upward to a dry chamber under the roots of a large birch; and here, where a few tiny holes were not likely to be noticed from the outside, two or three small openings, almost hidden by the moss and dead leaves, let in the air and an occasional ray of light. The big tree made a solid roof overhead, and the chamber was large enough, with a little crowding to accommodate a whole family of beavers.

There was only one other heavy task, and that was the gathering of the wood, which, with its bark, was to serve as food through the winter. This too was finally finished, and the very last things that the beavers did that fall were to put another coat of mud on the outside of the lodge, and to see that the dam was in the best possible condition. No repairing could be done after the ice made; and if the dam should give way at any time during the winter, the pond would be drained, and the entrances of the lodge and the burrow would be thrown open to any prowling marauders that might happen to pass that way. So it was imperative to have things in good order before cold weather came on.

There came a quiet, windless day, when the sky was grey, and when the big snow-flakes came floating lazily down, some to lose themselves in the black water, and some to robe the woods and the shores in white. At nightfall the clouds broke up, the stars shone forth, and the air grew colder and keener till long crystal spears shot out across the pond, and before morning a sheet of glass had spread from shore to shore. I do not think it was unwelcome. The beavers were shut in for the winter, or could only go abroad with considerable difficulty, but they had each other and there was a little world of their own down under the ice and snow. The chamber of the lodge was home, and just outside was their food storehouse — the big pile of wood which it had cost so much labour to gather. One of the entrances was shorter and straighter than the other, and through this they used to bring in sticks from the heap, and lay them on the floor between the beds, where they could devour the bark at their leisure. If they grew restless, and wanted to go farther afield, there was the bottom of the pond to be explored, and the big luscious lily-roots to be dug up for a change of diet. It was a peaceful time, a time of rest from the labours of the past year, and of growing fat and strong for those of the year to come. We have much goods laid up for many months; let us eat, drink, and be merry, and hope that the trappers will not come to-morrow.

Girls' Pets and How to Manage Them.

PIGEON-KEEPING.

THE first thing you must decide on if you are going in for pigeon-keeping is the kind of house your pets are to be kept in. Also, whether you intend to keep them confined or at liberty.

The birds must have quarters that are dry and draught-proof, or they will not thrive. Pigeons can stand the cold, being warm-blooded, but damp and draughts are fatal to their well-being.

A shed will do if you have one, and if you intend to let them fly out, an outside flight can easily be attached. But however you house them they must have roomy quarters, and not a stuffy little place like a doll's house. What may appear very snug and comfortable to you will not do for the pigeons.

We saw one very convenient pigeon-house last summer, though there were too many pigeons in it to be altogether satisfactory. The general arrangement and design, we think, may be followed with advantage. The house was 8 ft. long, 4 ft. wide, 7 ft. 6 in. high, and was made for the accommodation of six pairs of pigeons. The two sides, excepting about two feet, were framework covered over with a small meshed wire, the remaining space on either side and back being boarded. The front also consisted of wired framework, and a well-made door was in the centre. A weather-boarded roof covered the whole of the top, and the birds could get out through a hole let into the gable of the roof, and take their flights from a small ledge outside. At the back was a cote for six pairs, raised from the ground and fastened to the woodwork, so that the birds were safe from rats and mice. The floor was cemented, with gravel sprinkled over the surface. Let into the flooring was a stump of an old tree with some of the branches attached, and these served as perches. It was very simple – so much so, in fact, that any girl who is at all handy with saw, plane, chisel, and hammer could easily construct such a house at a very small outlay.

After all, every pigeon-keeper must adapt herself to circumstances, and do the best she can for the comfort of her pets. Take care, however, that the house or loft is inaccessible to the cats of the neighbourhood.

Start with birds of a good strain if you can; they are more profitable, though cross-breds are not to be despised, but they are, as a rule, unsaleable. Almost any local paper is a cheap and good medium in which to advertise your wants, and generally the replies come from someone in the neighbourhood who has for sale the class of birds you require. You can then go and choose for yourself and decide on the spot.

Before going into the question of feeding, we will describe some of the varieties of breeds of pigeons.

There is the well-known Carrier, a great favourite on the Continent. The principal colours are black and dun, which may be mixed by inter-breeding; blues, silvers, and pied birds, however, are often met with. The chief things to look at are the head properties – *i.e.* the beak, and eye wattles. The first should be long and light in colour, massive, and straight; and "the eye wattle should be ample, delicate and soft in texture, and of one width all round." While the wattle on the upper portion of the beak

should be of equal proportions on both sides, and extend down three-quarters the length of the beak; and though the one on the lower beak is not quite so developed, it must be similar in shape. "The neck must be slender, long, and graceful; the body substantial, and the flight and tail feathers of considerable length, the former extending almost to the end of the latter." The feathering altogether should be hard and close, the legs long and massive, and the bird should stand firmly upon the ground, with back flat and head erect.

Very similar in appearance to the Carrier is the Dragon, with this exception, that the face is shorter, and there is less eye wattle. The neck is also shorter and thicker, and the flight and tail feathers are not so profuse; while the shoulder-butts stand out from the sides. The colours are blue with black pencilled markings on the wings; Chequers and Grizzles (these birds should have dark-coloured beaks), yellows, reds, and whites, and the beaks of these three last-named should be flesh-coloured.

The Owl is a favourite bird with its large round head, and its peculiar bullfinch-like beak. On the breast is a cluster of to the eye to be a large bird, but this is owing to its profusion of feathers, rather than to the build of the bird itself. An important point to look for is the feathering on name given to this bird is derived from the peculiar sound it makes.

The Antwerp is to be found amongst the stock of almost all pigeon-keepers.

feathers, and the more these are developed the better the breed of the bird. The common colours to be met with are blues, and blues and silvers.

The Trumpeter appears the feet and the crown of feathers on the head. The usual colouring is black, though other colours are met with. For breeding purposes these birds are not recommended. The It is a big-framed bird with oval head and very short and thick beak, with well-shaped wattles. Silver-dun is the usual colour one sees in these birds, but blue and red Chequers are met with. This variety is very prolific, though apt to quarrel and show fight when shut up with pigeons of other strains.

The Homer is something like the Carrier, but smaller sized and well shaped. The colours vary, but white is seldom met with.

There are many varieties of the pigeons called Tumblers, so called because of their acrobatic performances, described as backward somersaults in midair, sometimes at a great height from the ground; other spring up a few inches from the floor of the house or loft, "turn one complete somersault, and alight on their feet again." These are called house Tumblers and the other variety flying Tumblers.

The colours vary.

The Runt is a large bird, and more often than not has been judged at shows by its weight rather than by its appearance. It is generally either blue or black. Its flesh is highly prized by those who have a taste for pigeon pies.

The Pouter's chief point is the crop, which he can blow out at will. This should be perfectly round, like an india-rubber ball, and should not present a baggy, lop-sided appearance. The legs should be long and feathered, while the girth round the waist should be slender. The best colours are blue, red, black, and yellow and white.

The Pigmy Pouter, as the name implies, is a smaller variety, but possessing the same points as the larger bird.

Our space will not permit us to mention all the varieties of pigeons, but we must not forget to include the beautiful Fantail. Its principal beauty lies in the tail feathers, and a good bird should have twenty-four or more of these; when spread out, they should form almost a complete circle, with the flight feathers, carried low, passing underneath it. The head should be small, and thrown well back to the tail. In these birds a slight tremulous motion of the neck is noticed, and this is a point to be looked for, and is found in all well-bred Fantails. The colours are varied; whites are to be preferred.

(To be continued.)

COMING OUT

BY E. EVERETT-GREEN.

"OH, Ella, you do look nice!" cried little Trix, dancing round her sister in an ecstasy of admiration and delight, "a real Cinderella – ready for the ball! Oh, do you think the fairy prince will be there to dance with you, and pick up your slipper when you drop it?"

"I hope I shan't drop mine," answered Ella, laughing, as she looked down at her pretty little embroidered satin toes peeping out from beneath the fluffy frill of the first really long-trained dress she had ever worn. Ella was just eighteen, but it was not very long since her hair had been down her back in a long tail, and her dresses reached only to her ankles. And now this first real evening gown, made in London, and so fresh and pretty in its pure whiteness and dainty simplicity, seemed a farther step upon the road towards womanhood, which she was half-longing, yet half-fearful of treading. Her eyes were sparkling with excitement and anticipation; but she strove to speak as though going to a ball were a matter of no such great moment after all. "I think satin stays on better than glass; and if any prince should be there, I don't think he'll take much notice of me. Think of all the pretty girls there will be there – Gracie and Lilian and Mysie and Mabel Stanley to start with, and the Bolton girls – oh! and ever so many besides. I shall be nobody there, you'll see, or, rather, I shall see. But it will be delightful to watch everybody even if I don't get many partners myself. I'm just going to have a lovely evening. If only mother could have gone with me!"

That was the only drop of trouble in Ella's cup. Her delicate mother had developed one of her bad sore throats two days ago, and it was impossible for her to attempt going out on a chilly spring night. But kind Mrs. Bolton was going to take

Ella in her train, and look after amongst her own bevy of daughters and at any moment she might be here to whisk her away.

"You're prettier than any of that crew!" stoutly cried loyal little Trix, as she led her sister in triumph to their mother's room to be looked at. Mrs. Duncombe, lying back in her easy-chair by the fire, and too hoarse to speak many words gazed fondly at the fresh and charming face of the blushing girl, framed by the soft cloud of softly rippling hair, and wished that she could have been there to see her make her debut into that sphere which marked, as it were, the rubicon between childhood and maidenhood.

Not that this function was anything very grand or fashionable. London folks would have smiled at the thought of beginning a dance at nine o'clock, and ending at twelve. But in Stillminster things were different, and early hours were in fashion yet, and when this dance for the young people of the place was arranged by Mrs. Stanley — the great lady of the town — she chose her own hours, which she thought far more reasonable and suitable than those which were becoming generally universal in "smart" society.

"I hope there will be plenty of dancing men!" cried Janet Bolton, as Ella, wrapped in her long white cloak, stepped into the supplementary fly which followed the Bolton carriage, bringing the two younger girls and their governess, who had been included in the invitation. "We are a fearful pack of girls ourselves, and only one of the boys available, and it's much the same with the Stanleys. The war has taken away such lots and lots of men. However, we'll hope for the best, and if men fail us we'll just dance with each other, for dance I must and will. You'll be my partner, won't you, Ellie? I'm big enough to do man for you. You're one of the fairy sort. I've run to bone and 'beef', as Fred calls it — he's more frank than complimentary."

The talkative sisters rattled away, leaving Ella no space to put her word in, and very quickly they found themselves driving up to the gaily-illuminated house decked with flowers, and thronged with people, where stout and beaming Mrs. Bolton marshalled them to the ballroom in her wake, and they found themselves in a very big room with a delightfully smooth floor, and nothing but flowers and rout seats round the walls to encumber the flying feet of the dancers. The musicians at the far end were already tuning up, and young men were bringing programmes and writing their names upon them, amid a great deal of laughter and chatter.

Harold Stanley brought Ella hers, and asked for a dance; and Fred Bolton and one other young fellow she knew also asked for dances. But Ella, whose quiet life with a delicate mother had not brought her into contact with many persons in the neighbourhood, found that she scarcely knew any of those who would be termed the "dancing men," and these certainly were far fewer in number than the girls thronging into the room. These seemed to know one another, and there was a great buzz of talk, ceaseless bursts of laughter, and interchange of a thousand little jests and pleasantries in which Ella seemed this, and then came her dance with Harold, and soon after with the son of the readily accorded.

But after that it seemed to Ella as though nobody noticed her. She sat beside Mrs. Bolton who was gossiping in ceaseless and animated fashion with another mother on her other side;

THERE WAS QUITE A LITTLE SENSATION IN THE COMPANY . . . TO SEE THE YOUNG CAPTAIN . . . DESCENDING THE STAIRS WITH A VERY PRETTY AND REFINED-LOOKING GIRL.

to have neither part nor lot.

At first she was too much amused by watching to mind house, who introduced her to another man, and he asked for a dance, which was and as for the Bolton girls, they were all over the room, dancing, or standing in knots together, criticising their neighbours and calling out jokes to them as they passed by, and never coming near their mother even between dances, nor seeming aware of the fact that Ella was sitting there as a spectator, too shy to try and float herself upon the stream of life, to which the other girls seemed to take like ducks to water.

Ella remembered how her mother had bidden her "not to be disappointed" if things were not quite as she expected; and now she began to understand the warning. Mrs. Stanley was a very kindly, young-looking matron, too young, it seemed, to be the mother of all those gay laughing girls; but her kindness did not take the form of keeping watch that her guests were all happy and amused. She thought it quite sufficient to ask them to her house, give them a good floor, good music, and a good supper. Young people must manage the rest for themselves, she thought, and her own girls certainly had a good time. Ella noticed that they all danced every dance — as daughters of the house always can do; and

as they were all pretty girls and daintily attired, it was no wonder they found partners easily; but Ella, sitting out dance after dance, whilst the music seemed fairly to make her feet ache with longing, said within herself —

"I think if this were my house, and I saw somebody hardly dancing at all, I should not like to go on dancing all the time, and not get partners for her. I don't want so very much, but I should like to dance just a little more."

The frock which had looked so pretty at home seemed eclipsed here by the numbers of other dresses similar in style and appearance. Some of them, indeed, were much finer and gayer, as their owners were smarter in their talk, and seemed to gain all the attention of the younger men. Ella would gladly have danced with one of the Bolton girls, as had been suggested, but nobody came near her. And presently she felt so disappointed and desolate, that she stood up and slipped away into the conservatory, where she could wipe away furtive tears without being seen.

She knew Mrs. Stanley's house quite well, and remembered that a glass passage from the conservatory led to a wing where the nurseries lay; and there Ella knew she would find the younger children of the house — dear little things, who would be certain to have a welcome for her. This thought cheered her up, and she sped along the glass passage to the foot of the staircase where she was suddenly almost knocked down by a little white flying figure, which she caught in her arms to stay the collision.

"Muriel! What a pace to come down! You will have a tumble if you don't take care. Why, childie, is anything the matter?" for Ella saw that the child was pale and scared and held her fast in visible agitation.

"Oh! come, come — please come! I don't know what to do and we're so frightened! I can't get anybody to answer the bell, and everybody's so busy they won't listen to me. I was coming to find mother or somebody; but there's a party, and I shall get into disgrace coming out like this. Oh! Do come — do come!"

Ella ran up the stairs as fast as she could. Plainly some child was in trouble, and the nurses all out of the way. Ella was confident that she could set things to right, and was delighted at finding something to do of a congenial nature.

"You don't think he is dead? You don't think he'll die?" panted Muriel, running at her side. "Oh, he looked so dreadful – I didn't know what to do!"

"Bernie?" asked Ella, knowing there was but one boy in the nursery. "What has he done to himself, poor little man?"

"Oh! It's not Bernie, it's Uncle Leonard, who's come back from the war. The Boers didn't kill him, though they tried; but he just looks as if he were dead now. Oh, do come quick!"

Ella was startled, but there was no drawing back now. They were close to the nursery door by this time. She had heard from the talk of the ballroom how Captain Conroy, Mrs. Stanley's brother, had been invalided home, and was in the house, though not well enough to appear at the ball. And now it seemed that something had happened to frighten the children, and she had been called to the rescue before she fully understood the case. Muriel threw back the door and ran forward. Ella followed more slowly, and with a beating heart, to find herself in the familiar nursery, with its comfortable plenishings and ruddy fireglow, where two small children in nightgowns stood clinging together and half crying on the rug; whilst upon the couch beside the fire was stretched a tall, motionless figure – the figure of a thin soldierly young man, with his arm in a sling, and a deadly white face and fast closed eyes.

"He was playing with us," sobbed Babs, the curly-headed baby girl. "We were having such a nice game. And then Bernie tumbled over and fell against his arm. And then he went backwards like that on the sofa, and he's never moved since, and we're so frightened we don't know what to do!"

This was lisped out in baby phrases, which were quite intelligible to Ella; and she saw at once that the young soldier had fainted, probably as the outcome of some jar to his wounded arm, which she had heard below had been badly shattered, and was slow to mend owing to the fermentation of abscesses.

A fainting fit in itself did not alarm Ella, who had often seen her mother in them. She knew exactly what to do, and, speaking cheerfully and confidently to the frightened children, she obtained and used restoratives which Muriel fetched her, knowing that farther attempts to summon aid at such a time as this would probably be futile.

Very soon her efforts were attended with success. A pair of rather hollow brown eyes opened slowly, and fixed themselves upon her face, at first with an amusing sort of dazed gaze, afterwards with a new look. And when that look of full comprehension was established, the young man suddenly moved himself, as though to sit up. But Ella interposed –

"No, please, don't move. You must keep quiet just a little longer," she said, in her sweet, gentle way. "You will be better very soon, but you must keep still. I can't get you any brandy just now, though I think you ought to have a little; but here is some sal-volatile and water. That is next best. Please drink it. I know it is horrid stuff, but it will do you good."

She spoke so winningly that he took the glass and drank its contents. Then the ashy pallor of his skin warmed into something more lifelike, and Bernie uttered a shout, and ran up crying —

"I thought you were deader, I did indeed. I thought I'd deaded you myself, and Babs said they would hang me for it. You're quite certain sure you isn't a deader, is you?"

"Quite certain sure, old chap. Only a bit of a muff — a very different sort of matter!" Then the dark eyes turned upon Ella with something half shy, half deprecating in their glance.

"Please do not trouble about me any more. I'm as fit as a fiddle. I can't think what it's all been about, nor why you are pressed into the service. It makes me awfully ashamed of myself."

Ella had been rather shy herself the minute before, for this yeomanry captain was so much younger than she had supposed. She had naturally fancied that Mrs. Stanley's brother would be a man getting on for forty, whereas he was barely six-and-twenty; but the consciousness that he was rather boyishly shy before her gave her back her confidence, and she sat down smiling and at ease, drawing Babs within the clasp of her encircling arm.

"You see, the children were frightened at your white face, and as nobody came for ringing, Muriel was flying down for help just as I was coming up to see the babies in bed. I see you have been aiding and abetting naughty ways; letting Muriel stay up to the unconscionable hours, and having these two mites out of bed in their nightgowns."

"Well, you see, the music and the stir kept them awake. Muriel had to go and watch the people coming in and describe the pretty frocks — she wouldn't have been a human child else. And these little shavers got so excited, it was no use trying to keep them in bed; so

we all had a bit of a surreptitious supper together. I foraged for that — I've had good practice in that sort of thing. And we were just having a bit of a scrimmage together, when — but really I don't quite know what it was all about, except that I seem to have made a stupid of myself, and you have missed a lot of your dances, and I daresay there are half a dozen fellows downstairs who would cheerfully cut my throat if they only knew the rights — or wrongs — of the matter."

"Indeed no," answered Ella, flushing up a little, and showing her almost blank programme. "I scarcely know anybody here, and —"

"But don't the girls introduce?" asked the captain, sitting up and looking just a little bit fierce. "They told me they were going to have a real good time themselves. Surely they see that their guests have the same?"

"Oh yes, I enjoyed it very much. I never was at a grown-up dance before, and everything is so pretty — the dresses, the flowers, and everything. And besides, I did dance a few dances at first. See!" and she laughed and held out her card.

"Oh! I see quite enough," returned the young fellow rather grimly. "They say that manners and customs change, and I don't think for the better. But if you haven't had a good time in the dancing line, do let me have the pleasure of taking you into supper. Give me just a quarter of an hour, and I'll be ready. I've not much changing to do, for I promise I'd put in an appearance then if I felt like it. And you must really give me that satisfaction."

It was in vain Ella remonstrated, thinking him quite unfit for the exertion. The young soldier was resolved, and he carried the day. There was quite a little sensation in the company that trooped across the hall to the supper-room to see the young captain, who was known to have won his D.S.O., descending the stairs with a very pretty and refined-looking girl, who, in her dainty coolness and fresh and untumbled raiment, presented a pleasing contrast to a great many of the other girls present, whose dancing had been of late degenerating almost into romping.

And somehow, after supper, Ella found that she was not to sit out at all. Partners seemed to flock round her, and her light feet flew round the floor with tireless activity. It was but a short while that was left, but it was packed with pleasure all through, and the last memory she had of that evening was being put into the carriage by Captain Conroy, and hearing his voice say with friendly satisfaction —

"I shall come and call upon your mother to- morrow, and thank her for having such a level-headed and clever daughter."

"Oh, Ellie!" cried Janet, "you had the best of every-thing. How did you come to unearth Captain Conroy like that? You are a lucky girl. Why, he absolutely danced the last Lancers with you. And he danced with nobody else. Isn't he hand-some and interesting?"

But Ella said nothing, and kept her tale for her mother's ear alone; glad that her talkative companions were fonder of asking ques-tions than of hearing the answers.

"Was there a prince, Ellie?" cried little Trix, just waking up from her rosy sleep as Ella came in softly in her ballroom finery`Ella flushed as she bent to kiss the little one, and answered —

"I almost feel as though there was."

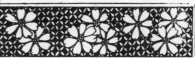

INTO THE SUNSHINE.

— ✺✺✺ —

DWELL who will in the valley below,
  I go up into the sunshine!
  Free and warm and glad is its play,
Light and life are in every ray,
  Burning to brighter and brighter day.
Let who will in the valley stay,
  I go up into the sunshine!

Mists are down in the valley below,
  Shadows and cloud wave to and fro;
The rivers go creeping, sluggish and slow,
  The very winds have forgotten to blow.
Dwell who will in the valley below,
  I go up into the sunshine!

On the golden summit the morning sings,
  Like a glad bird pluming his radiant wings;
The torrents flash like living things,
  Sparkling and foaming, the rivulet springs.
Every bright drop like a joy bell rings,
  I go up into the sunshine!

— ✺✺✺ —

J.T.Mitchell.

Cosy Corner Chats.

VI. – TELLING LIES.

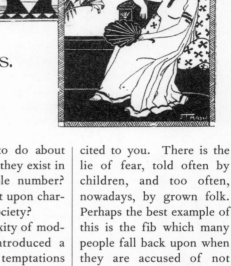

Y DEAR HELEN: I had the uncomfortable experience to-day of catching a young woman in a plain fib. We sat on the verandah, just beginning what promised to be a long and interesting talk, when three ladies came up the path. She said impulsively: "Oh, dear! How horrid of them to spoil our afternoon! I can't endure them!" Twenty seconds afterwards she rose graciously and greeted them with, "I am delighted to see you. Do come right up and sit down. How kind of you to come this hot day!" The words were scarce out of her mouth when she caught my eye, her colour rose, and she was as uncomfortable as you would wish to see any-one. Here is my text: What

are we really to do about social lies? Do they exist in any considerable number? Have they effect upon character or upon society?

The complexity of modern life has introduced a thousand new temptations to evade the truth. When life was very simple, and its social obligations comparatively few, it was pretty easy to be truthful and still protect one's personality from invasion and keep one's counsel. To-day it is difficult to do these things. Because it is difficult, we are growing, I think, more lenient to certain evasions of the truth; and one may almost classify the different kinds of lies for which people apologise. For example, there is the lie of good nature, like the one I just

cited to you. There is the lie of fear, told often by children, and too often, nowadays, by grown folk. Perhaps the best example of this is the fib which many people fall back upon when they are accused of not having answered a letter, and assure a correspondent either that they have never received it or that their own reply has miscarried. John Bull's mail-bag must have many holes in it if half of these mis-sent letters ever really get out of it. Then there is the lie of exaggeration. Sometimes it is not intended seriously to deceive, but oftener it is told to increase our own importance in the eyes of someone. How many times one hears a half-dozen girls matching stories of miraculous experiences, of hair-breadth escapes, of heart-broken lovers, and so on. Then there are fibs for the sake of keeping a confidence intact. I sometimes question whether anybody has a right to tell me a secret which he knows it may take a lie to protect. Again, there is the lie of silence – sometimes the most effective and cruel of lies. To utter no protest when my friend is maligned is often easy, but it is usually wicked.

Now, these are only a few kinds of untruth which result from the frictions of character and social life, and to which we are becoming lenient in others and in ourselves. We behave as if we thought they had no effect upon character, and were not really rendering the mind tolerant toward untruthfulness. The fact is, that it is impossible to let untruthfulness enter character by one door and shut it out by another. Truth is the basis on which all life rests. It is not the world which hears and believes or disbelieves the lies we tell which is really harmed by them; it is the head that conceived them and the conscience that ignored or pardoned them. It does not take many years for the whole structure of character to be weakened by those corroding stains. What is to be done about them? The only way to keep the character clear of the blot is not simply to avoid telling lies, but to cultivate a real love for the truth. The love of beauty shows itself in a hundred ways in its influence upon conduct: so must the love of truth become an actual and potent factor in our lives. A negative conviction always fails in keeping out lies. There must be a positive one. Do not suppose that truthfulness and tact are incompatible. It is not necessary to be brusque in the effort to be sincere. A genuine desire for kindliness and generosity may live side by side with a crystalline sincerity.

It is good for us occasionally to be found out in one of these little lies, and then to see how beautiful truth looks beside it. I told my young woman this afternoon that I wanted her to promise me for a week to review each day before she slept, and make a little note of the lies she had actually told. I believe the process would be salutary for a good many of us. The last and bitterest punishment for a long course of deceit is that finally one should be given over to believe a lie. Self-deception is the final penalty for the deception of others, until at last the victim of his own small sins goes out blind into a world whose only light is the light of truth.

HELOISE EDWINA HERSEY.

J.T.Mitchell

How to Make Cold Trifles for Supper.

THESE are very pretty cooking for any girl who has a *penchant* for the culinary art. Often quite a simple dish that takes only a few minutes to prepare will surprise one by its pretty appearance on the table; but take care that it tastes as good as it looks. There is a world of difference between a dish served carelessly and the same dish prepared daintily, so you should always aim at making your jellies, blanc-manges, or whatever it may be, as pretty and tempting as possible.

My recipes will be suit-able and practicable for any girl to choose from and make herself, and how proud she will be if on her birthday she provides the pretty supper herself at very little cost. A tea is always easy enough, but the supper looks so much more formidable. But if you are content to let your guests sit around the room and dispense with knives and forks, you can easily manage a delightful little supper.

Sandwiches are a *pièce de résistance* for such a supper and can be varied so easily. Order a sandwich loaf in time to have it a few hours old, then proceed to cut it up into thin bread and butter. Then, after spreading one slice with whatever you are going to put in it, cover with another, and so on; trim off the crusts, then cut into diamonds and fingers, pile on a paper d'oyley on a plate, with a few tiny sprigs of parsley to garnish, and a cardboard label prettily written or painted in quaint letters, with "Ham," "Cress," &c., on, finishes the pile. For ham sandwich-es, mince or chop your ham finely, and spread a little mustard on one side of the bread and butter. They are so superior to the usual slice of ham that has a tendency to leave the bread and butter behind and makes one feel very uncomfortable. Then, instead of the very ordinary tongue sandwich, I should get a *pâté* at the grocers — turkey and tongue or camp pie are very good, and there are others. These can so easily be eaten in thin slices, they do not need to be minced or chopped up. If you have no ham in the house you can get a variety of delicious sandwiches in this way. Then there is *foie gras*, which can be bought in large towns cheaply by the pound — a $1/4$lb. would go a long way, and is very easy to spread. Hard-boiled egg sandwiches are very nice also, especially if mixed with cress. When you have boiled your eggs long enough, plunge them into cold water; cut them carefully into thin slices, and spread the cress smoothly. Be sure to remember the salt. In the summer cucumber sandwiches are delicious. Cut your cucumber very thinly, and do not spread one slice over another but lay them carefully side by side, and put

salt on, not vinegar. Be sure to remember to have the slices singly or the top bread and butter will slip away, and eating the sandwich will be a trial. Then mustard and cress together will make nice little sandwiches, and there are always some people who are like rabbits in their fondness for green things. If you do not mind the trouble of peeling the shrimps, shrimp sandwiches are delicious. Put a little pepper as well as salt on them; it is a great improvement. You can prepare your sandwiches in the morning, then cover them all over with a damp new teacloth, and they will be as fresh as if you had only just cut them in the evening.

Having decided on your sandwiches, you can then choose your sweet dishes, and these it will be best generally to prepare the day before. You will not want to tire yourself out on the morning of your party. I shall not give you any recipes for pastry, although a little made into sausage rolls and tartlets is a great help to a supper; and if you use half as much butter or lard as flour your pastry

will be nice and short. Be sure to brush your sausage rolls with egg; it is such an improvement. There are one or two delicious fillings for tarts that I think I must give you, however, besides the ever-popular lemon cheese that can be bought at the grocer's and is so nice that it seems useless to make it. Chivers' brand is very good. A little strawberry jam mixed with an egg and some creamed butter makes bakewell tart, and is a novelty to most people; or the mixture can be spread over the jam. Marmalade mixed in exactly the same way is almost as good, and, if you like, you can sprinkle a little cocoanut on the top of both of them. These mixtures are a nice change from ordinary jam. Custards in glasses are nice if made nicely with eggs and not powder or cornflour. To a pint of new milk add two or even three eggs, well beaten, and two tablespoonfuls of sugar. If you put in cornflour, do not let it be more than a teaspoonful, but it is not necessary. Flavour with ratafia or any other flavouring you like after it is boiled. In boiling, stir it and let it boil slowly, and take if off before it bubbles or it will curdle. You can fill a few glasses with custard when it is quite cool, and put a ratafia biscuit as a floating island on each. Save quite a pint of custard (you must make two pints if you do this) to pour over the trifle, which is always a favourite dish. Get a moulded spongecake or some small ones and cut into slices, spread with raspberry or apricot jam, or dip into jam heated to a syrupy state or apricot juice boiled into a syrup with sugar. Lay them in a glass dish, add some ratafia biscuits, sprinkle well with sliced glacé cherries and chopped almonds, and when the custard is cool enough pour over the whole. Cream whipped with white of egg and castor sugar can be added as an improvement; if not, decorate the trifle by sticking strips of almonds and glacé cherries all over it; but, of course, the cream is nicest. Spread over, then decorate with glacé cherries and angelica in strips, and it will look lovely. If you have cream, you can save half for another pretty

dish – poached eggs. On slices of spongecake soaked in apricot syrup lay a tinned apricot, and surround it with cream. Arrange on a dish, and it will look very like its name. *Méringues* are improved also by a little whipped cream. Whisk two whites of eggs to a stiff froth, add 6oz. castor sugar, lightly stirring it in with a little vanilla as you are whisking the eggs. Have ready a tin lined with white buttered paper, take dessert spoonfuls of the mixture and drop on to the paper, do not let them touch each other. Bake in a slow oven, and take them out as they begin to colour. They can be eaten as they are, or two put together with a little cream between. Some may be tinted with cochineal.

Lemon sponge is a pretty dish, and only requires a little patience and a very little skill. Soak 1oz. gelatine in one pint of water for two hours, then put it into a saucepan; add the juice and the thinly-pared rind of two lemons, and $1/4$lb. sugar. stir until boiling with a wooden spoon. Strain into a large bowl.

When nearly cold add one white of egg (two if a small egg), and beat all for half an hour or longer with a whisk until completely frothed. It can then be poured into a wet mould and set in a cold place, or left a few minutes and then taken out in rough lumps into a glass dish. Some of it may be coloured with cochineal to decorate. This can also be made even more simply from a packet of Chivers' (or other maker's) jellies. Lemon, of course, in the same way. These packet jellies are very convenient and simple. When dissolved, pour into a wetted Yorkshire pudding tin, and when set slip off (dipping the tin into warm water first), then cut into strips or patterns for garnishing. Any flavour you choose, of course, can be used. Then some jelly chopped up looks pretty in glasses, and also for garnishing a dish in little heaps. Such decoration is charming work.

Cherry Cream or any other flavour is easily made with a packet jelly. Take any flavour – cherry, raspberry, or strawberry are best – and dissolve; then put in a basin until nearly set. Add half a teacupful of cream (or boiled milk cooled will do if cream is not to be had), beat well with a silver fork, and pour into a mould. This is delicious and so simple.

Orange Baskets are very pretty. Choose some unblemished oranges of equal size, cut in halves and carefully scoop out the inside, fill with any chopped jelly you have over, and make handles of angelica strips.

Macedoine of Fruit can be made any time of the year and very easily. In summer raspberries, straw-berries, currants, &c., together with a banana or two; in winter tangerine oranges, candied fruits, bananas, and tinned fruits can be used. Dissolve a packet of jelly in nearly a pint of water, when cool and just liquid, pour a very little into a mould, allow to set, then pile on some fruit and cover with more jelly; when this is set, repeat until the mould is full. When served, it can be garnished with candied fruits.

Charlotte Russe is a very pretty dish. Pour into a mould a little raspberry or cherry jelly, $1/4$in. about,

leave to set; get ready some Savoy biscuits by brushing the edges carefully with white of egg; when the mould is ready, place the biscuits on end round it, letting their edges join. Do this very carefully, and cut them down if necessary level to the top of the mould. Prepare some cream (as in the above recipe for cherry cream, well whisking it with the jelly), then fill the mould with it, being careful to keep the Savoys in their places. Cover, if you like, with a slice of spongecake to fit the mould, and leave to set. Be very careful in turning out so that the cream does not burst the case, which will be prettily fluted with a pink top.

Méringue for decorating can easily be made by whisking whites of eggs and adding a little castor sugar and flavouring, until it is foamy. It may be used as floating islands on goose-berry fool or custard, or piled high on a queen of puddings. The first is made by slowly stewing green gooseberries until pulp. If they are very young they need not be strained, but if the skins are visible this

should be done. Add a good deal of white sugar, and leave to cool. When a little cool add yolks of eggs, one or two according to quantity of fruit; beat together. When nearly cold pour into a glass dish and put on *méringue* in rough lumps. The queen of puddings is quite as easy. Soak two teacupfuls of fine bread-crumbs in a pint of milk, cream 1oz. of butter, add two tablespoonfuls of white sugar, and two yolks of eggs; whip together, then add the crumbs, milk, and a little flavouring. Pour some raspberry jam into a pie dish, then the mixture on it. Bake at once till the custard is set. Then pile the *méringue* on, and leave a few moments in the oven to set, and serve cold. Or the jam may be put on the top of the pudding when baked if liked better, and covered with *méringue*.

Fruit Salad is a luscious adjunct for a supper at any time of the year, and is made with any and as many fruits as you can get. In winter, tinned apricots, peaches, and pineapple (cut in dice), bottled cherries and raspberries, and bananas in tiny slices. Make a syrup of all the juices boiled together with sugar, and pour over the fruit.

Orange pulp and even desiccated cocoanut are good, too, in the salad. The pulp left from the "orange baskets" can be used up for it. In summer, currants, raspberries, strawberries, and grapes can be used for this delightful dish.

I am sure a dainty supper can be chosen from the recipes I have given in winter or summer, and I hope my readers will experiment for themselves.

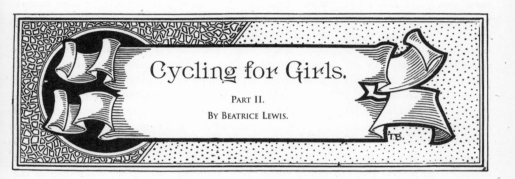

Cycling for Girls.

PART II.

BY BEATRICE LEWIS.

IF you are about to learn to ride, and you expect to be lucky enough to possess a free-wheel, don't make the mistake of starting to practise on the old type of fixed wheel. It is really no easier and you will have to learn the ways of the new machine all afresh. It's of no use practising the control of the back-pedalling action when you will never require to bring it into play on your new mount. Try and obtain the same kind of machine that you intend having, and pay special attention to the management of the brakes.

Now, everybody can learn to ride a bicycle, but just because the elements of riding are so easy to achieve, few persons realise that it requires a great deal of practice and perseverance to learn to ride well. We are very apt to imagine ourselves expert cyclists so soon as we can mount and dismount, keep our balance, ride straight, and turn corners without coming to grief. But if we are content to stop at this, we shall probably never attain to that perfect control of the machine, under all circumstances and in any emergency, which is the greatest safeguard, and, at the same time, the greatest pleasure of bicycle riding.

The certain knowledge of complete control cures all tendency to nervousness, when you know yourself to be safer on your machine than anywhere else. Almost every accident that happens to cyclists is preventable, since they arise nearly always from one of two causes — lack of capacity or lack of nerve. Cure these two failings, and we should read no more of the said "accidents to cyclists," which the papers delight in retailing to the distress of nervous parents and riders. Well, yes, I will admit two other causes. One is recklessness — unfortunately, as common amongst good riders as with beginners; and the other is the giving way of the machine by reason of the breakage of some defective part.

The latter reason is practically the only one that I admit to be "unavoidable," though even it would be of far less frequent occurrence if riders would take the trouble to understand the mechanism of their machines, or at least have them properly looked after and overhauled at reasonable intervals of time. So many persons imagine — and I'm afraid this remark is specially applicable to girls — that a bicycle, not being alive to eat oats like a horse, has no other needs, and will go on doing the work demanded of it indefinitely, and without receiving any special care. Now, a bicycle

starves for want of oil, as a horse for want of oats, and though it would not catch cold through neglect and wet, it will stiffen and rust. Everyone who wishes to get the best work and the best enjoyment out of their machine should try to comprehend a few simple facts about its mechanism and construction. Or, if that is too much trouble, they should employ some competent repairer to clean and keep it in order.

Now, if you want to be capable riders, and to have your machines completely under control, there is no better way than by practising a little trick-riding. Even the simplest manoeuvres will be found useful, especially for those who ride where there is any traffic. To be able to "tortoise" or "slow-race" is a most necessary achievement, and will save many a dismount. As for mounting and dismounting, every way should be tried, and many a sad accident might have been averted if the rider had been capable of a lightning or flying dismount under difficult circumstances. Try and accustom yourself gradually

to dismounting without slowing down, by degrees performing the feat while the machine is still in quite rapid motion. If your brakes went wrong going down hill, and you found yourself flying into another vehicle or a brick wall, think how desirable would be a flying dismount in time to avert the catastrophe. When such manoeuvres are tried in sheer desperation by unpractised riders the result is often as unfortunate as the peril which they have attempted to avoid.

Even so simple a feat as riding side-saddle might save you a long tramp home with a machine to push, in such eventuality as a broken crank. Or suppose some accident chanced to your own mount, rendering it quite unrideable, and no lady's machine, only a man's, was procurable. Well, attired as you are, in your ordinary skirt, you could ride it quite comfortably and elegantly — sidesaddle! It is wise to accustom yourself to be independent of the use of your hands on the handles. You can then not only arrange your skirt to set straight —

which, by the way, it rarely does of its own accord – but you can carry parcels or make any use of your hands for whatever emergency may arise.

Fancy riding is exceedingly good practice for steering, giving perfect command over the machine while riding very slowly. And it's by no means easy to steer to the inch between lines of traffic while crawling along at an enforced snail's pace. This is, indeed, one of the greatest essentials, and it's impossible to estimate how many mishaps and serious accidents might be averted if riders were only more expert in this. To be at home on your machine, to feel yourself so entirely mistress of the situation as not to mind what happens, or what other people and the rest of the traffic do, that is the desirable attitude. Riders and drivers do not always keep their own place on the road or behave exactly as they should in every way, so it's no use to expect it of them. On the contrary, make up your mind to expect nothing of anybody. Let other people do as they please. And though drivers hedge you in, though pedestrians block your path, though horses breathe down the back of your neck, and dogs dash right under your front wheel, know that it's your business and your pride to avoid them all and to come out smiling on top. Remember that in all cases of accident, it is invariably the cyclist who gets blamed, whether in fault or no, so make up your mind to provide absolutely no loophole.

But now let me again utter a word of warning against "showing off." There is a temptation, no doubt, when you can do clever things to exhibit your prowess, but it is very bad form, and should be sternly resisted, unless you are really riding for show in a gymkhana. Then by all means enter into the amusement thoroughly, and you will find the necessary practice and the event hugely beneficial to your ordinary riding.

How to be Strong.

SPECIAL EXERCISES
WITH THE SANDOW GRIP DUMB-BELL.

PART V.

IN the exercise that we have chosen for this month, you will notice one very important fact, which places this exercise in the front rank, and that is that nearly every one of the principal muscles of the body are affected by, and brought into play during, the performing of this exercise (No. 5). Whilst it is highly necessary, and, indeed, many of the exercises are specially designed in order to develop individual muscles, yet it is also highly necessary that the whole of

the muscles should be exercised in what we will term a collective exercise. The real aim of the exercise is that each muscle in the body should be developed in the same proportion, so that the

EXERCISE 5.

whole should result in a perfectly symmetrical figure. Such was the high standard laid down in days

of the old Greeks, and if you ever have a chance of visiting the collection know as the " Elgin Marbles," which were collected by Lord Elgin from the ruins of the Parthenon and brought to England, and now lie in the South Kensington Museum, you will see in some of the statues there examples of the Greek idea of perfect and symmetrical development.

Without further comment, therefore, we will at once describe in detail the present exercise (No. 5).

(1) Stand perfectly upright, feet apart and toes turned out, the heels being about one foot apart and the toes 15 inches apart, the hands, firmly grasping the dumb-bells, being held down at the sides. (2) Raise the hands erect above head, so that the dumb-bells touch. (3) Keep

the hands above the head, slowly bend the body (waist and back action) until you touch the floor with the dumb-bells. (4) Rise erect once more, returning the hands to the sides, and the cycle of exercise is complete. Repeat the operation, say, fifteen times, morning and evening, gradually increasing as in previous exercises. By this exercise you have thus brought into play the muscles of (1) the arms, sides and shoulders; (2) the waist and back; (3) and the legs. You will now have become fairly conversant with the whole of the preceding four exercises, and will find of great advantage to have, at intervals of about a week or ten days, an extra time for the drill, as a kind of "review day," in which to go though each of the exercises, say, about 15 to 20 times each. In this you will make sure of remembering what you have already been taught, in the same way as in many schools the system of a monthly examination is in force in order to ascertain what progress has been made with the students' studies, and how far the information imparted has been remembered.

A Bunch of Violets.

By Miss C. Measham.

ROBERT MILNE stood in the surgery regarding with a frown the contents of a note he held in his hand. It was merely a request to call at a certain house to see some children, but the house styled itself the Convent, the note was signed by "Elizabeth, Mother Superior, C.S.C". During the year that he had been in partnership with Dr. Wilson Robert Milne had never penetrated the inner world of the Convent, and he had no desire to do so.

It was a bright morning early in December when Robert rang the bell at the gate of the Convent.

"I am Dr. Milne," he said; "I believe I am expected."

"Come in," replied the portress Sister, in a studiously severe voice.

"I will tell the Mother you are here," the Sister vouchsafed.

In a few minutes the Sister returned accompanied by the Mother.

The Mother conducted Robert down a corridor, then through a door into a long passage, which brought them to a remote part of the building.

"This is the Orphanage," she explained. "We are afraid that two of the children have scarlet fever."

The two children were in bed in a dormitory,

spotlessly clean, but bare and chilly. A Sister rose and curtsied to the Mother when they entered.

"It is scarlet fever

HE HAD NEVER BEEN SO GLAD TO BE ALONE.

without doubt," Robert pronounced, after an examination of the patients.

"We do not want it to spread," the Mother said.

"We usually put any infectious cases in a cottage we have at the other end of the grounds. I suppose it will do the children no harm to move them-"

"Not if they are well wrapped up and taken in a closed carriage."

"We have a small ambu-

lance; I will send them in that."

"The room must be made thoroughly warm before they are put into it," said Robert, struck by the chilly air of the dormitory.

"Certainly. They will want a nurse, too." The Mother knitted her brow. She turned to the Sister beside her. "I scarcely know who can go," she continued. "Sister Lucy and Sister Catherine are both busy with cases in the town. I cannot take you or Sister Mary from the Orphanage."

"Does not Sister Prisca know something of nursing?" the Sister suggested.

"Yes; but she is so far from strong." The Mother considered a moment. "I think she might manage; we must send one of the elder girls with her as a help." She turned to Robert. "The entrance to the cottage is in Hutchin's Lane, Dr. Milne. I should be glad if you would call there this evening, see that everything is as you would wish, and give Sister Prisca your instructions."

Robert promised to do so.

It was about seven o'clock in the evening that

Robert paid his first visit to the cottage. The door was opened by a little black-robed figure. "Good evening," said a low voice, "will you come up and see the children?"

"Thank you," he replied. "Are you the nurse?"

"Yes." She led the way upstairs.

It required only a few minutes' conversation to discover that Sister Prisca knew her work.

Every day Robert included the cottage in his rounds. There was no fault to be found with the nurse, who did her duty thoroughly. She was always bright, and kept up the spirits of her patients; only when Robert gave his directions he would sometimes see an anxious look on the small countenance, a look which told him that her responsibilities weighed upon her.

Despite his approval of the nurse, Robert seldom left the cottage without a vague feeling of annoyance. The sick room did indeed proclaim strong views.

At first it appeared that the fever would prove a slight attack, but after the first two days the elder child developed more serious symptoms. When Robert called early one morning he found Sister Prisca looking heavy-eyed and paler than usual; her brow was clouded with anxiety.

"You have had a bad night," he said at once.

"Yes; Annie has been very delirious."

Robert found the child's condition was indeed somewhat critical. After he had given his directions and promised to call later in the day, he was about to go, but turned somewhat abruptly and faced the little Sister. They were standing outside the door of the sick room.

"Who is helping you with these children?" he said.

"I have Alice. She is a very good girl. She has had the fever herself."

"You mean the girl who opens the door to me?"

"Yes."

"She knows nothing of nursing. You cannot look after the child day and night; it is a sheer impossibility."

"I shall get some sleep during the day. Alice will stay with the children; she will call me when they want medicine, or if Annie is very restless."

"That does not sound very satisfactory," he said a little impatiently.

"I must try and do my best. The Mother was sorry she had no better nurse to send, but —"

"Good God, I don't mean that," he interrupted with sudden heat.

She gave him a somewhat amazed look. There had been no mock humility in her words. It had never occurred to her that she was other than the least able of creatures.

"You quite mistake me," he continued, more gently. "I want no better nurse; but I don't want you to knock yourself up. You are looking fearfully tired this morning. Don't you see, you make yourself ill if you try to go on without proper rest."

"Don't you think that if one is given a work to do, one is given strength to do it," she said, her pale face lighted up by the faith that was in her.

Robert looked at her, and found no reply. He could not cast himself down from the place she had given him as a fellow-Christian.

The next day brought no improvement in the child's condition. Robert had not expected it, but he believed the night following would bring the disease to a crisis.

"Do you think," the Sister asked Robert, "that the vicar should see Annie?"

"The Vicar!" he exclaimed. "Why should he?"

"You do not think then that there is any danger at present. The vicar has sent to inquire every day; he would, of course, wish to be with Annie if he thought – " She paused, and her lips trembled.

"I do not think it will be necessary. The child is very weak; each violent outbreak of delirium renders her more so; but after to-night the fever will probably abate, and, though she will require great care, I entertain no great anxiety. I will look in again in the afternoon."

He accordingly called in the afternoon, and then promised to come again the last thing at night.

It was ten o'clock when Robert arrived at the cottage. Annie was at her

worst; the crisis had come. For one minute he stood unseen in the doorway of the sick room, and watched Sister Prisca as she tried to soothe the frantic little creature. Some neglected bit of work seemed to burden the little one's brain. She called out from time to time that she must go downstairs, she must finish her work.

Sister Prisca held the child in her arms and tried to keep the bedclothes over her. "Oh, dear Jesu, give Thy lamb peace," she said aloud, her little face eloquent with supplication. "Make Thou all her bed in her sickness."

She caught sight of the doctor.

There was but little conversation between the nurse and the doctor. He insisted on taking at intervals her place by the bedside, making her rest in an armchair drawn up near the fire.

Sister Prisca was occupying the chair of rest when the church clock struck eleven. The child's voice had died away to a low murmur, and the sound of the bell lingered in the frosty air. The Sister rose at the first stroke. She crossed

herself with a sweet composure, and repeated in a low but clear voice: "Watch ye, therefore, for ye know not when the Master of the house cometh, at even, at midnight, at the cock-crowing, or in the morning. Have mercy upon us, O Lord, now and at the hour of our death."

About midnight the child was seized with a violent outbreak of delirium. She made every effort to throw herself out of bed, and it needed all the nurse and doctor could do to keep her there.

At last the child sank back exhausted; she lay quite still with closed lids. Robert felt the pulse. A long minute passed, then the child opened her eyes and saw the Sister standing beside her.

"Sister," she whispered, "I am very tired."

The nurse bent her head down to catch the words.

"You will go to sleep now, darling."

"I have not said my prayers."

"We will say them together."

She knelt by the bed, and holding one of the child's

hands, repeated in a low voice, a simple form of prayer. Before she had finished the little one was sleeping peacefully.

Robert's presence was no longer necessary. He bade Sister Prisca good night. A small black-robed figure filled his thoughts as he walked slowly home.

From that night the children began to recover. There was, indeed, an anxious fortnight, but the care and devotion of the nurse were exerted to the utmost, and no complications ensued.

Robert gradually ceased to find fault, even mentally, with the system that had at first so irritated him.

Two slight incidents, which, appearing slight at the time, were afterwards treasured as landmarks in their intercourse, marked the period of recovery.

One day when Robert called he found the vicar, who had been making inquiries, on the doorstep.

"Good morning, Milne," said the clergyman. "I am glad to hear from Sister Prisca that the children are going on so well."

The little Sister's name had not been uttered since the mother had first mentioned her. The children addressed her as "Sister" only.

After a few words the vicar departed, and Robert paid his visit.

Sister Prisca received his instructions in her usual grave but sweet manner. Robert meanwhile was oppressed with a distaste for her name.

"I wonder what made your mother call you Prisca," he said at last, somewhat suddenly.

"Prisca is my name in religion," she replied. "We don't always keep our baptismal names."

"Indeed," he said, pushed by a most potent curiosity to hazard offending. "What is your baptismal name then?"

"Violet," she answered, too innocent to be prudish.

"Violet!" He repeated the name softly. "Did you like the change?" He felt he was breaking down barriers when he talked to her of herself.

"The Mother wished it."

"And your own mother?" he risked further.

"She has been dead many years." She raised her eyes one instant to his as she spoke; it seemed to him that in that one glance he read a strange little history of desolation.

Violet! He should think of her by that name. Violet! The knowledge of her name made Robert picture her in some other than her present sphere, the picture was dangerously sweet.

It was in the late days of convalescence that the other incident occurred. His visits were less frequent, and when he did not include the cottage in his rounds, he felt he missed something. One day the Sister was not in the sick room when he entered it. It was some minutes before she appeared, in the act of removing a square of some white material from her head.

"I am sorry if you have been waiting," she said. "I did not know you were here."

"Have you been out?" he asked, thinking she was taking off some wrap.

"No; I was at vespers."

"Vespers! Saying some prayers?"

"Yes." Her face still wore the look of earnest prayer.

"You say a great many prayers. I suppose you have no fire; I am glad you put a shawl on."

"This is a veil," she said, her lips parting in a smile.

"Forgive my ignorance," he said, encouraged by the smile. "It is a nun's veil then?"

"Yes, a novice's veil."

"You are a novice. You have taken no vows yet?" There was a certain eagerness in his voice, but she did not detect it.

"We have to wait two years," she replied. Her face was quite grave again, the mouth had its frequent look of expectancy. He could not doubt but that she wished the time of waiting over. He was disappointed.

At last the day came when the children might return to the Orphanage; his visits must come to an end.

"It is good-bye then, Sister," he said. He held out his hand.

"Good-bye," she replied. Her small hand rested one instant in his, and she smiled at him in her simple friendly manner.

Robert realised in that moment that he did not wish

himself utterly forgotten. He seized the one means of keeping himself in her memory.

"Do you ever say a little prayer for me?" he asked, inwardly half-ashamed at his subterfuge.

"We all pray for our sick and for those who attend them." Her "we" had a chilling effect. It was just in the use of that pronoun that she was rigorously conventual.

"I don't want to know what 'we' do," his tone was very low, almost entreating; "will 'you' remember me?"

"In my prayers? Yes." So they parted.

The episode was closed. His case at the convent was past history. Probably he would never see Sister Prisca again. The experience had been somewhat unique. Would it sink to a level with other experiences that had been interesting in the past? He thought it would not.

On Sunday evening Robert decided to go to church. He had not been for years. He chose the church farthest from his house; it happened to be the one attended by the Sisters.

During the service he caught occasional glimpses of a certain small, black-robed figure, and surrounded as it was by others in like garments, he recognised it.

He lingered at the churchyard gate till the Sisters passed out. She did not see him, but he heard her speak a few words to her companion, and the low, sweet tones penetrated to his inmost heart.

In the calm morning thought Robert acknowledged to himself difficulties. The difficulties did not discourage or alarm him; his was a nature that delighted in something to overcome, that demanded long battle before attainment. He loved her. That was henceforth the sum total of life for him; the consummation of that love he would attain were she ten times sworn a nun. He must see her, must speak to her. Then he would tell her of his love, he would paint for her the joys of the life they should spend together, he would deliver her from the sway of her soul-subduing rule, would reveal to her the full meaning of youth and freedom.

THE VAGRANT.

The interview he sought was not easy of attainment. Ten days passed, and in spite of many efforts Robert did not gain his object. True, he saw her a second time at the church; once, also, he met her in the town in company with another Sister, but speech was on both occasions impossible. He was contemplating further measures when what is called chance threw the game into his hands.

Robert was paying a visit to an old woman, a shepherd's wife, who lived in a small cottage on the Downs.

The cottage stood quite alone, and the woman, who was crippled by rheumatism, led a very solitary life. From her Robert learned that it was Sister Prisca's custom to visit the cottage every Tuesday and Friday. The good woman was very fond of the Sister, and Robert gathered that these visits were her great consolation in life, and that she had missed them terribly during the illness of the children.

"I do count on her afternoons," the dame said. "She stays about an hour, reads a bit and then talks. She can talk beautiful, and she so young, too. I think sometimes when I listens as she ain't long for this earth, she seems so took up like with the other world."

Robert started slightly at her words. His practised eye had detected the little Sister's delicacy, but it had had no place in his love dreams. Now it flashed across him that she was indeed a frail little thing. He must not delay; the life she led was killing her, he must make haste to lift her out of it.

He walked back briskly across the Downs. The day was bitterly cold, the wind keen, the ground covered with snow. The end of January had brought with it a spell of particularly severe weather, and there were not many who would have cared for such a walk on such a day.

On Friday morning, as Robert was passing through the town, he caught sight of some pots of violets in the window of the nursery gardener. He paused to look at them, then went in and bought every blossom. They were placed for him in a small cardboard box, which he put in his pocket.

The afternoon came. Robert was delayed by patients until after three o'clock. Directly he was free he walked as quickly as possible towards the Downs. He mounted the hill and reached the tableland without encountering anyone. He looked across the expanse of snow towards the cottage; a small dark figure was approaching. He had intended to meet the Sister and turn back with her. Now that he saw her coming it struck him that it would perhaps be wiser to give the meeting an appearance of chance. Accordingly, he retreated to a small copse, the lower end of which straggled down to within a few yards of the footpath. He waited among the trees for what seemed an interminable time; a feeling of self-doubt, such as was unusual with him, grew upon him as the moments passed. At last a little figure was for a moment outlined clearly against the sky, then showed black with a background of snow, as the Sister began to descend the slope. The pathway inclined gradually towards the foot of the copse. Robert made his way through the trees, and came out just below her. He turned as though he had but then seen her, and, raising his hat, waited for her. His heart beat with great thumps; he looked at her anxiously, trying to gather whether his presence had startled her. There was, however, no sign of embarrassment in her face.

"Good afternoon, Sister," he said, steadying his voice with an effort, "have you been taking a walk on the Downs?"

"I have been to visit an old woman, a shepherd's wife," she replied.

"Ah, yes, old Mrs. Simpson. I was there a few days ago. How did you find her?" With some inward trepidation, he ranged himself beside her as he spoke.

She replied quite simply to his question as they went down the narrow pathway together. Now that his opportunity had come, Robert found it hard to make use of it. Her complete unconsciousness of the situation disarmed him. He made some further remarks about the old woman, then inquired after the children, but failed to give a personal turn to the conversation.

There was a short silence between them; then, with a slight tremor in his voice, he said, "Sister, do you know I cannot help wondering sometimes if you ever feel at all — at all — dull — or lonely?"

She turned her head towards him, her face wore a slightly puzzled look. "Oh, no!" she replied, "there are so many of us; we have so many things to do. I don't think we ever feel dull or lonely."

Here again was this "we." Would she never regard herself other than one of her community, never rise to individuality? It was discouraging, but they were drawing near to the high road; he must speak to her without further delay, must break through the barrier between them, must tell her all his desire.

"How long have you been at the convent?" he asked, finding it, despite the need of action, hard to proceed.

"I came when my mother died," she said. "I was seven years old. I have been there eighteen years."

"Eighteen years! Are you twenty-five? You look almost a child."

"I am very small," she said, deprecatingly.

"Eighteen years is a long time, you must have wanted to go away sometimes." She looked at him suddenly with a rather startled expression.

"When you were a child," he inserted hurriedly, "did you not?"

"I don't think so," she said, "not that I remember; they have always been so kind to me."

"And now," he added, with sudden boldness, for the high road was close at hand, "do you never want to see other places, or to try some other life?"

"Oh, no. I never want to go away. I should not like it." She spoke more quickly than was her wont. "I went once for a few days to stay with some cousins. I was so glad to get home. I am not used to many people; it was all so noisy, so different. I cannot explain, but I never want to go away."

They stepped on to the high road as they spoke. The way to the convent was not the way to the town. Must they part? There was no one approaching; he might yet tell her all that was in his heart. "Sister," he said, "I want to ask you something, can you spare me one minute more?"

"Yes," she said. She stood opposite to him, and he could see her full face. She looked utterly unsuspecting, still so entirely the little Sister.

"It is about something that concerns me very dearly," he began, "something that – "

A look of kindly interest rose in her eyes as he hesitated. "You have some trouble?" she queried, "I am sorry."

"Yes – well not exactly," he stammered, floundering hopelessly. The look in her eyes was so kind, yet so uncomprehending, he could not brave it. Suddenly he remembered the flowers, and fell back upon them as a sort of refuge. "I was only wondering if you would accept – if I might offer you these," he said valiantly. He drew the little cardboard box out of his pocket; then, opening it, displayed the violets.

Her face broke into its brightest smile. "How sweet they are," she said, for she loved all flowers as a child loves daisies. "How beautiful." She lifted a violet from the box, and held it up close to her nose, drawing in its fragrance.

"You will accept them," he exclaimed, with renewed hope, delighting in her smile, in her almost childish glee over his offering.

"Thank you. It is kind of you to give them to me." She smiled up at him, but the something he hoped for was not in the smile.

"I am glad you will have them. I am glad you told me your name is Violet; you are like them." He blurted the last words out abruptly, reddening as he spoke like any schoolboy.

She was looking at the flowers and not at him; she did not seem to hear his words, certainly she guessed not their significance. "I think," she said, "God gives us flowers to show us what perfect beauty is; to make us long for perfection."

She raised her head, her cheeks were flushed, in her eyes was the far-off look of those who love much, who

desire much, the things which are unseen. In that look Robert read the death-warrant of his hopes. "You like to think that," he said sadly. "Tell me, is your life a happy one?"

"Yes. I could not be happier in his world."

"In this world," he repeated, mournfully. Then he looked at the flowers. "Will you think of me sometimes?" he added.

"I shall never forget all your goodness to me and to the children. I often think of it," she replied.

He looked into her little face. The colour had left it, in the dim light it appeared to him pathetically weary. "You are tired and cold; I must not keep you longer." He offered his hand, and she did not withhold hers. For one second he held it. It was icy cold.

"Good-bye," she said, with her friendly smile.

"Good-bye, Sister. Good-bye, Violet."

He turned and strode away hastily, without looking back. One short hour had shut the door upon his vision of bliss. Yes, one hour, for Robert realised that he might, indeed, break down her ideals, he might rouse in her that latent desire which all have for what is new and strange, but could he hope to give her in some other sphere of life the satisfaction she found at the convent? She was happy in her delusion, for delusion it remained to him; would it not be cruel to destroy her happiness?

All that evening Robert told himself he was glad to think that no suspicion of the feelings he entertained had dawned upon her mind. The memory of her face wrapped him round like a magic atmosphere; it seemed a desecration to think of her as other than she was, to dream of an answering passion in those eyes so possessed with the love of the Eternal.

Love is indeed stronger than death, but of few is it demanded to prove this. Those who do love with an utter unselfishness rise not to that height in one short hour. Human desire dies hard. That night Robert could not sleep, as the hours dragged on a great contest raged within him. He wanted her. Should one failure mean despair? Every atom

of his being cried out for her. He could, he would, win her yet. Love strove with passion, till at last near morning he slept.

Sleep brought dreams. He wandered in an open wood, the air was laden with the scent of violets, he sought for a blossom but they were all hidden from him; again and again he put aside the sheltering leaves; his search was vain. At last he grew weary; he paused and rested against a tree. As his look wandered aimlessly round, he was suddenly aware of a violet just at his feet. It was partially sheltered by the leaves, but its little face was upturned to him. With a cry of joy, he knelt down to pluck it. His grasp was on the slender stem, when he felt someone touch him on the shoulder; he started, and looked round. All in white she stood before him, her golden hair, unloosed, fell down to her girdle, her face was lighted with a rapturous smile. The air seemed filled with music, strange words sounded in his ears. "A garden enclosed is my sister, my spouse, a spring shut up, a fountain sealed."

Before, in his amazement, he could kneel at her feet she was gone; when he turned to pluck the violet, it had withered. Then he awoke.

It was between eight and nine the next morning when Robert breakfasted. He had never been so glad to be alone. He was still looking through the morning's letters when the surgery bell rang violently. A note was brought to him. It contained a few hastily-written words, begging him to come to the convent at once.

Without a moment's delay, Robert obeyed the summons. On his arrival he was admitted very quickly. The Mother appeared at once; her face bore traces of tears.

"I sent for you directly we knew," she said. "When she did not come down to breakfast, I told someone to look for her. They called me; it must have been hours ago; it was her heart, we expect; it was always weak. My dear little one; quite alone – " Her voice broke.

Robert followed her in silence, his heart weighed down by an expectation that was all but a certainty. They mounted to a tiny room at the top of the house – a room plain, cold and cheerless. A crucifix hung just opposite the door, on a small table beneath it was a little jar of violets. Then his heart stood still.

They turned to the bed. She lay there, her eyes closed for ever on earthly things, her mouth beautiful with the smile of joy achieved. He could find no word at first, but touched lightly the hands that lay crossed on her breast. "Poor child," he said gently, "so young, so brave."

"Yes, you knew that at the cottage."

"It is hard to lose her," the Mother continued presently, speaking half to herself, "but one must be glad for her. She has heard the Bridegroom's voice."

Her eyes lighted on the violets. She took them from the jar and placed them on the little Sister's breast. "Rest in peace," she murmured.

Love which seeketh not her own rose supreme in Robert's heart. "Amen," he said, and bowed his head.

VII. – SPORTS AND RECREATIONS.

By Mrs. Hugh Price Hughes.

MY DEAR R. – You have set me a difficult task in spite of the fact that I suppose there is now no Christian society that looks altogether askance upon sports and recreations. The time was, in the days of our Puritan forefathers, when such things were indiscriminately consigned to the keeping of the devil and his servants, and were looked upon as the special portion of the ungodly and frivolous.

I do not suppose, however, that any thoughtful Christian to-day considers their creed, which was the outcome of the tremendous circumstances of their time and history, an ideal one.

We have but to look at

the world of nature to see the ideal of God. What is more joyous that the sunshine? Who can look at the golden daffodils this spring without thinking of those lines in Wordsworth's exquisite and unapproachable poem: —

"The waves beside them danced,
  But they outdid the sparkling
waves in glee;
A poet could not be but gay
In such a jocund company."

Who can watch unmoved the romping of three lively kittens with a grave, sedate old cat, and when we visit the monkey house at the "Zoo," or watch the proceedings of crabs and lobsters in the tanks of some aquarium, it is forced upon our minds that God has even introduced the idea of the comic into His creation. Recreation, in some form or another, is a law of our being, and with all young life it is an imperious law.

A child begins to act and play almost before it begins to speak. And to the healthy growing boy and girl, vigorous outdoor sports are, and ought to be, a necessity. We hail with joy all efforts made in the present day to bring healthy outdoor games within the reach of the children and young people of our cities, and long for the playgrounds and open spaces to be infinitely multiplied, and for more and more cheap and easy access to the country around. This is just as it should be, excepting, of course, that insane tendency which exists in our older universities and public schools to make certain sports the object and aim of existence. The worship of cricket and football that exists in some of these educational centres is simply puerile and contemptible, and defeats the very object of true, healthy recreation.

Turning, however, from outdoor sport and recreation to social pleasures and amusements provided for young people, either privately or at public places of amusement, there is a difficulty which comes home to every thoughtful youth and maiden. The difficulty, I think resolves itself into a question expressed roughly in these words, "Is it possible for me to enter into certain forms of amusement, which are a great source of pleasure and enjoyment, without doing moral harm to myself and others?" If there is one question that I have been asked oftener than another, especially by young people who have received some amount of education, it is this: "Is it right to dance? Is it right to go to the theatre?" and it is a question that I always refuse to answer.

Christ gives us certain broad, all-embracing principles, which are the same always and true for all time. The carrying out of these principles varies continually according to the age in which we live, the circumstances of the time, and the surroundings of the individual life.

The one thing that He does distinctly and emphatically forbid in his followers is the worldly spirit. Against this we all need ever to watch and pray, as the most deadly enemy that can assault the soul. Some people think that if they avoid certain amusements such as balls and theatres, they are safe from all harm in this direction, and that in giving up "worldly amusements," as they call them, they have nothing to fear in that quarter.

There could be no greater delusion. I have known people who would be horrified at the idea of entering a ballroom or theatre, as thoroughly worldly in spirit as many a one who did; and I have known others, on the other hand, who frequented such amusements, who were amongst the most unworldly people I have ever met.

What is, therefore, the essence of the worldly spirit – what is this secret inwardness and root of evil against which we have to watch and pray? St. John says it is "the lust of the flesh, the lust of the eye, and the vainglory of life," and these, when reduced to their elements, can be expressed in one word – selfishness.

Now in the choice of our recreations we must answer the questionings of our conscience by the application of this broad Gospel principle:

"Do I, or do I not, in gratifying my taste for certain pleasures, minister to my own selfishness, sacrificing thereby the good and well-being of others, and also sacrificing the usefulness and power for service in my own life?"

We must look at our recreations and everything else from the standpoint of the one tremendous purpose that we have before us; and if we feel in our conscience that any recreation hinders us in some path of usefulness to which God has called us, our duty is plain before us.

This question will be answered very differently in different lives. What proves the hindrance to usefulness in one life is often the opportunity of another.

I cannot conceal from my mind that dramatic power is a gift of God, as much as any other art, and is intended by Him to be used

for the happiness and good of mankind. Dancing, also, is a natural instinct implanted by Him; and in these things, in themselves, there is no more harm than there is in music or walking. I believe the time will come when these amusements, natural and healthy in themselves, will be purified from the associations that in the present day so frequently render them harmful. That day, alas! has not dawned yet, and in the meantime we stand face to face with many difficulties and perplexities.

Our only safeguard is to make our consciences keenly alive to the poison of the worldly spirit. If, in our choice of recreations, we do honestly in every deed and word seek not only our own but also our neighbour's good, if we make them minister to our highest and noblest purpose in life, we shall not go far astray.

Girls' Pets and How to Manage Them.

PIGEONS – II.

URCHASING requires care and judgment. Suppose you make a start with two or three pairs. They must be quite young birds, or "squeakers," as they are called, and should be about six weeks old. If you buy old birds they are liable to fly away home at the first opportunity, and some dealers look for the return of their birds a few weeks after they have been sold. This will explain the need for starting with young birds. These, by the bye, should not, if you can possibly help it, all come from one stock.

After they are eight or nine months old, the birds may be mated. This is usually done about March by shutting a pair up for a few days together. They can fly out after this, and you will soon observe if they are good friends by many little attentions they will pay to one another. Pigeons breed from about March till the end of August.

The nest boxes should be partly prepared by yourself, and before placing in the straw lay down a handful or two of pine sawdust; it keeps away vermin, and is not objectionable to the birds. Nest pans are preferable and these can be bought at any dealer's.

The hens will lay two eggs, an interval of a day taking place between the two. When the second one has been laid the birds will take their turns in sitting for a period of seventeen to eighteen days, though the hens will do the larger share of the sitting.

When the young are hatched the parent birds feed them, though it is safest to keep an eye on them, to see that they do not neglect this. Sometimes the parent birds cannot feed their offspring, and it is as well you should know what to do either in this case or on account of the loss of one of them. Mr. Lewis Wright gives the following advice :— "The simplest, easiest and quickest way is to chew small mouthfuls of plain "milk" biscuit into a smooth pap, and feed the little squeaker from your lips, into which its beak must be inserted." You will thus be required to act the parents' part, and you must remember your responsibility, and not neglect the feeding times. When the orphans get out of the pap stage, which they will do after a few weeks, you must give them soaked grain or peas, by pouring hot water on to them and give just warm, putting the food into the birds' beaks with your fingers until their crops are full.

Before giving advice about feeding, you might as well know that when you have to hold a pigeon there is a proper way to do this, so that you will not hurt the bird or injure it plumage. The breast part should rest in the palm of the hand, the head to the little finger, with the legs passed through between the first and second fingers, the thumb resting across the back. By holding the bird in this manner, firmly but gently, you can turn it in any way you choose, and make any necessary examination.

FEEDING

The food that suits for winter will not do for summer time. Heating foods, slow of digestion, are suitable for cold weather, such as tick beans, tares or old grey peas; but for summer feeding you must include occasionally a supply of green food. Give grey peas instead of beans, mixed together with wheat and maize, and only during breeding time a few grains of rice may be put with this mixture; it is good for the young squeakers. Do not change the food suddenly, but gradually substituting the summer for the winter feeding, and *vice versa*.

It has been calculated that for a flying-out bird a pint to a pint and a half of grain is sufficient for one week's food, so that when making your purchase at the corn chandler's you can multiply this according to the number of birds you keep.

New grain of all sorts is bad, for it will purge your birds and make them very ill. Fresh water in plenty for drinking purposes and bathing must always be at hand for their use; a pie dish will do for a bath. The bath is absolutely necessary to preserve healthy stock.

One word more before leaving the question of feeding, and here the value of a hopper comes in. See that the sparrows are excluded from your loft by using small meshed wire in its construction; the sparrows select the best grains, to the disadvantage of your pigeons. By using the hopper, sparrow feeding is done away with, and the benefit is in the saving effected. Old mortar rubbish should be given to the birds to peck over.

DOCTORING

We are enabled to give you a specialist's advice regarding the treatment of the more common ailments of pigeons. He says:— "Do not forget that proper attention to the comfort and feeding of pigeons is essential, not only to keep disease away, but to aid in curing a sick bird. There is no more unsatisfactory patient of any kind that I know than a sick pigeon; but a person may have a very valuable bird, and wish to do all in his power to aid it. No matter how trifling the ailment may seem, even if only a common cold, the bird should be removed from the loft, because you never know what it may turn to. Take it and put into a pen by itself, and place this pen in a warm corner where it can have fresh air. Now give it daintier food, softer grains, such as barley, rice, wheat &c., tender green

food, fresh water, and a few handfuls of hemp. Nurse and keep clean. When you have fulfilled these instructions you have gone half-way towards removing the trouble, if, indeed, there be a remove for it.

"Diarrhoea is a far too common and a troublesome complaint. Give a few drops

PORTABLE PIGEON-HOUSE
WITH FLIGHT.

of warm castor oil, or castor-oil capsule, with four or five drops of laudanum. This for one dose. Put plenty of gravel down, and mix prepared chalk with grains.

"Cold. — Nostrils or eyes, or both, run. Give castor oil, or a pinch of Epsom salts in water. Bathe eyes and nostrils frequently, and keep in an extra warm place

at night, quite away from draughts. Give hempseed.

"Going Light. — This is a term used to express a very dangerous and very often fatal disorder in young pigeons, in which emaciation is one of the principal symptoms. If there be diarrhoea, try to stop that by the means I have just advised; then give a few drops of cod-liver oil frequently, and also a few drops of Parrish's chemical food. It is thankless work treating a bird in this complaint, which has been compared by some to consumption, and by others to distemper in dogs.

"Inflammation of the Eyes. — Bathe frequently in warm milk and water; use at first a weak solution of alum, three grains to the ounce, as an eye-wash, and afterwards put into each eye half a drop of vinum opii (opium wine). Keep the bird free from draughts.

"Constipation is the reverse of diarrhoea. Green food will remove it, or a little warm treacle.

"Spouts is the absurd name given to the cracks or excoriations in the wattles of some birds. It requires a little surgical operation – namely, paring or clipping off the wrinkles that cause the mischief. Afterwards use an ointment of oxide of zinc made with vaseline.

"These are a few of the more common complaints to which the pigeon is liable, with remedies for the same, which, simple though they appear, will, nevertheless,

be found efficacious in most cases."

[*By kind permission of Messrs. Spratt's, we are able to illustrate one of their Portable Pigeon-Houses, which we can thoroughly recommend.*]

In the Doctor's Sanctum.

EXCESSIVE TEA-DRINKING.

THAT tea-drinking has become a gigantic social evil no one will deny. In America alone one million pounds, and in England even more, are expended every year in the purchase of the drug; and the evil is growing at an alarming rate. Into Britain tea to the value of £11,000,000 is imported every year. We are indebted for the following lucid and convincing utterances upon the subject to that brilliant medical writer, J. H. Kellog, M.D.

The fact that when a person drinks strong tea and coffee the sense of hunger is allayed has given rise to the idea that tea and coffee are foods. Medical textbooks and physiology have for

many years been teaching that tea and coffee, if not exactly foods, are to some extent substitutes for them. A thorough-going investigation, however, has shown the very opposite to be the case. It has been proved conclusively that tea and coffee are not foods in any sense whatever, and that they diminish the appetite for food simply by diminishing the ability to digest it.

There are many things besides tea and coffee that diminish the appetite for food. Many a man would rather have his pipe of tobacco or a cigar than his dinner. Heavy smokers scarcely know when the dinner hour comes, except by the clock or by a weakness of the knees. Alcohol

operates in the same way. The man who uses alcohol can relieve his hunger by a toddy or a glass of whisky, for the effect of alcohol as well as of tobacco is to diminish the power of the stomach to digest food.

We know that tea, coffee, and other kindred drugs are not foods, because a person cannot live upon them. Anyone who undertakes to work upon the strength of tea and coffee, and eats no other food, diminishes in weight about as rapidly as if he ate nothing at all. There is no food power and no real energising power in either tea or coffee. They do not support the ability to work, but they do increase the disposition to work. The man who is tired or exhausted takes a cup of tea or coffee, a glass of whisky, or a small dose of cocaine, and is relieved of his weariness. He feels greater ease in labour, but his muscles have not recuperated; no new energy has been put into them; he has simply lost his sense of weariness. Now, this sensation of fatigue is a danger-signal — a beacon-light. If the light of the lighthouse is extinguished the ships may run upon the rocks and be wrecked. So the man who, under the influence of a drug, is no longer conscious that he is going beyond the limits of safe exertion, may continue working harder than ever, but as a final result the exhaustion that he experiences exceeds that which attended his former efforts. When a man takes tea or coffee as others use alcohol, he has to put forth a greater effort, and greater exhaustion is experienced every time he repeats the use of the drug. This shows that these drugs waste energy, and that the waste of energy is greater at each effort — this is a physiological deduction.

The fact is, that alcohol, tea, and coffee belong to the same class of stimulants. To emphasise this is of special importance, because it is a very singular fact that, while it is generally recognised as true that the habit of alcohol-drinking or using intoxicating liquors of any sort is injurious, there is an almost universal belief that tea and coffee are whole-some. I am satisfied that this favourable opinion with reference to these drugs is due to ignorance of their character.

Natural foods encourage digestion. One kind helps the digestion of another. For example, the acids in sugar and fruits serve to stimulate and call forth the gastric juice, which is necessary for the digestion of the albumins, as of nuts; and the fats which the nuts contain are useful and necessary, again, in stimulating the process by which the food is moved along the alimentary canal, also encouraging the action of the liver. No wholesome food ever interferes with digestion, but carefully conducted experiments show beyond all cavil that the use of tea and coffee has a most pernicious effect upon digestion, because of the injurious substances which they contain. Tea contains tannin; if you add a little iron to tea, it becomes black. No one would think of making tea in an iron tea-kettle; it would be as black as ink. If you take a strong cup of tea and stir it with an iron spoon, it soon becomes black; this is because of the combination of the tannin of the tea with iron, a combination that makes ink. Leather is made by soaking hides in a decoction of oak bark, which contains tannin. The tannic acid combines with the connective tissue of the hides or skins, and thus produces leather. So when a man eats a piece of beefsteak and drinks a strong cup of tea, the tannic acid of the tea combines with the connective tissue of the steak, and the latter is converted into leather. Certainly, if one understands this, he cannot imagine that tea would have a very favourable influence upon digestion. If one were to soak his beefsteak in a strong cup of tea for half an hour he would find it as impossible to chew it as to chew sole-leather. So when a person eats beef and drinks tea, the leather-making process is started in his stomach.

Now, some writers say that although tea and coffee are a positive hindrance to the digestion of fats and albuminoids, they, nevertheless, in some mysterious fashion or other, encourage the digestion of starch. This is by no means the case, as can be shown by a very simple logical demonstration. For what digests starch is saliva, therefore what hinders saliva hinders the digestion of starch. It is also a well-known fact that the tannin contained in tea hinders the production of saliva — that is to say, hinders the digestion of starch.

The demand for tea and coffee is purely artificial; if it were a natural demand it would be universal, which it is not. Now, the demand for food is absolutely universal. Yet you can hardly find a boy or girl who would drink tea or coffee were it not for the cream and sugar accompanying it. It is not until the natural taste has been vitiated that such things can be tolerated.

Not only is it true that tea and coffee contain no nourishment and serious ly interfere with digestion, but it is true also that they are actual poisons. One proof of this is that they will kill animals. Distil tea or coffee by placing it in a dry retort, and a poison in it is crystallised in the form of needles; this poison can be separated from tea or coffee by various means. The amount of poisonous matter (thein) contained in tea is about 6 per cent., and in coffee about 1 per cent., the thein of tea and the caffein of coffee being the same thing. One-eighth of a grain of caffein or thein will kill a frog; five grains will kill a rabbit; and seven and a half grains will kill a cat. There is more than an ounce of poison in a pound of tea, enough to kill seventy rabbits or fifty cats. It takes only about ten grains of thein to make a man sick. Professor Lehmann, a German physician, some years ago, gave each of several men from eight to ten grains of thein, and they were so much affected by it that they were not able to do any work on the day of the experiment, nor yet on the next day; but,

as I have stated, one single half-ounce of ordinary tea contains from ten to sixteen grains of thein — of this very poison. It takes only two cup of "good, strong tea" to make some people more or less intoxicated.

Another evidence that tea is poisonous is its individual influence upon the man or woman who drinks it. Many a person cannot sleep at night if he takes a cup of tea in the afternoon.

Some time ago there was a woman in the Midlands who had acquired the habit of tea-drinking, who carried her mania so far that she had the teapot on the stove all the time, and drank thirty or forty cups a day. In consequence of this habit she was finally sent to the lunatic asylum. There was another woman who had delirium tremens as a result of tea-tippling. She drank no alcohol or intoxicating liquors, so-called, of any sort. She had simply taken great quantities of strong tea. She was a tea-drunkard. In many an English cottage home you invariably find a pot of villainous tea brewing on the hob all day long. The neurotic and hysteric tendency, which is such a marked feature of life among all our classes at the present day, is mainly attributable to tea-tippling. The impaired digestions and decayed teeth which cause so many of our recruits to be rejected that the matter has become a question of national importance — this, too, is largely the result of foolish tea-swilling; for men are becoming quite as bad as women in the matter.

The two following authentic stories will show, in fact, that the blame may be distributed pretty evenly between the two sexes:—

A few years ago some girls in a tea factory were arrested on the charge of being drunk and disorderly. It was found that they had used no alcoholic liquors, but had chewed tea constantly; they had free access to the drug, and they carried it in their pockets, chewing it all the time, and, as a result, became intoxicated. Not long since, in London, there was a club of newspaper reporters who used to get together every Saturday night and have a spree on tea. They would sit up until midnight and after, drinking tea; they would drink and drink until they became insensible.

Athletics for Girls.

FENCING. – II.

ANOTHER thing must be guarded against. The idea that quickness is vital to fencing is true to a great extent, but the beginner generally errs by being too quick. She will parry before her opponent has formed his attack, thus laying herself open to a thousand new dangers. She will lunge without consideration, letting her foot move before her hand, and then she will wonder why the point of her foil is nowhere near her master's body. She must grasp the fact that her hand is the most important part of her mechanism, and her foot must follow its lead, as her hand must follow the directions of her head.

The next movements to be learnt after the guard and the lunge, are the advance and retreat. To advance, the right foot is moved forward and the left follows, and both are still at right angles to each other, and their original distance apart. The advance should be made smoothly and quietly, and without attracting your adversary's notice, unless you wish to startle him into retreating in order that you may carry out some plan of attack. Italian fencers have a way of advancing which is surprising, and sometimes effective. They spring off the ground with both feet and land about a yard nearer their opponent. To do this successfully needs practice, and it should not be attempted until you feel that your knowledge of fencing justifies you in playing tricks with it.

A good master will insist upon his pupil thoroughly understanding these preliminary movements before she learns the attacks and parries; and I cannot attempt to teach the latter here, for they can only be properly learnt from demonstrations and practice.

There are eight simple parries; prime, seconde, tierce, quarte, quinte, sixte, septime and octave. The two of them most in use are quarte and sixte, which defend the part of the body most likely to be attacked, that is from the collar-bone to the chest; and they are the quickest and the simplest to make. In fencing, as in most things, the simplest course is the best, and though it is very gratifying to be able to make elaborate parries, to bring them off successfully wants about five years' hard work. Of course, they must be learnt, but after all they are more for ornament than for use.

A fencer who is perfectly at home with her quarte and sixte parries and their counters may feel sure of herself when she engages in loose play. The parry of quarte defends the left side of the body, and sixte the right side. It is usual to come on guard in quarte — that is, with your blade inside your opponent's; but should the position of the blades be reversed (that is, in the sixte) then to parry quarte the foil hand is moved across the body just

ENGAGE.

To retreat, the left foot is drawn back and the right follows it, still keeping their respective positions. This backward movement is meant to be seen, and to lure your opponent on; therefore the right foot should touch the ground sharply but not heavily.

Two enthusiasts might try to carry them out according to a book of instructions, but the result would be of no real use. All I can hope to do here is to give a general idea of the parries, counter-parries, attacks, feints, and ripostes, and of the way they should be done.

enough to cover it, and the upper part of your blade (the forte) comes sharply against the lower part (the foible) of your opponent's. The parry of sixte is the same movement on the right side. Some masters say the and octave the right side. They are made by dropping the point of the foil, but the hand is not lowered; then, if an attack is made in septime from quarte it is parried by dropping the point, the hand remaining the wrist, and parrying with the foible instead of with the forte, which will result in the point of your foil being some feet outside your opponent's body, instead of where it ought to be, aiming straight at

PARRY OF QUARTE.

wrist should be slightly turned in parrying quarte, and I think it does add to the ease and quickness of the parry.

The parries most in use after quarte and sixte are septime and octave. They defend the lower part of the body, septime the left, stationary. Prime, seconde, tierce, and quinte are variations of these four principal parries and are seldom used in loose play. In parrying, the faults to be avoided are: wide or heavy parries, which are a waste of energy besides being dangerous; using the arm instead of the chest.

There are more varieties of attacks than of parries. The simple disengagement is the first, as it is the most important, to learn. It is made by dropping the point of your foil under your adversary's hand, and going in on the other side.

The arm is straightened at the second movement, the instant before you lunge, not before, in case your attack is parried before you have time to finish it. After the disengagement comes the one–two (or double disengagement), the one–two–three (a triple movement), when the point of your foil should creep nearer and nearer to its goal; the double, when you encircle your opponent's blade; and the cut over, the beat, press, and graze, which explain themselves.

Feints are false attacks to put your adversary off her guard and to deceive her. Thus, instead of making a direct beat and lunge, we will imagine that you beat in quarte, and, when the other blade returns to oppose yours, you disengage and attack in sixte. A riposte is a parry and attack without moving from the position of guard; it is an immediate return after the attack has been parried, and while the attacker is on the lunge. In attacking, the principal thing to remember is that no lunge should be made at random on the chance of making a hit; every attack should be considered and deliberate, unless, of course, a sudden opening gives a sudden chance.

There are many other things to be said about fencing, but they are best discovered for one's self after a long acquaintance with it. It is one of its beauties that there is always something new to learn in it. When you are allowed to begin loose play, you will find pleasure and health in mastering the technicalities of fencing, in devising combinations of attack and defence, and in knowing that you are training your brain and your body both in harmony together for your present and future benefit.

The Adventures of A LOON

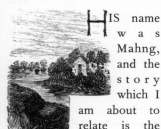

HIS name was Mahng, and the story which I am about to relate is the story of his matrimonial career — or at least of a portion of it.

One snowy autumn night, three years ago, he was swimming on the Glimmerglass in company with his first wife — one of the first, that is. There may possibly have been others before her, but, if so, I wasn't acquainted with them. It was a fine evening — especially for loons. There was no wind, and the big, soft flakes came floating lazily down to lose themselves in the quiet lake. The sky, the woods, and the shores were all blotted out; and the loons reigned alone, king and queen of a dim little world of leaden water and falling snow. And right royally they swam their kingdom, with an air as if they thought God had made the Glimmerglass for their especial benefit. Perhaps He had.

It was very, very lonely, but they liked it all the better for that. At times they even lost sight of each other for a little while, as one dived in search of a herring or a young salmon trout. I wish we could have followed Mahng down under the water and watched him at his hunting. He didn't dive as you do, with a jump and a plunge and a splash. He merely drew his head back a little, and then thrust it forward and downward, and went under as simply and easily as you would step out of bed and with a good deal more dignity. It was his feet that did it, of course. They were not good for much walking but they were the real thing when it came to swimming or diving. They were large and broad and strongly webbed, and the short stout legs which carried them were flattened and compressed that they might slip edgewise through the water, like a feathered oar blade. The muscles which worked them were very powerful, and they kicked backward with so much vigour that two little jets of spray were often tossed up in his wake as he went under, like the splash from a steamer's paddles. And he had a rudder, too, for in the after part of his body there were two muscles just like tiller ropes, fastened to his tail in such a way that they could twist it to either side, and steer him to port or starboard as occasion demanded.

With his long neck stretched far out in front, his wings pressed tightly against his sides, and his legs and feet working as if they went by steam, he shot through the water like a submarine torpedo boat. "the Herdsman of the Deep," the Scottish Highlanders used to say, when in winter a loon came to visit their lochs and fiords. Swift and strong and terrible, he ranged the depths of the Glimmerglass, seeking what he might devour; and perhaps you can imagine how hastily the poor little fishes took their departure whenever they saw him coming their way. Sometimes they were not quite quick enough, and then his long bill closed upon them, and he swallowed them whole without even waiting to rise to the surface.

The chase thus brought to a successful conclusion, or perhaps the supply of air in his lungs giving out, he returned to the upper world, and again his voice rang out through the darkness and the falling snow. Then his wife would answer him from somewhere away off across the lake, and they would call back and forth to each other with many a laugh and shout, or, drawing closer and closer together, they would cruise the Glimmerglass side by side, with the big flakes dropping gently on their backs and folded wings, and the ripples spreading out on either hand like the swell from the bow of a ship.

Once Mahng stayed down a little longer than usual, and when he came up he heard his wife calling him in an excited tone, as if something had happened to her. He hurried toward her, and presently he saw a light shining dimly through the throng of moving snow flakes, and growing brighter and brighter as he approached until it was fairly dazzling. As he drew nearer still he caught sight of his wife sitting on the water squarely in front of that light, and watching it with all her eyes. She was not calling now. She had forgotten Mahng, she had forgotten to paddle, she had forgotten everything in her wonder at this strange, beautiful thing, the like of which had never before been seen upon the Glimmerglass.

She herself was a rarely beautiful sight – if she had only known it – with the dark water rippling gently against her bosom, her big black head thrust forward, and the feathers of her throat and breast glistening in the glare of the headlight, white as the snow that was falling around her.

All this Mahng saw. What he did not see, because his eyes were dazzled, was a boat in the shadow behind the light, and a rifle barrel pointing straight at his wife's breast. There was a blinding flash, a sharp, crashing report, and a cloud of smoke; and Mahng dived as quick as a wink. His wife would never dive again. The bullet had gone tearing through her body, and she lay stretched out on the water, perfectly motionless, and apparently dead. And then, just as Mahng came to the surface a hundred yards away, and just as my partner put out his hand to pick her up, she lifted her head and gave a last wild cry. Mahng heard it and answered, but he was too far away to see what had happened. He dared not return till the light had disappeared, and by that time she was gone. She had struggled violently for a moment, and had struck savagely at the hunter's hand, and then she had as suddenly collapsed, the water turned red, and her eyes closed for ever. Did you know that among all God's creatures the birds are the only ones whose eyes close naturally in death? Even among men it is not so, for when our friends die we lay our hands reverently upon their faces, and weight their stiff lids with gold. But for the bird Nature herself performs the last kindly office, and as the light fades out from the empty windows of the soul, the curtain falls of its own accord.

During the next two or three days Mahng's voice was frequently to be heard, apparently calling his wife. Sometimes it was a mournful, long-drawn cry— "Hoo-WOOOO-ooo"— that might have been heard a mile away — a cry that seemed the very essence of loneliness, and that went right down where you lived and made you feel like a murderer. And sometimes he broke into a wild peal of laughter, as if he hoped that

that might better serve to call her back to him.

His children had gone south some time before. They had seemed anxious to see the world. Perhaps, too, they had dreaded the approach of colder weather more than the older birds, who had become somewhat seasoned by previous autumns. Anyhow, they had taken the long trail toward the Gulf of Mexico, and now that his wife was gone Mahng was entirely alone. At last he seemed to make up his mind that he might as well follow them, and one afternoon, as he was swimming aimlessly about, I saw him suddenly dash forward, working his wings with all their might, beating the water at every stroke, and throwing spray like a sidewheeler. Slowly — for his body was heavy, and his wings were rather small for his size — slowly he lifted himself from the water, all the time rushing forward faster and faster. He couldn't have made it if he hadn't had plenty of sea room, but by swinging round and round in long wide circles he managed to rise little by little till at last he was clear

of the tree-tops. He passed right over my head as he stood away to the south — his long neck stretched far out in front, his feet pointing straight back beyond the end of his short tail, and his wings beating the air with tremendous energy. How they did whizz! He made almost as much noise as a train of cars. He laughed as he went by, and you would have said that he was in high spirits; but before he disappeared that lonely, long-drawn cry came back once more — "Hoo-WOOOO-ooo."

In the course of his winter wanderings through the south he happened to alight one day on a certain wild pond down in Mississippi, and there he found another loon — a widow whose former husband had lost his life the previous summer under rather peculiar circumstances.

Beside a small lake in Minnesota there lives an old Dutchman who catches fish with empty bottles. On any calm, still day you may see a lot of them floating upright in the water, all tightly corked, and each with the end of a fishing line tied around its neck. They seem very decorous and well-behaved, but let a fish take one of the hooks and begin to pull, and immediately that particular bottle turns wrong end up, and acts as if it had taken a drop too much of its own original contents. Then the Dutchman paddles out in his little scow, and perhaps by the time he has hauled in his fish and rebaited the hook another bottle is excitedly standing on its head. But never before nor since have any of them behaved as wildly as the one that a loon got hold of.

The loon — not Mahng, you understand, but the first husband of his new acquaintance — had dived in search of his dinner, and the first thing he saw that looked as if it might be good to eat was the bait on one of the Dutchman's hooks. He swallowed it, of course, and for the next five minutes he went charging up and down that pond at a great rate, followed by a green glass monster with the name of a millionaire brewer blown in its side. Sometimes he was on the surface, and sometimes he was under it; but

wherever he went that horrible thing was close behind him, pulling so hard that the sharp cord cut the corners of his mouth till it bled. Once or twice he tried to fly, but the line caught his wing and brought him down again. When he dived it tangled itself around his legs and clogged the machinery; and when he tried to shout, the hook in his throat would not let him do anything more than cough. The Dutchman got him at last, and eventually Mahng got his widow, as you shall see.

She had her children to take care of, and for a time she was very busy, but after a few weeks they flew away to the south, as Mahng's had done, and she was free to go where she liked and do what she pleased. For a while, she stayed where she was, like a sensible person. Minnesota suited her very well, and she was in no hurry to leave. But, of course, she could not stay on indefinitely, for some frosty night the lake would freeze over, and then she could neither dive for fish nor rise upon the wing. A loon on ice is about as helpless as an oyster. And so, at last she, too, went

south. She travelled by easy stages, and had a pleasant journey, with many a stop, and many a feast in the lakes and rivers along the route. I should like to know, just out of curiosity, how many fish found their way down her capacious gullet during that pilgrimage through Illinois and Kentucky and Tennessee.

Well, no matter about that. The Mississippi pond was in sight and she was just slanting down toward the water, when a hunter fired at her from behind a clump of trees. His aim was all too true, and she fell headlong to the ground, with a broken wing dangling helplessly at her side.

Now, as you probably know, a loon isn't built for running. There is an old story, one which certainly has the appearance of truth, to the effect that when Nature manufactured the first of these birds she forgot to give him any legs at all, and that he had started off on the wing before has noticed her mistake. Then she picked up the first pair that came to hand and threw them after him. Unfortunately, they were a

THEY WENT UP, AND UP, AND UP.

misfit, and what was, perhaps, still worse, they struck his body in the wrong place. They were so very short and so very far aft that, although he could stand nearly as straight as a man, it was almost impossible for him to move about on them. When he had to travel on land, which he always avoided as far as he could, he generally shoved himself along on his breast, and often used his wings and his bill to help himself forward. All his descendants are just like him, so you can see that the widow's chances were pretty small, with the hunter bursting out of the bushes, and a broad strip of beach between her and the friendly pond.

But she was a person of resource and energy, and in this great emergency she literally rose to the occasion, and did something that she had never done before in all her life, and probably will never do again. The astonished hunter saw her lift herself until she stood nearly upright, and then actually run across the beach toward the water. She was leaning forward a trifle, her long neck was stretched out, her two short legs were trotting as fast as they could go, and her one good wing was wildly waving in a frantic endeavour to get on. It was a sight that very few people have ever seen, and it would have been comical if it hadn't been a matter of life and death. The hunter was hard after her, and his legs were a yard long, while hers were only a few inches, so it was not surprising that he caught her just as she reached the margin. She wriggled out of his grasp and dashed on through the shallow water, and he followed close behind. In a moment he stooped and made another grab at her and this time he got his arms around her body and pinned her wings down against her sides. But he had waded out a little too far, and had reached the place where the bottom suddenly shelves off from fifteen inches to seventy-two. His foot slipped, and in another moment he was splashing wildly about in the water, and the loon was free.

A broken wing is not necessarily as serious a matter as you might suppose. The cold water kept the inflammation down, and it seemed as if all the vital forces of her strong, healthy body set to work at once to repair the damage. If any comparative anatomist ever gets hold of the widow and dissects her, he will find a curious swelling in the principal bone of her left wing, like a plumber's join in a lead pipe, and he will know what it means. It is the place where Nature soldered the broken pieces together. And it was while Nature was engaged in this soldering operation that Mahng arrived and began to cultivate the widow's acquaintance.

"In the spring a fuller crimson
comes upon the robin's breast,"

and in the spring the loon puts on his wedding garment, and his fancy, like the young man's, "lightly turns to thoughts of love."

But speaking of Mahng's wedding garment reminds me that I haven't told you about his winter dress. His back and wings were very dark brown, and his breast and underparts were white. His head and the upper portion of his neck were black; his bill was black, or blackish, and so were his feet. His coat was very thick and warm, and his legs were feathered right down to the heel joint. More than five feet his wings stretched from tip to tip, and he weighed at least twelve pounds, and would be still larger before he died.

As to his nuptial finery, its groundwork was much the same, but its trimmings were different and were very elegant. White spots appeared all over his back and the upper surface of his wings, some of them round and some square. They were not thrown on carelessly, but were arranged in gracefully curving lines, and they quite changed his appearance, especially if one were as near him as one is supposed to be during a courting. His spring neckwear, too, was in exceedingly good taste, for he put on a sort of collar of very narrow vertical stripes, contrasting beautifully with the black around and between them. Higher up on his neck and head the deep black feathers gleamed and shone in the sunlight with brilliant iridescent tints of green and violet. He was a very handsome bird.

And now everything was going north. The sun was going north, the wind was going north, the birds were going, and summer herself was sweeping up from the tropics as fast as ever she could travel. Mahng was getting very restless. A dozen times a day he would spread his wings and beat the air furiously, dashing the spray in every direction, and almost lifting his heavy body out of the water. But the time was not yet come, and presently he would fold his pinions and go back to his courting.

Do you think he was very inconstant? Do you blame him for not being more faithful to the memory of the bird who was shot at his side only a few months before? Don't be too hard on him. What can a loon do when the springtime calls and the wind blows fresh and strong, when the new strong wine of life is coursing madly through his veins, and when his dreams are all of the vernal flight to the lonely northland, where the water is cold and the fish are good, and where there are such delightful resting places around the marshy ponds?

But how did his new friend feel about it? Would she go with him? Ah! Wouldn't she? Had not she, too, put on a wedding garment just like his? And what was she there for anyhow, if not to be wooed, and to find a mate, and to fly away with him a thousand miles to the north, and there, beside some lonely little lake, brood over her eggs and her young? Her wing was gaining strength all the time, and at last she was ready. You should have heard them laugh when the great day came and they pulled out for Michigan — Mahng a little in the lead, as became the larger and stronger, and his new wife close behind. There had been nearly a week of cooler weather just before the start, which had delayed them a little, but now the south wind was blowing again, and over and over it seemed to say —

"And we go, go, go away from here!
On the other side the world we're overdue!
'Send the road lies clear before you
When the old Spring-fret comes o'er you,
And the Red Gods call for you."

And the road was clear, and they went. Up, and up, and up; higher and higher, till straight ahead, stretching away to the very edge of the world, lay league after league of sunshine and air, only waiting the stroke of their wings. Now, steady, steady! Beat, beat, beat! And the old earth sliding southward fifty miles an hour! No soaring — their wings were too short for that sort of work — and no quick wheeling to right or left, but hurtling on with whizzing pinions and eager eyes, straight toward the goal. Was it any wonder that they were happy, and that joyful shouts and wild peals of laughter came ringing down from the sky to tell us poor earthbound men and women that somewhere up in the blue, beyond the reach of our short-sighted eyes, the loons were hurrying home?

Over the fresh fields, green with the young wheat; over the winding rivers and the smiling lakes; over — shut your eyes, and dream a little while, and see if you can imagine what it was like. Does it make you wish you were a loon yourself? Never mind; some day, perhaps, we too shall take our wedding journeys in the air; not on feathered pinions, but with throbbing engines and whizzing wheels, and with all the power of steam or electricity to lift us and bear us onward. We shall skim the prairies and leap the mountains, and roam over the ocean like the wandering albatross. To-day we shall breathe the warm, spicy breath of the tropic islands, and to-morrow we shall sight the white gleam of the polar ice-pack. When the storm gathers we shall mount above it, and looking down we shall see the lightning leap from cloud to cloud, and the rattling thunder will come upward, not downward, to our ears. When the world below is steeped in the shadows of coming night, we shall still watch the sunset trailing its glories over the western woods and mountains; and when morning breaks we shall be the first to welcome the sunrise as it comes rushing up from the east a thousand miles an hour. The wind of the upper heavens will be pure and keen and strong, and not even a sleigh ride on a winter's night can set the live blood dancing as it will dance and tingle up there above the clouds. And riding on the air, alone with the roaring engines that have become for the time a part of ourselves, we shall know at last what our earth is really like, for we shall see it as the loons see it — yes, as God and His angels see it — this old earth, on which we have lived for so many thousand years, and yet have never seen.

But, after all, the upper heavens will not be home; and some day, as we shoot northward, or southward, or eastward, or westward, we shall see beneath us the spot that is to be for us the best and dearest place in all the world, and, dropping down out of the blue, we shall find something that is even better than riding on the wings of the wind. That was what happened to Mahng and his wife, for one spring evening, as they came rushing over the pine tops and the maples and birches, they saw the Glimmerglass just ahead. The water lay like polished steel in the fading light, and the brown ranks of the still leafless trees stood dark and silent around the shores.

They chose a place where the shore was low and marshy, and there, only two or three yards from the water's edge, they built a rude nest of grass and weeds and lily pads. Two large greenish eggs, blotched with dark brown, lay in its hollow; and the wife sat upon them week after week, and covered them with the warm feathers of her broad, white breast. Once in a while she left them long enough to stretch her wings in a short flight, or to dive in search of a fish, but she was never gone very long. It was a weary vigil that she kept, but she sat there in daylight and darkness, through sunshine and storm, till at last the day came when there were four loons instead of two at the Glimmerglass.

(To be continued.)

Girls' Pets and How to Manage Them.

BY A WELL-KNOWN BREEDER AND EXHIBITOR.

GENERAL MANAGEMENT AND BREEDING OF RABBITS.

AS this article is written for girls who probably have not a great deal of money to spend, I shall try to point out the best way to keep rabbits healthy and well with as little expense as possible.

The first point for a beginner to consider before purchasing her pets is where she shall keep them. It is best, if possible, to have a shed to keep the hutches under; but, if that is not obtainable, she should cover the top of the hutches with sheets of galvanised iron (which is very cheap now), and take care that it projects six inches to a foot over the front and back, to keep the rain from blowing in as much as possible, and to carry off the water. This roof should be sloped from front to back.

The hutches can be made very cheaply by getting bacon boxes or good-sized cases from the grocer. The front of these should be half covered with wire, and the other half boarded; the door usually makes the latter half. A rabbit is very fond of getting in a darkened corner sometimes. The hutch should be, roughly, two feet square for single rabbits, but it must be larger for breeding does, and at least eighteen inches high. The breeding hutch should have two compartments, with a door to each. In the partition there should be a hole large enough for the rabbit to get through quite easily, and the sleeping compartment should be quite dark except for the light admitted through this hole.

The hutch is best raised from the ground two or three feet. Very good hutches can be got from various firms who make this kind of thing, and if a girl is a good carpenter she can obtain their catalogues, and make herself a more elaborate hutch than the one described.

Having got the hutches ready, the fancier should consider the question of feeding, and have food in readiness for her pets when they arrive. Rabbits are best fed twice a day. The best dry food is oats, of which they are very fond, and a good big handful twice a day will be enough, but with this they must have a good handful of hay at the evening meal, and at both meals they should have a little green food.

The fancier should always be careful to see that all dew or rain has dried off this before she gives it to her rabbits, or they will most likely become affected with a disease most expressively called "Pot-belly." Almost any green stuff from a garden will do for them; the waste leaves from cabbages, mowings from the lawn, lettuce leaves, grass from the roadside, dandelions, &c., &c., — all these will help to feed a rabbit and

they get the chance will always drink some, so it is, perhaps, best to let them have the chance occasionally. A doe should always have water with her when about to litter down, as they get very thirsty then, and if water is not supplied, frequently eat their young ones. When a doe has

the damp sawdust and manure can be scraped out, and a little fresh sawdust added. Then, once a week, all the sawdust should be scraped out (the rabbit first being removed), and a little disinfectant, such as Sanitas powder, sprinkled over the floor, and left for an hour or two; then fresh sawdust can

By kind permission of]   PROZE-BRED FLEMISH GIANT.   [*"The Stockkeeper."*

cost nothing. In the winter, when green food is scarce, a few mangels, swedes, turnips or carrots may be bought, and small pieces given to the rabbits, care being taken that they do not get frost-bitten.

Rabbits can live altogether without water, but if

young ones, she should have a saucerful of bread and milk every day.

Hutches should be cleaned out every day, and the best bedding is a thin layer of sawdust; this can be bought at about sixpence to a shilling a sack, and is very healthy. In the morning all

be put down, and the rabbit put back.

Every three months the inside of the hutch should be lime-washed all over. If a fancier is thinking of breeding rabbits, she should be sure the doe is over six months, and healthy, and well nourished. If the doe is young, it is best for the buck to be of mature age, and *vice versa*. The doe should always be placed in the buck's hutch. March or April is about the best time to start breeding, and if the young ones are wanted for showing, three litters a year will be plenty. If they are for profit, five or six litters may be got from a doe with safety, and allow for a short rest in the winter.

The doe goes thirty days before littering down, and the young ones suckle the mother for a month. The doe may be put to the buck when the young ones are a fortnight old. The young ones are born blind, and open their eyes about the seventh or eighth day, when they begin to run about.

Great care should be taken not to disturb the doe when the young are first born, and for about a week after, as nervous does will often eat their young if frightened at that time.

The young ones should be taken away from their mother about a month to five weeks old, and should then be put into a large hutch all together, separating them as they get to be three or four months old, according to their sexes. At about six months those that are wanted for breeding or show should be put in separate hutches, whilst the others may be sold for killing, or killed for home consumption. The usual way to kill a rabbit is to knock it on the head, but

some people bleed them. This latter method has the disadvantage of spoiling the skin and fur where the blood runs over it. The smaller breeds will be quite fit to kill when required, but larger varieties should be shut up in a small hutch for about a week and well fed.

If the fancier wishes to show her pets there are many varieties to choose from, but if she thinks of keeping them for profit and eating she should choose a large cross-bred. A cross between the Belgian hare and the English rabbit is very good. For a fancy rabbit, the Dutch is very pretty, neat, and clean, and the badly marked ones, though small, have plenty of flesh on when eaten.

Cosy Corner Chats.

VIII. – THE READING OF FICTION.

MY DEAR HELEN: Ought you to give up novel-reading? By no means. The novel has come to stay; and, the sooner we all acknowledge that fact, and make the best of it, the better. Undoubtedly, clandestine novel-reading has had a bad effect on girls, both mentally and morally. It is high time that we should all recognise the force which we have to deal with in modern fiction, and should turn it to good use instead of bad use.

You were always fond of statistics. So I will tell you that, from some observations I have made of girls, in summer and in winter, in school and out of it, I have calculated that, in the nine years of education from twelve to twenty-one, the average young gentlewoman reads a novel more than an hour a day. Thus she gives one and one-third years of solid working days to this occupation. Nearly one-eighth of the entire period covered by a girl's education is to-day spent in novel-reading. We try to fill the girl's hours and days with the ablest teaching, with discipline by mathematics and the clas-sics, with acquaintance with statesmen and generals, with the company of "the ever-living, high, and most glorious poets"; and, meantime, in spite of us, she passes a large fraction of her precious educational years under the potent sway of the novelists. They may be good or bad, indifferent, stimulating, depressing, or degrading; they have their grip upon her, and she cannot shake them off. For my own part, I welcome the fact that fiction has come to play so large a part in the life of our young women. It had its frightful dangers, and I see many a girl yielding to them; but it is also a beneficent force — a force whose good results we scarcely yet have begun to estimate. I want you to recognise this force, and make it do your bidding.

The old charge against novel-reading was that it enticed us into a world of unreality and one which unfitted men and women for ordinary daily life. Undoubtedly, there are certain classes of novels of which this is true. It was indeed true of many of the early English novels written by women. You will remember how delightfully Mr. Stockton ridiculed these in "Rudder Grange," when he made Pomona retire from her cooking and dishwashing to a world peopled with dukes and duchesses, where coronets, elopements in high life, murders, balls, and garden parties made a combination as interesting as it was absurd.

In glancing the other day over a list of novels, I came upon the following titles in three pages:— "Changed Brides," "The Bride's Fate," "The Missing Bride," "The Unfaithful Bride," "Cruel as the Grave," "Tried for her Life," "I forbid the Banns." Now, the titles of these books are enough to know about them. It should not be necessary to warn any intelligent girl against them anymore than to warn her against eating half-ripe fruit or mouldy cake. They are unreal, over-emotional, and set up false standards of life and conduct, dangerous, pernicious.

There is another class of novels which is unreal. These are not as demoralising as the first, but character does not thrive on their namby-pamby flavour. They are "goody" books, usually written especially for girls; often the medium for so-called "heart-to-heart" talks. In them ordinary life is wrapped up in rose-leaves. Opportunities for splendid self-sacrificing achievements grow on every bush. Religion and love are charmingly confused, and young clergymen are likely to be the heroes.

For you, however, I fancy that a greater danger lies in the novels of the third class. In these a blind fate sits on the throne of the universe. Men and women struggle, toil, aspire and suffer; and there is but one end for them all — failure. These novelists preside over an earthquake country. No matter what verdure may grace it, or what noble architecture may adorn it, destruction is assured for it. Of course, you know who are the arch-offenders in this way. The later Hardy and the later Henry James have much to answer for in the destruction of the moral poise of those who have read them. Reliance on a ruling beneficence is the first requisite for a healthy moral life. I must believe in the solidity of the world under my feet. I must believe that God, and not the devil, sits on the throne of the universe. Every book which weakens or threatens or ridicules that belief is by so much dangerous to the structure of character, and to that skill and steadiness of hand which we need to acquire.

Now, this substantially ends my case against the novel. That work of fiction which is false by virtue of its over-emotionalism or of its cynic pessimism is dangerous. Anything which is false is dangerous. To read all novels indiscriminately is just as unsafe as to eat without discrimination; but I am not going to abjure fish because some family dies of poisoning from stale fish.

Let us turn to the brighter picture, and see what the novel has to offer us for the increase of that refined skill which our girl must bring to her life. Every day she is set to some new task requiring a light touch, from the reorganising of a working-girls' club to the making of salad-dressing, from the smoothing out of an irritating friction in a church committee to the saving of a baby's life by courage and skill in a critical moment. "The proper study of mankind is man." In the able novelist we have a matchless guide to the mysteries and subtleties of human nature.

I speak now of the master of the art. The people of his creation are as substantial, as true to life, as the folk among whom we move; but they have one interesting distinction from our next-door neighbours. Mr. Smith and Mrs. Brown put up sash curtains at their windows and lock up their hearts, and endeavour in every way to shut us out from that knowledge of motive and conduct which will help us really to know them. The imaginary characters of fiction, on the other hand, are eager to show us complicated motives, busy brains, and throbbing hearts. It goes without saying that we understand hundreds of fictitious characters better than those of our dearest friends. Hamlet, around whom has raged the fiercest battle of criticism for three hundred years, is better known to us to—day than his modern counterpart, General McClellan.

Nothing can be more necessary to our young woman than the ability to read human nature. We set her at work on a problem in algebra, and she successfully determines the one unknown quantity by the aid of the two that are known; but the problems of life reverse the ratio, and we force our girl, in all good faith, to reduce the equation of life where she knows, at most, herself only, and perhaps not even herself. We do not inflict upon our friends her piano performance until fingers, ear, and musical sense have all been trained by years of practice; but she begins her service in the world in surroundings where the most complex conditions are found, and when she has had no experience in dealing with real men and women. The fifteen-year-old girl is scarcely expected to select the colour of a feather for her hat or the stuff for a gown; and at twenty we expect this girl to cope successfully with the most difficult social and moral questions. For crises there is no practice school. There is, however, one place where a fair idea may be had of how people should act and how they do act, in the varied and severe strains of life. This is the novel. I do not mean that all the heroines are, or should be, models of the virtues. Sometimes the most pointed sort of teaching is teaching "how not to do it"; but I mean that the springs of conduct, the methods of conduct, and the results of conduct are set forth, and that teaching by example is brought to its highest perfection in the novel. I cannot, for example, imagine that a girl who has once read "Middlemarch" carefully and thoroughly, and with a wise teacher looking over her shoulder, would ever make the mistake of thinking a marriage of duty right, not to say noble and self-sacrificing.

In the second place, the novel not only shows us by example how we must act, but it makes us desire to act as the novelist says it is right to act. We love persons, not theories.

Again, fiction enlarges our acquaintance, quickens our sympathies, removes us from the immediate circumstances of ordinary domestic life, and so makes us better able to bear its irritations when we must go back to them. The woman who has no resources is likely to be a fretful woman. Deliver me from the tongue of her who has no acquaintances except the men and women of her "set." George Eliot, Anthony Trollope, Thackeray, Hawthorne, lead us into good society. In their volumes the doors of a thousand hospitable houses are always wide open. They are ready to cure narrowness and provincialism — those social diseases to which women have been so susceptible. Aristotle said long ago that "the office of tragedy is to cleanse the mind with pity and with terror." So with the novel. Gracious drops are the tears which fall over the fortunes of people created by a master in his art, and deep and effective are the resolutions made by many a girl in a hammock as she passes a June morning over a novel.

The novel, like any great force, has its dangers and its victories. Its dangers lie in that emotionalism which is the menace of our age and our sex. Its promises are of greater skill, wiser tact, more ready hands and loving hearts for the world which waits in weakness and weariness for our touch. The future of the novel is immense. More and more will the novel glorify its office; and so more and more will it enlighten the mind, quicken the intuition, and deepen and broaden the sympathy.

HELOISE EDWINA HERSEY.

Athletics for Girls.

SWIMMING.

BY "NEPTUNE."

IT is only during the last decade or so that swimming, as a pastime for women and girls, has become admittedly desirable. But that it is one of the best for all who are not the victims of any constitutional weakness of heart or circulation, which makes bathing unwise, is being more and more recognised both by would-be swimmers themselves and by those who have to do with physical education.

Swimming is one of the very few pastimes in which a normally strong and healthy girl starts with distinct (if slight) advantage over her brother; owing to the extra lightness and natural buoyancy of her body. This fact alone should encourage all

AN IDEAL SWIMMING COSTUME.

who as yet cannot swim to learn to do so as speedily as possible.

As to the advantages of swimming, a prominent member of the Brighton Ladies' Swimming Club expressed the following opinion in a recent interview:—

"As you know, I am an enthusiastic supporter and advocate of swimming. I can scarcely say when I did not swim, having been taught when quite a mite of a child, and being able to swim quite well by the time duty and object in life was to look pretty, if born so, and at all events cultivate their figures and good looks to the highest degree; and never, by any chance, betray the fact that they were capable of enjoying pionships, won many prizes, and spent many pleasant and healthful hours in the element to which most people seem to have an antipathy that is simply incomprehensible to those who can swim."

WITH FINGERS AND THUMBS OF HANDS TOGETHER AND PALMS SLIGHTLY HOLLOWED.

THE BACKWARD DIVE.

I was seven or eight. I remember that my first "suite" – made very like a little boy's serge suit – was thought highly improper by a maiden aunt, whose idea of girls was that their sole sports, pastimes, or pursuits which would entail the admission that they possessed what she was pleased to call "lower limbs."

I have, since those days, held several club cham-

"You believe in swimming, evidently?"

"I cycle, play golf, cricket, hockey, and, when I was at school, played a mild game at football, and have run many an – as my aunt would say — 'unbecoming' mile, paper-chasing; for I don't believe in developing one portion of the body at the expense of the other. But swimming will undoubtedly do more for what is commonly known as one's 'figure,' than any other one sport that I know. Of course, I am not considering gymnastics, which are in reality a series of correlated exercises, and not a sport at all.

"Ask any swimming instructor, and she will tell you the same. Thin girls who swim regularly and judiciously soon become more plump, and strangely enough, fat ones frequently become more well-proportioned. Of course, I admit that swimming cannot be indulged in all the year round by many; there are not baths in every seaside town even, and in comparatively few inland ones. But the number is yearly increasing, and during the seaside holiday, which thousands of women and girls get every year, there is ample opportunity for them to learn and even benefit considerably by so doing.

"Costume certainly is an important matter. Bathers may, perhaps, be best divided into three classes — the 'bobbers' or mere paddlers, who can wear a costume the elaborateness of which a swimmer would find a nuisance and impediment; the poor swimmers — who possibly will never be anything else — who may content themselves with the ordinary shop suit; and the swimmers proper, who, whilst liking naturally to look smart, will place comfort and convenience first, and who will probably pin their faith to a jersey costume of "combination" type, either of merino or serge, or if a Frenchwoman, possibly of silk. The real swimmer's costume should be sleeveless, with the knickers quite short above the knees, and, as to the jersey part, although cut away round the neck, not too much so, as that would cause the upper portion of the costume to fill, and impede progress. Such a costume I have myself worn for the last five or six years, and I do not wish for a better."

As was stated in the interview, swimming baths have increased of late years to a very encouraging extent; and there are now quite a number in the metropolis, as well as in the larger provincial towns, where the elements of the art may be very wisely acquired by a short course of lessons before the annual visit to the seaside. Indeed, to learn in the comparative privacy and comfort of a bath is a very desirable thing in itself, for it is only on calm days that the novice can hope to comfortably acquire the art in the open sea. Nothing can, of course, compare with the bracing effect of the sea itself. But on a rough morning the learner would have very grave doubts as to the advantage of "open" water, and would be very liable to suffer from loss of nerve, which would militate sadly against her making rapid progress.

Before determining to become a swimmer, it is of the greatest importance that medical advice should be taken as to whether or no the particular person is likely to find bathing beneficial or the reverse. Not a few of the lamentable accidents which occur each season are directly attributable to the omission of this precaution. Some unsuspected weakness of brain, heart, or circulation often exist; the unfortunate bather suffers from its lows:— When bathing at a strange place (more especially if from a tent placed at any considerable distance from other bathers), never omit to ascertain the tendency of the tide, the depth of water, and the existence before breakfast it is wise to drink half a glass of milk and eat a biscuit half an hour or so before going in. Do not remain in the water too long — twenty minutes to half an hour is usually quite long enough, and even

DIVING INTO DEEP WATER.

LEARNING TO FLOAT.

effects; and — well, the rest is often summed up in the verdict, "drowned whilst bathing."

A few maxims which everyone should remember may be briefly put as fol-

or likelihood of holes or sudden shelving of the beach.

Never bathe immediately after a meal — the best time being about the middle of the morning. If bathing

this time should be curtailed on the first suspicion of chill or tiredness. Never bathe alone, if it is possible to avoid doing so. Everyone is liable to cramp, even good swimmers; and if you get it do not struggle aimlessly nor lose your presence of mind. Make an effort to at once throw yourself on your back, kicking vigorously with your legs (as cramp may often be warded off by so doing), and call for assistance.

On going to the assistance of bathers taken with cramp, remember to keep clear of and not allow them to catch hold of you. The best means of assisting them to the shore is to either push them in front of you or tow them by the hair. If you are a good swimmer either way will be equally easy if the victim of cramp will simply float, and not struggle or attempt to assist. Drowning people are often terribly difficult to help, as invariably they are only semi-conscious, though often not sufficiently far gone to render them unable to struggle.

The hints regarding going to the assistance of persons suffering from cramp apply also to the case of the drowning. Some excellent instructions for saving them, and afterwards restoring consciousness, are issued by the Royal Humane Society, and these should be read and studied by everyone who bathes. Never overtax your strength by swimming out to sea half as far as the whole distance you can easily accomplish. Remember that the return half will be proportionately more tiring, as you will not be as "fresh" as when you started. After dressing, take a sharp walk if the least feeling of chill is noticeable; and on returning home it is well to thoroughly rinse the face, neck, and arms in fresh water to remove the salt, which will have a roughening tendency upon the skin, and, if the latter be delicate, possibly cause painful chapping.

Swimming is so essentially a practical pastime that it is not an easy matter to learn it from a book, but there are some elementary hints which may be given, and even prove profitable if carefully followed.

The most favourable spot at which to learn to swim is a sandy beach gently shelving from quite shallow to deeper water. The assistance of a companion — if possible, one who can swim at least a little — is very helpful until the idea of swimming is somewhat mastered. Stand in water a little less than shoulder deep, facing the shore, in the position shown with the fingers and thumbs of the hand close together, and the palms slightly hollowed. The arms should then be stretched out to the fullest extent straight in front of you, making the hands like scoops with the knuckles upward; then twist the wrist of each hand slightly inward so that, when the arms are swept backwards and outwards, the hands push against the water, and not merely cut it with their sides as they would if held perfectly flat.

Take as much "grip" of the water as possible. The arms should then be separated and thrust back to their fullest extent, until they are almost at a right angle to the body, when the elbows should be gradually and slowly bent till they are close against the sides. The hands should now have assumed, by means of an inward twist, a position close in front of each breast with the thumbs uppermost. They should then be again thrust smartly upwards and forwards, with their outside edges turned gradually up, till they have once more assumed the position with which they started.

A point to be remembered: The hands in making the stroke must never be allowed to pass behind the bend of the elbow. To throw the arms farther back from the position, almost at a right angle to the shoulders, referred to, is to materially retard the stroke, and, when actually swimming, will probably cause your head to dip unpleasantly.

It is wise also to recollect that the stroke should be kept about an inch below the surface of the water, in practice, except when thrusting the arms forward from the chest to recommence the stroke, when they will in their upward course almost rest upon the surface. These movements mastered, it will be necessary to acquire the ones controlling the legs, so that the two may ultimately be combined, and the act of swimming thereby performed.

It is with the leg movements that the advisability of friendly assistance becomes most apparent.

If learning in a swimming bath, the rope running round the edge will provide all the support necessary, but we are supposing that the reader is learning in the sea. You should retire to somewhat shallower water than for the arm movements, so that the friend (who will firmly grasp you by each wrist) will be able to stand firmly, with the water not much more than waist deep. You should now hollow the back slightly, and rising from your feet (which should have been placed almost close together) bend both knees, and draw them well underneath the body, leaning the chest on the surface of the water.

You will find that this act of bending the knees will force the body away back from the person supporting you. The next movement is a smartly made kick, with which the legs should be opened to the highest and widest extent possible with comfort, the heels meantime being turned downwards, the toes being pointed upwards, and the feet assuming a "spread-eagle" position. Next, describing an almost complete semi-circle with each leg, the toes will be found to gradually drop as they reach the widest point of separation. Now, continuing the backward and circular movement, the legs — which should be stiffly extended — will almost touch at the completion of the stroke in a straight line with the body, the toes pointing to the rear. During all these motions the back should be kept as flat as possible, consistent with making them properly, and not humped up.

It is well for the learner to recollect that the object of the exercises is to propel the body through and not out of the water. Each time the movements have been completed, the feet should be allowed to rest on the bottom, and a new start made without hurry. When you find that you are actually travelling forward, you should endeavour to so perform the movements that there is no appreciable pause between the drawing up of the knees and the kick outwards of the legs, but a continuous action.

The combining of the arm and leg action is swimming. This will be best acquired in slightly deeper water than that previously entered. A hand placed just beneath the learner's chest, will usually be found to afford all the support necessary.

To commence the stroke the hands should be brought close in front of the chest, elbows to the sides, and fingers and thumbs closed, palms slightly hollowed and turned downwards. The arms should then be shot out straight in front, and swept slowly backwards as directed in the remarks on the arm movements. Simultaneously, the first of the leg movements – the drawing up of the knees – is being carried on. As the legs come into position the hands will have come close together and just under the chin, the palms being together, fingers touching and pointing straight out.

The hands are now again shot out straight as the legs are kicked open, and as far apart as possible, by straightening the knees. When the arms have reached their utmost limit of extension the thumbs are turned down again, and the arm stroke is completed by

the backward sweep, the legs being kept rigid the while. The latter are then quickly bent and brought into the first position for a fresh attempt.

It is well to remember than in learning swimming hurry is greatly to be deprecated. It is often the cause of acquiring a bad style (which cannot be easily altered), and does much to retard the would-be swimmer. One should try to swim as low as possible, as to do so is to gain power and speed. The breath should be expelled when the hands are extended in front supporting the head, and inhaled when they are brought back, breath being taken through the nose as much as possible. The head should be thrown back so as to keep the mouth and chin clear of the water.

Of the side-stroke, swimming on the back, and other forms of fancy swimming, space will not permit us to write; but it is only necessary to add that much of these will present no insuperable difficulties once the breast-stroke has been satisfactorily mastered.

It is not likely that the swimmer will long be con-

tent to enter the water in the prosaic manner of walking into it, when the opportunity for diving presents itself. A few words upon this subject, aided by the illustration, may therefore well conclude the present brief paper.

One word of caution. Never dive into any water until the fact that the depth is sufficient has been satisfactorily ascertained. Many serious mishaps occur every season for want of this simple precaution. First attempts should always be made from an inconsiderable height (say, from the stern of a row boat, or from the edge of a diving raft), which may be gradually increased until a reasonable height (say, ten to twenty feet) has been attained. The minimum depth will vary with the skill of the diver, but it may be here remarked that much harm may result and no real good can come of foolhardy diving into excessively shallow water.

The modes of entering deep and shallow water vary considerably. In the former the dive is made with the body entering the water at a sharp angle; in the latter case the entry is made at a more oblique one, the object being to keep as near the surface as possible after entering the water, and also to gain as much impetus from the send-off as can be. To dive into deep water the knees should be bent and both arms stretched

the object from which the dive is taken, the farther out must the diver jump so as to attain the right angle by which to enter it. In diving into very deep water it is frequently necessary to swim a few strokes upwards to assist the body to regain the surface, as the lack of touching bottom to gain

the arms hanging a little to the rear. The knees should be slightly bent, and the arms swung to the rear to gain impetus. The body is then launched forward and downward, head first, at an oblique angle by stiffening the knees suddenly, and at the same time shooting forward the hands to the fullest extent, the toes giving a last push against the edge. The legs should be kept quite rigid, with the toes pointing rearwards.

The learner should attempt to acquire a graceful, quiet style, which may be modified to suit her individual liking as experience is gained. Diving feet first is a favourite method with many lady swimmers, the main object being to drop as perpendicularly as possible. The diver should stand erect, with the head back, toes pointed, knees stiff, and arms as rigid and straight down, close to the sides, as possible.

WATER POLO.

over the head with the fingers pointed, the diver falling over into the water as it were, the legs being straightened with a jerk as the body approaches the surface. The hands are kept straight until it is desired to return to the surface, when the palms must be turned back and an upward kick or two given with the legs. The higher above the water

an upward impetus will cause it to take longer than anticipated to return to the surface.

In shallow plunging the feet should be placed together on the very verge of the bath, plank, or raft, as the case may be, so that the toes may have a good grip with which to give the body a send-off. The body should be bent forward with

Of fancy forms of diving and plunging, such as the Belgian jump and backward dive, it is not here possible to write. Most of them can be best and most easily acquired by watching others. But even with the acquirement of trick swimming and fancy diving the resources of the pastimes are by no means exhausted, as there yet remains the excitement and interest of racing and water-polo playing for the expert and for those who wish to pursue the sport to further lengths.

The latter is, of course, a favourite pastime with swimming clubs who have the entrée of baths, and although lady swimmers have not as yet taken up polo very seriously, the time is no doubt coming when they will do so.

How to be Strong.

case of many ladies to-day, but is firm and column-like, rounded off in graceful curves to the shoulders and chest. No part of the body receives such little attention to-day as the

PART VI.

IN my last chat I made mention of the Greek statues at the Museum as being splendid examples of perfect symmetry and grace. This applies more especially to the female figure studies, and is nowhere more noticeable than in the décolleté parts, *i.e.*, neck and throat, shoulders and chest. In these "studies," the neck has not the appearance of being "just stuck on," as is the

EXERCISE 6.

neck and throat and its development, with the con-

sequent results. Nothing is more noticeable, and detracts from a woman's personal appearance, as a thin, "scraggy" neck. The perfect head of hair and charming features are often marred by an absolutely unshapely neck, much to their possessor's annoyance.

It is to obviate such a reproach as this, and (in the case of those who, unfortunately, have this defect) to cure it, that the remaining exercises in this series of chats have been devised, and I feel sure that the truth of the above remarks is so well known and appreciated that they will be followed with great interest and complete success to those already needing it, as well as the means of preventing such disfigurement to others who at present have not noticed the defect.

The exercise (No. 6) is performed as follows:— Stand erect, with head and shoulders well back, dumbbells firmly grasped in each hand, and arms by your side. Slowly raise your right hand to your shoulder, keeping the muscles in tension, and inhaling your breath the whole of the time, until the arm is in a horizontal position at right angles to the body. Lower the arm to the side again, at the same time raising the left hand to the horizontal position, like the right was raised previously. Continue this exercise about 20 or 25 times morning and evening. At the end of each two motions, raising and lowering the right hand and raising and lowering the left hand, the breath which you have been inhaling during this period should be exhaled, so that with the commencement of the next motion you commence to fill the lungs with air. By taking a long and continued inhalation, striving to get as much air as possible into the lungs, they become expanded to their fullest degree, and your chest development will speedily begin to increase, as well as your muscles in arms, shoulders, and neck, and the hollow places to fill up. There are two very important points in this exercise which it is well to point out, as follows:— (1) Careful attention should be paid to the instruction to perform the exercise, raising the arms slowly. It is this gradual expansion and contraction of muscle that really does the effective work. All swinging or jerkiness of action should be avoided in this exercise. (2) Whilst you are instructed to return your arms to your side, it is intended that you should avoid touching or striking your body with the dumbbells. Attention to these two points will increase the efficiency of the exercise.

(To be continued.)

Athletics for Girls.

SKATING.

BY CHRISTINE HANDLEY, M.A.

KATING is an accomplishment which British maidens have unfortunately all too little opportunity of acquiring. So provokingly fleeting are the visits of the Ice Fairy that skating enthusiasts are fain to fly from perfidious Albion across the sea to Switzerland or Holland (the home of skating) for practice in their beloved art. And in very sooth, which of us, having once tasted the delight of skimming on steel-shod foot over ice-bound lake or river,

does not long for more? In the gay time of the Stuarts, even the practical Pepys, watching the graceful gyrations of the ladies and cavaliers of St. James's, felt constrained to admit, when he "did see the people sliding with their skates," that it was a "very pretty art."

To become adepts in this desirable accomplishment, it is best to begin on an up-to-date basis, having due regard for the mighty principle of evolution — that is to say, by making one's earliest essays in childhood's happy days, when monkeyish propensities and consequently the blindly-imitative faculties

are at their strongest. But to a self-conscious maiden, what can be more galling than to feel herself absolutely ungraceful and awkward and helpless, and to find her efforts at a graceful, easy glide end in ignominious downfall on the hard ice? Her body gets painfully bumped, certainly, but worse than the ache of the bruise is the smart of wounded dignity. Therefore the girl desirous of adding skating to the list of her accomplishments would spare herself much needless pain by leaving her dignity at home for the day. Then moral agony, at any rate, will be spared her, for fall she certainly will, and that right early and often, be it said.

While divesting herself of her dignity, let the would-be skater not forget to put on warm stockings and sensible lace-up boots. The salient features of the "sensible" boots should be — (1) Low, flat heels; (2) strong soles; (3) roomy square or rounded toes. In very pointed boots the toes are crushed together; consequently the blood is unable to circulate, and exquisite pain is the result.

The question of boots is indeed a most important one for the novice in the art of skating. No one can learn to skate whose feet are cold and aching. Under such conditions the muscles lose their elasticity and the ankles their strength. Therefore, O maiden desirous of learning, do your best, as far as in you lies, to aid the circulation by having suitable foot-gear. Your boots should not err upon the side of largeness any more than on that of undue tightness. The uppers should be laced up sufficiently tight to give a sense of support

to the ankle.

Having disposed of the question of boots, we now come to that of skates. They may be roughly divided into two classes — the old-fashioned variety, partly made of wood, and attached to the boot by means of a

OUTSIDE EDGE BACKWARDS.

screw and straps, and the newer American skate, fashioned entirely of metal. The latter certainly bears off the palm for convenience, but for the beginner the balance of comfort lies with the old-fashioned wooden skate, which screws into the heel, and is strapped round the toes and ankle. To

the unaccustomed ankles of a beginner the weight of a metal skate is very tiring, and therefore the wooden variety is to be recommended till some degree of proficiency is attained. For figure-skating it is best to have a pair of blades fastened by a Mount Charles fastening to a pair of boots specially reserved for skating. It is important that these blades should be neither too much curved nor too flat, where they come into contact with the ice.

But to return to the preliminaries of skating. A beginner feels much more comfortable on a pair of skates whose blades have had the keen edge taken off them by use than on a brand-new pair. Therefore let the aspirant after prowess in skating, having obtained an already-used pair, wend her way on her sensibly-shod feet to the ice, and there have her skates securely screwed and strapped on. Then, by the aid of a helping hand, let her rise. She will feel a desperate inclination to cling to that hand, but she must screw up her courage, relinquish it, and learn to stand alone till she feels fairly steady. She should then try to walk on her skates. Her feet will make wild dashes for liberty and try to glide from under her, but she must do her best to keep her ankles rigid, and a good heart. The beginner should bear in mind the fact that it is in the study of the law of balance that the whole art of skating lies. To acquire an insight into that law, the tyro will find it a great help to stand feet together, leaning rather forward than backward, get someone to push gently behind, and so, without any attempt at striking out, be propelled at a gentle rate over the ice. Care must be taken to keep the feet parallel, otherwise inelegance and disaster will ensue.

After a few doses of intelligent help, one feels a courageous desire to master the mysteries of, at any rate, the ordinary inside edge, and starts off proudly alone. The proverbial fate will surely ensue; but, by bearing in mind one or two simple laws, serious disaster may be avoided. Always remember to keep the weight of the body forward.

So you will avoid testing the strength of the ice with the back of your skull. Secondly, think of what you were told so often when a little girl, and turn your toes out. This will render it impossible for the feet to go very far astray. In the third

EIGHT.

place, don't be afraid, when striking out on one foot, to lift the other off the ice, holding it just behind the performing foot. If you feel yourself falling, you can always put your reserve skate down, and so regain your tottering balance. Fourthly, keep the ankle as rigid as possible.

After a little practice you invariably find that that you are much better on one foot – either right or left, as the case may be. Then it behoves you to devote all your attention to the erring member. Endeavour to make your strokes perfectly equal; above all, keep on one foot as long as possible. Lay your weight well on the foot you are striking out with, so as to make it describe a proper curve. Don't brandish the unoccupied foot ungracefully in front or at the side, but hold it behind the other with the toe turning well outwards, so as to be ready to begin a new stroke at right angles to the end of the previous one. Each stroke on the inside edge should describe a quarter of a circle. Should you commit the blunder of sliding along the ice on the flat of your skate-blade, a proper curve will not be described. Avoid the error, therefore, by turning toes well out and pushing off alternately to the extreme right and left. Above all, take warning by Mr. Kipling's "Eathen," who "keeps his side-arms awful

and leaves 'em all about."
A windmill may be a pleasing addition to a landscape; but don't play at being one. Remember you were not built for the purpose. Sometimes one sees a really good lady figure-skater looking absolutely unpleasing to the eye, simply because of her windmill propensities.

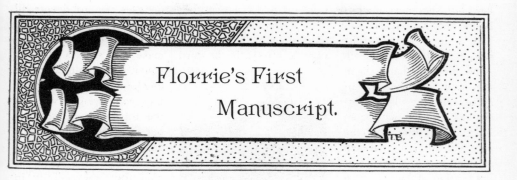

Florrie's First Manuscript.

IT was kept in the drawer of an old washstand among the attic lumber. Ever since Emily Wallflower had lent her one of Mrs. Ratcliffe's tales of skeletons and haunted castles, and she had read it in the dinner-hour at school, there had come over her a desire to write a book; and this pile of paper was the result. There was a preface at the beginning, and a line of dots at the end, to divide the "Finale" from the main story.

Florrie was always at the head of the spelling-class at school, but somehow between spelling through her mouth and spelling through her fingers, there was a difference. As to the plot — that had all seemed to come to her in the last half-dozen pages. To save expense she had written on both sides of the paper, and had spent most of her pocket-money at the stationery-store buying up packets of the very best cream-laid note. She reasoned, not unnaturally, that, if she received those twenty golden sovereigns for the copyright, two shillings and sixpence would not be such a very extravagant sum for paper. So six long months Florrie wrote on, giving up her playtime for the benefit of "Rookwood Parsonage," and fondly dreaming her mother and sister knew nothing about it. But one fine Saturday afternoon she took the manuscript, all punctuated and packed, out of the drawer, and sent it by post to London, while her mother and Louie were out marketing.

Then she and Bertha

Green climbed into the apple-tree, and began to sketch boys and girls with round eyes, and hands like under the limb of the tree. The birch-plantain up the rampart and the old flour-mills, whose sails turned to Florrie nor Bertha was an artist; and long before the wind dropped and the mill-sails stood still, the

FLORRIE.

the prongs of a toasting-fork, many subjects for the exercise of their genius in free-hand passing directly the time and tune of the passing winds, made an excellent background for their picture. But neither product of their genius had been torn to scraps and scattered in the lane below. Then Florrie said "good afternoon" to her friend and went off to her dormitory at the top of the house, to set down the things she would buy when those twenty golden sovereigns came.

There were three things she could not do without – a writing-desk, with pigeon-holes for her MSS.; an ink-stand, on lion's claws; and a delicious batch of the very best cream-laid note-paper. Then it would be nice for her to make some little acknowledgment to friends, such as a silk mantle for mother, and an ivory-handled umbrella for aunt, a pair of kid gloves for cousin Bell, a blue dress and parasol for sister Louie, a cap and apron for Hannah the maid, and a new smock for the milkman, whose old one she had lately noticed was getting sadly out at elbow. She liked that straw hat in Miss Phillpot's window also: besides, she really needed a summer hat, and a plaid frock, like Sally Rover's green one, would strike all her school mates with awe when she entered the class-room Monday mornings!

When this list was moneyed out it looked a formidable affair, and left only one solitary half-crown to carry her forward till her next manuscript should be sold. She had already jotted down the title and a bit of the preface of another work, called "Nightshade Abbey," but so far there had been a slight haziness about that part of it which Louie called "the plot." When writing "Rookwood Parsonage," it was far better, she had thought, to let the story tell itself – all real geniuses did that – but in her present advanced state of experience, she began to see a little through the mist, and finally she concluded she would dream a little longer on the apple-bough days, and lie awake longer at nights talking to her characters, as one of the other great authors did, before she dipped her pen in ink any farther. And so, between planning and dreaming and going round to shop-windows to have everything selected before her twenty sovereigns came, days and weeks passed unconsciously away, and the Wednesday morning arrivedwhich brought matters to a climax.

It was well she ate a good breakfast that morning, for a great bull with horns awoke her at dawn of day, trying to rob her of her manuscript. She heard the church clock strike eight just as she finished plaiting her hair, and then she resolved to take a seat in the apple-bough and try to fix her attention on the page of poetry she had to learn before meeting Miss Spookes. In fifteen more minutes the postman would come along, so she turned her face toward that point in the lane where his head would pop up first, and waited and waited.

Yes, there he was at last. A very silly young man, too, she thought, for he always seemed to whistle loudest when he happened to be carrying bad news. He was whistling now, and swinging something in his right hand that appeared to hang by a string.

Several women came out to their doors to ask if there was anything for them, and then – oh, horror! – on by the orchard fence still whistling he came, and the identity of Florrie's brown paper parcel could no longer be mistaken. He paused under the apple-bough to scan the address, as if not quite sure such a portentous communication could be intended for so small a person as Miss Florence Whitherington,

Alas! in one mind at least there was no doubt about it whatever; and the wonder is that the poetry book didn't drop down there and then through the branches to the postman's head.

Meantime that individual gave vent to another form of expression, halfway between a whistle and a chuckle, and walked soberly up to the house.

Yes, it was indeed her manuscript. That label, and the little nest of stamps half-covered with black marks in the right hand corner, swam like a dreadful shuddering mist before her eyes. A shower of November meteors seemed to rise in the sky and fall to the ground in a thin vapoury dust – the dust of those twenty golden sovereigns. She would have cried if she could have found tears. But no, a heavy stone seemed to have shut down the relief-valves of her heart.

She hardly remembered what happened next, except that her mother came along the garden path to gather parsley for stuffing, and spoke up quietly into the tree –

"Florrie dear, the postman has brought you a parcel. I put it in your drawer right away; and I think you'd best leave the looking into it until you come back from school."

Kind, thoughtful mother! She always did the very best thing that could be done with every thing, even when it chanced to be a rejected manuscript.

It was quite two days before Florrie summed up courage to go to that drawer again, and then under the cruel brown paper she found a little surprise – not a cheque, but a real editor's letter, bit bold characters containing a very kernel of good counsel inside a shell of encouragement, all written down in the space of half a page, with the photo of a publishing house standing sentry at the top.

"Dear young friend," it said, "allow me to hope you will have the good sense to rise above this apparent failure. To be able to persevere under difficulty is better for us than to achieve sudden and unmerited success. Try again. Learn as much of the things about you as you can. Catch a butterfly, examine it, and let it take to its wings again, and finally set down all you have found out about it on one side of one sheet of paper, before you attempt to write all over twenty. I shall be pleased to consider anything you may send after you have taken my advice, and done your best."

Then followed publisher's name and address, and a list of books it would be well for her to read.

She often wished afterwards she had kept that letter. But no, it was far too stinging, and Florrie's opinion of herself and her works was very different then to what it became after ten years' training. Consequently five minutes later, the unfortunate copy of "Rookwood Parsonage," the good editor's letter, the title page and preface of "Nightshade Abbey," and all that had found a place in that dreadful washstand drawer, were a heap of fluffy, smouldering ashes under the grate in "Mount

Everest" kitchen, and Florrie's first conception of what martyrdom meant was being sobbed out among the pillows in her bedroom.

She was more sympa-thetic after that, and didn't leave the pots to wash themselves quite so often, and — "Did she ever write again?" you ask. A first lesson in grammar, or spelling, or any other branch of learning, usually implies a second and a third; so also does a first manuscript.

GRANNIE.

Cosy Corner Chats.

IX. – THE STUDY OF ENGLISH LITERATURE.

MY DEAR HELEN: You seem a little worried that you are to leave your father's generous library, where you have read at your own sweet will since you could read at all, to pursue the study of English literature in a regular classroom, with written examinations looming up to prevent your taking your daily pleasure in Shakespeare and Thackeray and Emerson. Let me see if I can do a little to prove to you that you should find the faces of our old friends more attractive, and not less so, under these new condi-tions. The study of English literature has fallen into dis-repute among a good many right-minded folk. I think this is for several reasons. Two of them are, perhaps, worth our notice. The teaching of literature has often been given over to fact-mongers — the most delusive of educators. They have told us a great deal about the facts of the writers' lives, and the dates and order of publication of their works, and very little about the works themselves. Or literature has been pre-sented in critical lectures or essays, which leave the student's mind in the condi-tion of that of the famous young lady who had not seen Niagara, but had heard it very highly spoken of.

Now literature, properly studied, makes its first appeal directly to the perception, just as truly as does botany or geology. The great books are the data to be viewed through the conditions of life preceding them. The study of them differs from the study of a bit of rock or a quartz crystal only as the study of a butterfly differs from that of the flower which feeds it. It is a higher form of life, and all the better fitted for the scientific method. Here the materials for the study are not dumb chemicals or fossilised animals, but the most vital truths told by the deepest thinkers. The first step toward the proper teaching of literature is to put into the hands of the student the specimen to be studied; the second is to subordinate to the specimen itself all talk about it. It is of no importance when one reads "Prometheus Unbound" that one should know anything about Shelley's habit of being late at dinner or his original interpretation of the obligations brought by marriage; but it is of importance that we should understand his passionate sympathy with the French Revolution, his revolt against the iron-bound system of education which had turned him out of university, and his profoundly religious view of the universe, which the English Philistine knew no better than to call Atheism.

Observation, however careful and painstaking, is the beginning only of that education which prepares us for complete living. The memory is all that gives dignity to observation. The cat which purrs about a strange piece of furniture or investigates from a distance with her sharp glance a newcomer, observes better than you or I, but she does not remember or judge, save in exceptional cases.

Royal roads to a good memory are legion nowadays, if we may believe the words of their discoverers. I shall continue to think, however, that the best way to learn to remember is to memorise; and that the best material for memorising is the greatest words of the greatest masters. Hamlet's soliloquies seem to me more practical material for strengthening the will than all the chronologies ever compiled. I would even go so far as to hope that holding great lines in the memory may have a certain regenerative effect upon character. I should like every young man to know by heart Hamlet's characterisation:—

. . ."Give me that man
That is not passion's slave, and I will
    wear him
In my heart's core, — ay, in my heart
    of heart."

The effects of a busy life might well be counteracted by Wordsworth's reflection:—

"The world is too much with us."

or by the matchless lines setting forth for all time the riches of the imaginative life:-

"To me the meanest flower that blows
    can give
Thoughts that do often lie too deep
    for tears."

Perception and a strong and accurate memory are not all we require of a girl. For "complete living" we must have, in just measure, the power of comparing and judging. These powers are easy enough to exercise in simple matters. A child can tell the difference between a kitten and a puppy, but it is not on such simple questions that the conduct of life turns. But among the pages of the great writers there is scope for the practice of the keenest discrimination. One must choose, judge, compare, when the question of the real value of a poem or a play is at issue. One must even learn to suspend judgment — a task still more difficult than to form judgment. Practice makes perfect. It is possible to gain a vision so clear that it cannot be deceived. How much this clear vision is needed may be seen, for example, by the rapid change of opinion in regard to the works of Walt Whitman in the last ten years. Literature is manifold. There is no coming to the end of its combinations. We are bound to keep the eye clear, the standard high, and the judgment practised. In doing this, we shall make, not only a better race of critics, but a race of better men and women. Perhaps you are wondering if all this work done on the masterpieces of literature is not sacrilegious. Nothing could be worse than using the greatest imaginative lines of literature for carpenter-shop display. But to the work which may be done by the reverent pupil that thinks the master's thoughts after him, the great books yield their treasures. They lay open their very hearts for the sympathetic gaze of youth. Why should we keep young minds laboriously building houses of clay and plaiting straw when real timber, stones, and mortar lie ready to their hands? Leading an eager class through the wonders of "Macbeth" makes all the plodding among the dry books of studies whose material is not thus fascinating seem pathetically dull. I remember hearing one of my teachers say that he believed that in heaven every man, woman, and child would be a teacher of English literature. I suppose that the pupils in that case would be the angels!

There is no royal road to learning but this; it is pos-sible to choose those subjects for investigation which shall unfold and vitalise all the parts and powers of the mind. In the great realm of literature, in the work of Shakespeare and Shelley and Lamb and Emerson and Carlyle and Browning and Tennyson, every power of our mind may find its stimulus. Am I dull and unresponsive? The fascinating story of Spenser and the tragedy of Shakespeare shall arouse me. Am I slip-shod in mind? The matchless lines of the great poets beguile me to a reverent and accurate memory of them. Am I slow to read the secrets of human character? The men and women of Shakespeare and Thackeray and Hawthorne will first interest me, and then stand still while I study them and learn from them how to understand the folk among whom I live. Am I rude of taste and faulty of judgment? The highest excellence in minds as far apart as Tennyson and George Eliot, or Chaucer and Browning, compels my admiration and forces open my blinded vision; and, while all this is going on in my intellectual development, my spirit is refreshing itself at the great springs of human thought. Thus I think the study of English literature ought to send you back to that beautiful and generous library all the more eager to know it and all the better fitted to love it.

HELOISE EDWINA HERSEY.

Girls' Pets and How to Manage Them.

THE POODLE.

By Mrs. L. S. Baker, Ladies' Kennel Association.

F the numerous different breeds I would recommend for girls, I would certainly name the Poodle. If in his present queer fashion of train and headdress as the encumbered "corded," or in neat tie-ups and short frocks of the now exceedingly fashionable "curly," he is one of the quaintest of dogs; he is also one of the most intelligent, one of the most responsible, and one of the best knockabouts as a breed in the whole long list of the breeds of dogs.

You can never, unless he has been spoiled as a puppy by teasing and unkind treatment, and rarely then, get him bad-tempered. He is always anticipating new things in the way of walks and fresh adventures, which he thinks your brain is maturing for his benefit, and if there comes along that *dies irae* which comes to youth, when skies are grey and influenza is fierce, and things are wrong in the whole, whole house, there isn't any curly doggy head more jolly and kind and comfortable and sympathetic to rest in condoling inquiry on your lap, nor any colder nose with the "Oh, it'll be all right to-morrow" touch about it, than a poodle's.

Poodles, as a breed, are owned mostly by ladies. I know two ladies who own eleven well-known poodles, seven of which are kept as companions in the very large house. Their kennel is considered one of the best in England. All its members are well known to the Curly Poodle Club, which fixes their points, arranges what classes shall be offered for them at the chief dog shows, and generally rules curly poodledom. I am personally acquainted with two "corded" champions, and also know their owners. However, as I don't wish to grow mysterious, and the limits of an article are not the least bit elastic, I plunge at once to tell you that there are two distinct divisions of the poodle family to be seen at our shows, and of these I give you illustrations. Please remember, the "Russian or corded poodle" and the "French or curly poodle." The popularity of the two breeds waxes and wanes for various reasons. Sometimes, as happens with all breeds, a great celebrity owns one, and society papers get hold of the fact and journalists generally write about it, and possibly you see it stated: "Curly poodles (or corded poodles, as the case may be) are becoming the fashion." Then lots of people who've got poodles begin to show their dogs, and, finding they are not what they thought they were — that is, not up to club standards of points — they buy others that have been bred to these points, and so sales become brisk in the breed. Then the "doggy press" and the doggy columns of the society papers, and the odds and ends columns of the evening papers, and here and there

an enterprising daily (for in these days even dailies that do not devote an occasional line to dogs are held to be behind the times), all are found to contain little notices about the breed which is becoming the

CHAMPION CLIPPED POODLE – LA POUPÉE.

curly." I am going to be guilty of paradoxical statements, but the best authorities assure me that there is absolutely no difference in the two breeds. If, from the time "the curly-headed baby" in your kennel begins

fashion; and there sets in that strange mysterious American wave which is called "a boom." As soon as a boom in dogs begins, you must know the best dogs almost invariably always go off to America.

The present fashion in poodles leans towards "the

to run about and get himself gloriously dirty on a muddy day, you rub and brush and comb his coat out, but continue to do this always (determining with the same to have him clipped), he will delight you as "a curly." If you don't brush and comb his coat out but leave it to its own quaint devices, the old hair hangs on to the new, and there grow longer and longer those queer-looking ropes which dance and shake as he runs, like *une robe de danse grotesque*, which are his "cords." A corded poodle's pride, and that of his owner, naturally lies in the length and size and the abundance of these. He also, to meet the demands of fashion and his own convenience, poor chap, must be shaved. The operation is an art, and is known as "poodle clipping." There are several very well-known adepts at this work in England, but the cleverest of all these is a lady. She is named Miss Dallin, and many lady owners of poodles get her to come to their houses to clip the dogs and to advise about the treatment of the coat. She has the wonderful gift which some dentists possess (very few, I do admit) of making the patient feel that he doesn't at all mind the operation. Not that it hurts in the least, but many dogs are exceedingly nervous of the advent of the clipper, just as a terrier will slink in terror into a corner and try to hide as he

sees the bath appear on the scene for his tubbing, though he will plunge into the pond without a murmur, and even seek the pleasures of a swim. One of the bad practices of the trade is said to be that of drugging the dogs to keep them quiet, and though this does not obtain, possibly, among the most reputable of the profession, it is given as a reason that you should know your clipper. Some ladies, therefore, take lessons and do it themselves. The eleven poodles I speak of are clipped by their mistresses and the maid.

In France, where the poodle is the national dog, poodle clipping is quite the first of the *petits métiers* of Paris and the big cities. You can meet the *tondeur des chiens* with his little box on his shoulders at every turn on his way to his clients' houses. You can see him on a fine morning on the banks of the Seine preparing for his day's work, and you can sit and watch him take a dog and sponge and lather him, and send him for his rinsing in the river while the owner waits. You can see the dog rubbed half dry after he has shaken himself, see him

wrapped in his *peignoir de bain* while the clipping and shaving are going on, and the owner directs the fashion in which it shall be done; and you see the finishing touches of drying the ears and wiping between the toes and under the armpits, and the manicuring of broken and long nails, as well as the cleaning of the teeth, if the bath is a luxurious one.

The care and attention to the wants of a pet dog, and to the exigencies of his toilet and all the details of his feeding and exercise and consequent health, are a good experience for a girl as well as a healthy little moral training. She learns to exercise care, to be observant and thorough, to be thoughtful and kind for other than herself, and to be independent of others for the carrying out of little everyday necessary duties. She acquires and exercises all this through a good motive channel, *i.e.*, affection.

A poodle, and, in fact, any dog, to be kept in health must be fed regularly and exercised thoroughly. A dog who is the friend of the family or the companion of any member of the household generally gets fed three times a day, and this is not too often under circumstances of frequent and untrammelled exercise or walks twice daily; but he should have two small meals and one good one, and this last should be given at night, when he should be let out for his final run, and then sent to bed. To keep your poodle in health give him at least four ounces of good meat a day, vegetables occasionally, and now and then liver, sheep's head, or tripe to make a change. Allow plenty of milk, if he will drink it, and dog biscuits or hound meal, sometimes dry, sometimes soaked, make a very useful variation. The water bowl should always be full, and the common practice of putting a piece of sulphur in this is of no value, because sulphur is quite insoluble in water. All poodles require warmth, and are rather prone to internal chills, so, if caught in the wet, must never be allowed to lie about in a damp condition. You may thus save them much. Have always a kennel advice card in your cupboard of requisites — it

will cost about 2s. 6d. — and chiefly be careful not to wash your dog on the coldest day of the week, never immediately after a meal, and always to dry him well. Let him have the run of the house and the freedom of the grounds. I think I would say: If he falls ill, call in a vet.

It is one of the main things in showing a dog successfully — after condition, which is your daily charge — to show him well groomed. The foundation of this is the bath, and the main thing in washing a dog after you have got him clean is to dry him well. This should, of course, be done with soft, dry bath towels. The poodle's coat must be brushed with a stiff, not too hard, brush, and then the hair must be gently and very carefully combed out to its proper fluffiness. His legs are dried, his feet are always nicely wiped and dried between the toes during the rubbing process; he is gently and carefully rubbed under the armpits, and wherever the wind might chafe the skin or the cold strike home a chill. If he is kept well exercised, he does not require the manicurist; but

his teeth are cleaned with a soft tooth-brush by the expert, and this you can always be, because the first difficulty is removed; the dog doesn't mind your doing it, because he loves you.

I would not advise you to take your poodle to the nearest river to wash him. The schoolroom floor is a capital place for the whole operation, and I should recommend two big baths — one for washing and the other for rinsing — some of the scullery canvas cloths to take the sloppings, and a bath blanket to do the drying on. You want at least three towels of fair size, a bath thermometer, a sponge, some good liquid dog soap, your brushes, and an ear sponge. First catch your dog. Put him into the first bath, which should be a warm, not a hot, bath. Sponge him to wet his coat all over, except the head, pour some of the liquid soap on his back, and rub it well in with the hand until all his body is in a good lather. When you are quite sure his body and legs are clean — and, of course, you will do each leg separately, teaching the dog to keep still in his bath while you do this, and rubbing always with the hand — you must attempt the head, and here you have got to be deft or you will cause the dog much annoyance and some pain by letting the soap into his eyes. I always find it best to quickly squeeze the sponge, dipped into clean warm water, twice over the head, keeping it close and not making a douche of it, and then a few drops of soap on the poll and rub well with the hand up from the back of the head round the ears, and rinse and wipe with the clean water sponge again. Then transfer the dog to the other bath, which must be tepid water, rinse him well, wring out the sponge, and as he stands in the bath wipe the wet off him, and press it out from the coat with the hand. Remove him from the bath on to the drying blanket, and wrap him in the biggest towel, which can stand for the *peignoir de bain* of the French *tondeur des chiens*. While he stands in this, dry his head, wipe his eyes, his ears (inside and out), and use your little

ear sponge, and sprinkle the least powdering of boracic acid in the ears. Dry his neck and under the ears, where the trouble known as glandular swelling takes place; dry him under the armpits, and his legs and feet, and rub him (still with his peignoir over him and using it as a towel) with both hands along the body till the gentle friction has produced a comfortable glow and this part of the toilet is practically complete. Use a second towel in the same way — a warm one in winter, and before the fire. If you can teach the dog to roll himself in a spare sleeping blanket at this stage while you clean his teeth and comb and brush his head and forelegs, &c., it is a good plan; and perhaps when you let him run out into the garden it is best to put his coat on.

The chief points of the curly poodle, as agreed to by the Curly Poodle Club are:

General Appearance. — That of a very active, intelligent, smart, elegant-looking dog, well-built, and carrying himself proudly.

Head. — The head to be

long, straight, and fine, the skull fuller looking than in the corded, and not so peaked.

Muzzle. — Long (but not snipy) and strong, not full in the cheek, teeth white, strong, and level, gums black, lips black and not showing lippiness.

Eyes. — Oval shaped, very dark, full of fire and intelligence.

Nose. — Black and sharp.

Ears. — The leather long and wide, low set, and hanging close to the face.

Neck. — Well proportioned and strong, to admit of the head being carried high and with dignity.

Shoulders. — Strong and muscular, sloping well to the back.

Chest. — Deep and moderately wide.

Back. — Short, strong, and very slightly hollowed, the loins broad and muscular, the ribs well sprung and braced up.

Feet. — Rather small and of good oval shape, the toes well arched and close, pads thick and hard.

Legs. — The forelegs set straight from shoulder with plenty of bone and muscle. Hind legs very muscular and well bent, with the hocks well let down.

Tail. – Set on rather high, well carried, never curled or carried over back.

Coat. – The coat should be very profuse, and of hard texture, of even length, and to have no suspicion of cord in it, and can be either curly or fluffy.

Colours. – All black, all white, all red, all blue, all brown.

The White Poodle to have dark eyes, black or dark-lined nose, lips, and toenails.

The Red and the Brown Poodle to have dark amber eyes, dark-lined nose, lips and toenails.

The Blue Poodle to have dark eyes, lips and toenails

All other points of coloured poodles should be the same as required in a black curly poodle.

'TWAS EVER THUS.

DOWN a winding pathway,
　　In a garden old,
　　Tripped a dainty maiden,
But her heart was cold.

Came a prince to woo her –
　　Said he loved her true;
Maiden said he didn't,
　　So he ceased to woo.

Came a perfumed noble,
　　And, dropping on one knee,
Said his lover was deeper
　　Than the deepest sea.

But the dainty maiden
　　Said his love was dead;
And the perfumed noble
　　Believed just what she said.

Came a dashing stranger,
　　Took her off by force;
Said he'd make her love him –
　　And she did, of course!

HILDA'S HEROISM.

BY EDITH METCALFE.

OT very far from the road stood the little cottage at Whitgate, where Hilda's grandmother lived. Delicate tea-roses and purple clematis climbed over the trellised porch, and at the back there was a rambling, old-world garden, well stocked with fruit trees and full of old-fashioned flowers planted in broad borders round the beds of vegetables.

Hilda thought it was the most charming place in the world, and was never so happy as during the long visits she paid to her grannie. Her home life, indeed, was rather dreary, for her only sister was much older than herself, and her father was a silent, undemonstrative man, fond of his children, it is true, but always rather puzzled how to share in the life and interests of his motherless daughters. So he acquiesced gladly in his mother's wish to have Hilda constantly with her, and Hilda, in her turn, was as much at home at Whitgate as she was in Kensington.

It often happens that the baby of a family is very fond of little children, and Hilda was no exception to the rule. She constituted herself the friend and play-mate of all the children in the little seaside town, and it was pretty to see how they ran to meet her when they saw her coming, and how carefully she watched over them when they were playing near her on the beach. Her greatest delight was to be asked by some poor woman to mind her baby for her, and the patience and good-humour with which she would tend and amuse the tiniest infant were inexhaustible.

Of all the children who thus formed Hilda's court, the most devoted and the most loved were those who lived in the coastguard station, about half a mile from the town on the west cliff.

They were all so clean and tidy, and brought up in an atmosphere of discipline that made them quick and obedient and easy to look after. The coastguard station was itself a favourite resort of Hilda's, who liked its precise neatness, its whitewashed walls, and tarred outhouses, its bright green doors and shutters and closely-mown strip of lawn, from which the great flagstaff rose. Almost every morning after her bathe in the sea, Hilda would climb the cliff and call at some one of the coastguardsmen's houses for a glass of milk and a big slice of home-made cake; then she would romp upon the lawn with all the little ones who were not at school, and dry her long hair in the hot sunshine before running home for her midday dinner.

Her morning swim was an indispensable part of the day's routine. Mrs. Simpson was a firm advocate of all sports in moderation for girls, and paid as much attention to their having healthy bodies as she did to their having healthy minds. Two or three times a week old Sergeant Casey, the Irish

drill instructor attached to the Whitgate volunteers, came to the house to drill her and give her lessons in fencing and singlestick, and every day she bathed from the same machine, which she grew to regard as her very own, sometimes going quite far out of her depth when followed by some fisherman in his boat, in case she should become unduly tired. Thus she developed into a strong and healthy girl, firm of flesh and straight of limb, with the clear complexion and bright eyes that always belong to those who are not afraid of the open air and shrink neither from sun nor rain. And all the time love for her grand-mother and devotion to the children in the place were making her sweet and lov-able as well.

Whitgate is an oddly fashioned town. All the fisher folk live down in the east side, where there is a small harbour for their fleet of boats; in the west side are the shops and the few villas of the gentry, but the popu-lation all told is very small, and there is an air about the place as if it had been left

behind in the march of progress. At the extreme west of the town, and just below the new coastguard station is a decrepit and ruined breakwater; perhaps it was once intended to be a fashionable pier. However that may be, it is a melan-choly piece of masonry, running straight out into the sea for perhaps a hundred yards without any apparent object, and, on the left hand, where it is exposed to the full fury of the winter storms, falling into hopeless ruin. Its upper surface is rough and neglected, and there are even gaps in it, through which a careless person might have a fall on to water-washed lumps of rock and concrete twenty feet below.

Possibly because it is so dangerous, it is the spot most frequented by the Whitgate children, and Hilda often came her, too, to read and enjoy the salt spray beating in her face and the sun making her cheeks tin-gle as it dried the spray again.

It was after tea one afternoon that she was sit-ting at the far end of the pier, engrossed in reading

Kingsley's "Water Babies." The book held her imagination, and she was wrapped in one of those delightful and by the funny barking of a very young puppy. She looked around, and saw little Peggie Robb, the With Peggie was her greatest treasure, her very own retriever pup, at present little more than a woolly

THE LIFEBELT FELL WITH A SPLASH BY HER SIDE, AND, PUSHING PEGGIE'S BODY THROUGH IT, SHE LET GO HER HOLD.

day dreams, in which the mind seems to be detached from the waking body, when suddenly she was recalled to her actual surroundings by light footsteps three-year-old child of one of the coastguard's men, trotting towards her, and gravely saying "Mind! mind!" as if warning herself to be careful how she came. ball with bright eyes and a fluffy tail, and a firm conviction that everything in this wonderful world was expressly devised for its especial entertainment.

Hilda, too, called out to Peggie to "mind," but she felt no real anxiety, for the little maid had often been upon the pier before. Some little way from her, however, the puppy stopped to examine something that struck him as curious, some fossil shell in the stonework, or some old crevice in the concrete; and, just as he was pausing there, the water lapping against the side of the pier ran into some hole below and made a hollow gurgling noise that aroused his curiosity still more. He ran to the edge of the pier to discover what it might be, and without any warning fell over the side, yelping with terror, and splashed into the sea below. Peggie saw him disappear, and, bursting into tears, ran wildly to the spot.

Hilda screamed to her to stop, but the child never heeded her; even if she heard the call she could scarcely have stopped in time. As fast as her fat little legs could carry her she ran to the unprotected side of the break-water, and still calling wildly to her pet, fell headlong after it into full five fathoms of water.

Hilda dropped her book and sprang to the point whence Peggie had fallen. She closed her eyes for a second, and an agonised, inarticulate prayer for help burst from her very soul. Then she nerved herself to look down, and a sob shook her as she realised how unnecessary was the frightful risk the child had run in her unselfish but unreasoning devotion to her pet, for already the puppy had managed to scramble on to a projecting block of masonry, and was standing on it, dripping and shivering with fright, but absolutely safe and within easy reach of anyone with any nerve to climb. But Peggie, who in her baby innocence had no idea of danger, was caught in the side current, and, vainly beating the water with her chubby arms, was being carried every minute farther away from the pier.

Never was there a moment when a girl's presence of mind and healthy development of body did better service for a fellow-creature than Hilda's did for little Peggie now. She turned to the shore, and, putting both hands to her mouth, called shrilly towards the coastguard station for help, using the Australian bushman's cry of "Coo-ee," because she knew how far that sound can carry. Twice and three times the cry rang across the intervening space, and something in the terror of her voice sped it to wondering ears. A woman came and looked over the boundary wall, and Hilda murmured a prayer of thankfulness. She snatched her scarlet stocking cap from her head and waved it wildly, pointing all the time to the sea, and then, flinging her cap upon the pier and kicking off her canvas shoes, she put her arms high above her head, and without the slightest hesitation, dived bravely into the sea.

She rose, breathless but unflurried, and struck out in the direction where she had seen Peggie's body last.; the tide helped her a great deal, but she had never swum before in her clothes, and her fisherman's jersey and blue serge skirt felt like leaden weights. The jersey she could not undo, but she managed to slip off her skirt, and with firm, steady strokes gained upon the almost drowning child. Hilda had never realised before what slow progress even a good swimmer can make, and her heart felt like bursting with the tremendous effort she was making. She turned on to her side and used an overhand stroke to increase her speed, but even when she was almost within reach of Peggie she seemed unable quite to catch up with her; and just as, at last, she made a grab at the unconscious body it rolled down again, pulling her with it.

Yet when Hilda came again to the surface she was grasping Peggie firmly, though whether dead or alive she could not tell. It was all to their advantage that the baby was unconscious, for she did not hamper Hilda by any frantic struggling; and, though Hilda had done so much, there was more to do ere she could know if life remained for either or both of them. She pushed Peggie across her back, holding her with one hand and trying to keep her head out of the water, and then turned painfully towards the shore, making westwards that the current might help her on. So it was that she did not see the help that came from her.

The woman upon the cliff had understood, and almost before Hilda had reached the child every man in the station was tearing wildly down to the beach. With marvellous speed they launched the patrol boat, and the stout oars bent as the determined fellows, with set teeth, strained every muscle to lift the boat along. In the stern stood Matthew Robb, Peggie's father with a life belt and a line in his hands, directing the others in their course, and with a look upon his face that was in itself a prayer.

"We're coming, missie; we're coming," he shouted. "Don't give up yet, we're coming," and then, with a fierce roar to the men: "Shove her along, mates, pull; oh, God, let us be in time! We're coming missie."

And Hilda heard, She was too tired to seem to care, but there was Peggie, and she tried to keep going just for Peggie's sake. Ahead of the boat the lifebelt fell with a splash by her side, and, pushing Peggie's body through it, she let go her hold, and rolled helplessly downwards.

God let them come in time. Matthew Robb leaned over the side of the boat, and, plunging his arm into the water, seized Hilda's, and dragged her up again. Tenderly he lifted her into the boat, with tears rolling down his cheeks, while in the bows another man raised Peggie's still form, and handed it over the thwarts to her father.

Hilda opened her eyes, and Matthew Robb bent over her.

"The puppy," she whispered, and relapsed into complete unconsciousness.

At the coastguard station things were ready for them. British seamen are not called handy men for nothing. Warm blankets and fires were waiting, and a doctor had been sent for ere ever the boat was launched; and when, a long time afterwards, as it seemed to the anxious onlookers, life and consciousness returned to Hilda and Peggie, the puppy was sorrowfully licking the last drops of salt water from his fluffy coat.

That was the first time Hilda Simpson saved a life, but it was not the last, and she holds more than one medal from the Royal Humane Society. Her name is known far beyond that Kentish village, and yet in Whitgate itself she is never called by it; to the children she is simply "Missie," and by the coast-guardsmen, whose lives are hers if they could do her service, she is called "Grace Darling."

WELSH WOMEN.

Cosy Corner Chats.

X. – MAKING A HOME.

Mrs. G. S. Reaney.

MY DEAR R. — May I lovingly and tenderly point out to you your personal privileges and responsibilities in regard to making a home? In olden times, more even than to-day, we spoke of the husband as the "bread-winner," and associated him in his character and life as the actual home-maker. But we must remember "Man does not live by bread alone, but by every word which proceedeth out of the mouth of God." There are influences which are so closely associated and intertwined with the making of a home, that to forget their importance would be to ignore their value; and these influences, in the main, are the direct utterances of the young wife's life. And this thought brings me straight away to the fact that what you are in your own heart-life, such will be your power in making your home bright and beautiful. "As a man thinketh in his heart, so is he." As a woman thinketh in her heart, so is she.

Trials, disappointments, and difficulties are not necessarily "evils." They are among the "all things" which "work together for good." See that you give your own heart its full share of spiritual food; your body its legitimate portion of rest. The need of at least one leisure hour in the day to call your own, for rest of body and culture of mind, should be established at the onset. It is due to yourself; due to your home. Banish for ever from your mind the idea that it is selfish to look after your own interests. You are God's property, and your life can only be lived at its best when you are your best. To be over-wearied will mean enfeebled powers. To find no time for self-culture will mean to degenerate. In this, as in many things which definitely concern others, you will daily find the need of being unselfish enough to be selfish.

And now for a few suggestions about making a home. I take for granted you are starting your married life with a husband who unites with yourself in the desire to establish a home free from intoxicating drinks. Let me urge you never to relax your determination to keep your home clear from a presence and power which have so terribly broken into other homes, as happy in their beginning as your own. Lose no opportunity of reading up-to-date temperance literature; so shall you be strengthened in your principles, and made more firm in your efforts to induce others to join a good cause.

However thoughtful and in earnest your husband, it will rest largely with yourself, my dear young friend, to make it possible for him to establish "Family Worship" in the home. You will be wise to devote much care to the planning and cooking of meals. However kindly disposed your husband may be, if his food is habitually, from one cause or another, indigestible, he will grow in time to be fretful and moody. Badly cooked food is accountable for many home discords. Study variety, and dismiss from your mind the thought that meat is an essential at every meal. To many a young wife this has been a serious difficulty. Lacking knowledge – to be obtained by reading vegetarian literature and other, supplied by any good bookseller – in her effort to provide the table with "good food," the young housekeeper has made larger demands upon her purse than it could meet; expenditure exceeded income, debt gathered, troubles came.

A word here. To keep your heart free from unnecessary care, let me beg you never to run into debt. Wherever possible, pay for everything as you have it. Let me suggest a plan. Get seven little bags, and every week place a certain proportion of the money entrusted to you to spend into each. Thus:– No. 1, rent, coals, and gas; No. 2, food; No. 3, clothing; No. 4, wear and tear of furniture (renewing things as wanted, making good damage); No. 5, wholesome literature and recreation; No. 6, a rainy-day reserve; No. 7, church funds and gifts to the poor. By this systematic plan the habit of thriftful forethought will be cultivated, and the healthy little question, "Can we afford it?" will restrain expenditure where wisdom suggests the need.

I hope you do not think a home thus made would be too "prim and proper" to be happy. Try the experiment. Order is heaven's first law. No home can be lastingly happy which is not orderly. And it will rest with you far more than your husband to make this order and to keep it. Home is never so restful to a hard-working man as when it is orderly. To ensure this orderliness there must be true method in work, and where there is method there will be attention to details which hold their own special points of usefulness. "A stitch in time saves nine." "A place for everything, and everything in its place." Where orderliness reigns we usually find the mistress of the house the possessor of a calm, unruffled spirit. Nothing really wearies as much as the fret and worry of an ill-planned and ill-managed home.

You will long to keep your house free from dust, and you will spare no care in this respect. Do not forget that with you will rest the power to keep pure and free from the dust of discord, gossip and slander the atmosphere of home life. Be on your guard. Let your home be the abode of kindliness. By the way, in your desire to keep out the dust, do not shut out fresh air: in your anxiety to preserve your pretty things unspoilt, do not keep away the sunlight. Better dust and faded curtains, than pent-up rooms and an unhealthy dwelling. A home to be happy must be healthy.

As the chosen companion of your husband, and the possible mother of children, the home you make must be all that is invigorating and cheerful. As one essential to this, I beg you to cultivate a bright spirit. There is a way of taking all the bitterness out of trial and sorrow.

The cheerful heart seems to find speech in those bright little touches which some homes have and others lack. Make your home pretty. A plant here, a vase of cut flowers there, a twisted ribbon, a bow-tied antimacassar — what tiny touches these, yet how they combine to breathe out fragrant memories of home which those dear to you will treasure up.

Finally, my dear young friend, remember the greatest power in making a home happy and beautiful is Love. Love which, seeking not her own, thinks and plans and contrives for others. Love which never wearies. Love which grows in faithfulness to its high ideals as time advances.

How to be Strong.

PART VII.

I WAS reading a very interesting article some time ago relating to the importance of physical exercise to the boys and young men who are in the future to be the backbone and support of the nation, and, as I firmly believe that the girls and women of this country will play a no less important part in future progress of the British Empire, I make no apology for quoting some of its "points" in this month's chat, feeling sure that it will have its interesting (and, I trust, its profitable) side for yourselves.

The first point was of the responsibilities of being a citizen of this great and ever-increasing British Empire, and of the necessity of equipping oneself men-

tally and physically for the proper discharge of the duties involved. Of course, the educational system of the nation is responsible for the mental development, but what about the physical? The writer, a well-known authority on physical education, went on to say: "When

EXERCISE 7.

the rush was on for volunteers to go to the war in South Africa, out of 21,000 young men who volunteered, 18,000 had to be rejected, leaving only 3,000 who were considered strong enough to enter the army." So you will see what a serious thing it is for the coun-

try. Rifle clubs are very good things in their own way, but the writer goes on to say: "Before you teach a man to carry a gun, you ought to see that he is strong enough to carry it." The day will probably never come when the women of the country will have to "carry a gun," but the point of it all is equally applicable to you. We want a sound, healthy, and educated mind in a sound, healthy, and educated body. Those of you who have been working steadily at these exercises know what a difference it makes to your health and happiness to know that, although women are called "the weaker sex," you are enabled by these exercises to be relatively as strong and "fit" as your own brothers! When you look at it from an Imperial point of view you see how very important it is. The nation is made up of the individual!

This month's exercise (No. 7) is specially adapted for producing an erect and well-developed figure. It is performed in the following manner:— Stand erect, with arms close to sides. Bend the arms at the elbow until the dumb-bell is level with the shoulder. Lunge forward about 30 inches with the right foot, planting it firmly on the ground. Slightly raise the left foot on the toes, and vigorously thrust out both arms straight in front of you, exhaling your breath. Return the arms to the level of the shoulders once more, this time inhaling the breath, and returning the right foot to its original position; then repeat the whole operation again, thrusting forward the right foot and extending both hands outwards from the shoulders. Repeat the exercise about 20 times.

(To be continued.)

Athletics for Girls.

PING-PONG PLAYING.

BY BEATRICE LEWIS.

THE intense fascination that the game of ping-pong exercises over young people of both sexes and the rapidity with which it has spread and popularised itself in all parts of the world are surely sufficient arguments in its favour. No foolish or worthless pastime, no mere amusement lacking in scope for the display of cleverness and individuality would ever attain the pinnacle of success to which ping-pong has undoubtedly climbed during the past year. There are various reasons besides the mere pleasure of the actual game which go to form active factors towards its triumph.

First and foremost amongst these must be counted the fact that the exercise of playing is exhilarating and beneficial above anything hitherto induced by an indoor game. Then, it is inexpensive and accessible to all classes and all means. Essentially a social pastime, it is equally suitable for afternoon and evening play, and can be enjoyed in any kind of dress. The only restriction I would lay down in this latter respect is with regard to the wearing of tight things, especially tight-fitting sleeves, which would certainly impede the play and distress the player. But since tight garments are harmful, under any conditions it is scarcely a special exaction of ping-pong to demand their avoidance.

I should here to like say a few words to young girls on what I may call the ethics of game-playing, and the position and importance that should be accorded to it in one's daily life. It is a habit amongst many people to decry the playing of games as childish and to scoff at all signs of earnestness and enthusiasm expended upon them. "Oh, it's only a game! How absurd to take it so seriously!" Now, this appears to be an entirely false spirit in which to enter upon any pursuit.

Games, especially if they give scope for healthful exercise, hold a legitimate place in the lives of all young persons, and are therefore well worth entering into heartily. At the same time, it should never be forgotten that play must not be allowed to usurp the place or the time of work and duty. If the ardour for play leads to scamped lessons, to the scurried and untidy performance of the necessary needlework task, to a forgetfulness of mother's instructions, or an ungracious manner in lightening her labours, and in rendering her thoughtful assistance in the household work, be sure that an ugly phase of selfishness is setting in which must be checked without delay. Pull yourself up, take yourself to task promptly and severely,

PICKING UP A BALL WHICH HAS ROLLED OVER NET WITHOUT ANY BOUNCE.

and try to let duties and pleasures respectively find their proper level in the scheme of your daily life.

But, granted that your playtime is not allowed to encroach upon higher duties, let me beg you not to be ashamed to throw yourself thoroughly and heartily into the pastime of the moment. Use your brains, concentrate your attention, and do your best to excel. When it does not annoy me, it makes my heart ache to see young girls joining feebly and listlessly in pastimes and pleasures, instead of displaying a healthy and vigorous enthusiasm. It is my experience, and my sincere conviction, that thoroughness permeates the character in work and play alike, while a listless indifference destroys the moral fibre, and will prove a bar to success in all things small and great.

Therefore, while you are playing, play with heart and soul, and do the very best you are capable of.

Ping-pong, like all other games, can be played prettily and gracefully, or the reverse — very much the reverse! It's really as easy from the beginning to cultivate a graceful style as to flounder and fling oneself about with arms and legs going like a distracted windmill. Some girls contract an ugly habit of standing with the legs apart, back bent and elbows squared. Such a pose, together with a countenance engraved with a fierce and anxious glare, would render the prettiest of girls an unattractive spectacle. I do not mean to suggest that you should be ever thinking of appearances, but a good carriage is very important, and exercise loses more than half its value if carried on in an awkward and slovenly manner.

If due attention is paid to the pose, ping-pong will be found really beneficial to the figure. So try to stand while serving and waiting, with one foot slightly forward and well-balanced hips, with chest expanded, shoulders back, and waist well in, the head and whole upper part of the body thrown slightly forward in a natural attitude for reaching out in any direction. Quiet play should be aimed at, but don't carry this idea to the

STRETCH AFTER A SCREW BALL.

extent of resigning all balls that require to be reached after.

As well as a good carriage, ping-pong gives scope for the display of a generous spirit. There is always a risk lest, while getting very interested in one's game, we should be tempted to snatch at every advantage and to be greedy of one's points. This is, unfortunately, a very common failing, and a far from engaging one. And where, after all, is the satisfaction of merely scoring points when not resultant from genuinely fair and good play? If you want to be a popular, as well as an expert, player, make up your mind to be the first to concede a doubtful point, don't argue the score on your own behalf, don't grumble at the bad strokes played by yourself, or mutter discontentedly at the good ones played by your adversary wherewith you are bowled out. A reputation for sweet temper and a "good sportsman" character is easily won or lost at ping-pong, and a bad loser or a grumbler will soon find that her company is not greatly sought by her playing companions.

Another habit to be sedulously avoided is that of screaming, exclaiming or emitting "zoological noises" in the excitement of play. Resist the temptation to dis-

persist in addressing the players and think it quite disagreeable and uncivil when, in their absorption, they fail to reply. I am afraid I cannot conscientiously counsel such amiability as would be requisite to carry on the conversation

content with easy victories over beginners, but always try as far as possible to find your adversary in a superior player, for only this way will your own style improve. And it's really far more interesting to be well beaten by an expert than to smash up all to nothing a merely indifferent performer.

RETURNING BALL WITH BACK TO TABLE.

cuss points or to converse about the game, or any other subject, while playing. It will spoil your own play, distract your adversary, and inevitably put out the scorer. Concentration is an absolute *sine qua non* and a wandering mind can but direct wandering and ineffective strokes. It is very tiresome and worrying, even during a quiet home game, when the onlookers

under these circumstances, for one's game would simply go all to pieces in the attempt.

In the very early stages of play, of course, the object is to serve the ball over into the opposite court, and to return it there when served to yourself. But this phase is very quickly worked through, and the play soon develops along far higher lines. Don't be

Since the commencement of its popularity the game has undergone considerable developments and evolved a far more scientific character than appeared at first possible. In its early stages the object of the players was centred in passing the ball backwards and forwards over the net, and the longer the rally the more wonderful the play was deemed. If this class of game had not been summarily ousted by something more interesting and brilliant, the entire pastime would soon have died a natural death, for, confined to those lines, it soon became tiresome in the extreme both to participators and to onlookers.

It is undoubtedly the public tournament play that has brought the game up to the high level of excellence that it has now attained.

Clever children seem specially adapted to excel at

since the conditions of play and players vary so greatly that no "best" racquet has been universally agreed

est place in popular favour at the time of writing is the rubber-covered wooden bat, which certainly has a wondrous knack, when wielded by expert fingers, of delivering the most untakable cuts, screws and spins. But the plain wood racquet, which almost completely superseded the once universal vellum, still retains its place, though many players have a fancy for covering it with various materials. A short handle is now almost universal, as it proved easier to turn and twist the bat expeditiously

BACK-HANDED CROUCH STROKE TO RETURN BALL THAT SHOOTS WITHOUT BOUNCING.

this pastime, for they have recently ousted many of their older and expert antagonists from their positions of vantage.

I want to say a few words on the important subject of the racquet, though it is impossible to lay down any law as to the "best,"

upon. Fancy and habit go a long way in determining the choice, and the majority of players find themselves at a terrible disadvantage when compelled to dispense with the services of their own pet implement!

Perhaps the make of racquet that holds the high-

if the handle does not protrude much beyond the palm of the hand. It is wise to experiment with several different racquets before fixing your choice on one, and that which suits your friend's style of play may not necessarily best adapt itself to yours.

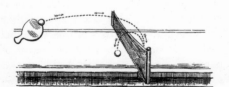
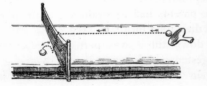

A SCREW-BACK BALL THAT BOUNCES BACK TO THE SIDE WHENCE IT CAME.

A BALL TO BE PICKED UP AT QUICK HALF-VOLLEY.

The Adventures of a LOON

PART II.

OST of the chicks were very smart and active, and they took to the water almost as soon as they were out of the shell, swimming and diving as if they had been accustomed to it for weeks instead of hours. In some ways, however, they required a good deal of care. For one thing, their little stomachs were not quite equal to the task of assimilating raw fish, and the parents had to swallow all their food for them, keep it down till it was partly digested, and then pass it up again to the hungry children. It made a good deal of delay, and it must have been very unpleasant, but it seemed to be the only practicable way of dealing with the situation. I am glad to say that it did not last very long, for by the time they were two weeks old the young loons were able to take their fish and reptiles and insects at first hand.

When they first arrived the chicks were covered all over with stiff down, of a dark, sooty gray on their backs, and white underneath. But this did not last long either. The first feathers soon appeared, and multiplied rapidly. I can't say that the young birds were particularly handsome, for even when their plumage was complete it was much quieter and duller of hue than their parents'. But they were fat and plump, and I think they thoroughly enjoyed life, especially before they discovered that there were enemies as well as friends in the world. That was a kind of knowledge that could not be avoided very long, however. They soon learned that men, and certain other animals such as hawks and skunks, were to be carefully shunned; and you should have seen them run on the water whenever a suspicious-looking character hove in sight. Their wings were not yet large enough for flying, but they flapped them with all their might, and scampered across the Glimmerglass so fast that their little legs fairly twinkled, and they actually left a furrow in the water behind them. But the bottom of the lake was really the safest refuge, and if a boat or a canoe pressed them too closely they would usually dive below the surface, while the older birds tried to lure the enemy off in some other direction by calling and shouting and making all sorts of demonstrations.

Generally these tactics were successful, but not always. Once some boys cornered the whole family in a small, shallow bay, where the water was not deep enough for diving; and before they could escape one of the youngsters was driven up on to the beach. He tried to hide behind a log, but he was captured and carried off, and I wish I had time to tell you of all the things that happened to him before he was finally killed and eaten by a dog. It was pretty tough on the old birds, as well as on him, but they still had one chick left, and you can't expect to raise all your children as long as bigger people are so fond of kidnapping and killing them.

Not all the people who came to see them were bent on mischief, however. There was a party of girls and boys, for instance, who camped beside the Glimmerglass for a few weeks, and who liked to follow them around the lake in a row boat and imitate their voices, just for the fun of making them talk back. One girl in particular became so accomplished in the loon language that Mahng would often get very much excited as he conversed with her, and would sometimes let the boat creep nearer and nearer until they were only a few rods apart. And then, all of a sudden, he would duck his head and go under, perhaps in the very middle of a laugh. The siren was getting a little too close. Her intentions might possibly be all right, but it was just as well to be on the safe side.

The summer was nearly gone, and now Mahng did something which I fear you will strongly disapprove. I don't want to tell you about it, but I suppose I must. Two or three male loons passed over the Glimmerglass one afternoon, calling and shouting as they went, and he flew up and joined them, and came back no more that summer. It looked like a clear case of desertion, but we must remember that he had stood by his wife all through the trying period of the spring and early summer, and that the time was at hand when the one chick that was left would go out into the world to paddle his own canoe, and when she would no longer need his help in caring for a family of young children. But you think he might have stayed with her, anyhow? Well, so do I; I'm sorry he didn't. They say that his cousins, the Red-throated Loons, marry for life, and live together from the wedding day till death, and I don't see why he couldn't have done as well as they. But it doesn't seem to be the custom among the Great Northern Divers. Mahng was only following the usual practice of his kind, and if his first wife had not been shot it is likely that they would have separated before they had gone very far south. And yet it does not follow that the marriage was not a love match. If you had seen them at their housekeeping I think you would have pronounced him a very good husband and father. Perhaps the conjugal happiness of the spring and early summer was all the better for a taste of solitude during the rest of the year.

As I said, the time was near when the chick would strike out for himself. He soon left his mother, and a little later she too started for the Gulf of Mexico. Summer was over, and the Glimmerglass was lonelier than ever.

Mahng came back next spring, and of course he brought a wife with him. But was she the same wife who had helped him make the Glimmerglass ring with his shouting twelve months before? Well, I — I don't quite know. She looked very much like her, and I certainly hope she was the same bird. I should like to believe that they had been reunited somewhere down in Texas or Mississippi or Louisiana, and that they had come back together for another season of parental cares and joys. But when I consider the difficulties in the way I cannot help feeling doubtful about it. The two birds had gone south at different times and perhaps by different routes. Before they reached the lower Mississippi Valley they may have been hundreds of miles apart. Was it to be reasonably expected that Mahng, when he was

ready to return, would search every pond and stream from the Cumberland to the Gulf? And is it likely that, even if he had tried for weeks and weeks, he could ever have found his wife of the previous summer? His flight was swift and his sight keen, and his clarion voice rang far and wide over the marshes, but it is no joke to find one particular bird in a region covering half a dozen States. If they had arranged to come north separately and meet at the Glimmerglass, there would not have been so many difficulties in the way, but they didn't do that. Anyhow, Mahng brought a wife home. That much, at least, is established. They set to work at once to build a nest and make ready for some new babies; but, alas! there was little parental happiness or responsibility in store for them that year.

If you had been there you might have seen them swimming out from shore one bright, beautiful spring morning, when the sun had just risen, and the woods and waters lay calm and peaceful in the golden light, fairer than words can tell.

They were after their breakfast, and presently they dived to see what was to be had. The light is dim down there in the depths of the Glimmerglass, the weeds are long and slimy, and the mud of the bottom is black and loathsome. But what does that matter? One can go back whenever one pleases. A few quick, powerful strokes will take you up into the open air, and you can see the woods and the sky. Aha! There is a herring, his scales shining like silver in the faint green light that comes down through the water. And there is a small salmon trout, with its gray-brown back and his golden sides. A fish for each of us.

The loons darted forward at full speed; but the two fish made no effort to escape, and did not even wriggle when the long, sharp bills closed upon them. They were dead, choked to death by the fine threads of a gill net. And now those same threads laid hold of the loons themselves, and a fearful struggle began.

Mahng and his wife did not always keep their wings

folded when they were under water. Sometimes they used them almost as they did in flying, and just now they had need of every muscle in their bodies. How their pinions lashed the water, and how their legs kicked and their long necks writhed, and how the soft mud rose in clouds and shut out the dim light! But the harder they fought the more tightly did the net grapple them, winding itself round and round their bodies, and soon lashing their wings down against their sides. Expert divers though they were, the loons were drowning. There was a ringing in their ears and a roaring in their heads, and the very last atoms of oxygen in their lungs were almost gone. Death was drawing very near, and the bright, sunshiny world where they had been so happy a moment before, the world to which they had thought they could return so quickly and easily, seemed a thousand miles away. One last effort, one final struggle, and if that failed there would be nothing more to do but go to sleep for ever.

Fortunately for Mahng,

his part of the net had been mildewed, and much of the strength had gone out of the linen threads. He was writhing and twisting with all his might, and suddenly he felt something give. One of the rotten meshes had torn apart. He worked with redoubled energy, and in a moment another thread gave way, and then another, and another. A second more and he was free. Quick, now, before the last spark goes out! With beating wings and churning paddles he fairly flew up through the green water toward the light, and on a sudden he shot out into the air, panting and gasping, and staring wildly around at the blue sky, and the quiet woods, and the smiling Glimmerglass. And how royally beautiful was the sunshine, and how sweet was the breath of life!

But his mate was not with him, and a few hours later the fisherman found in his net the lifeless body of a drowned loon.

Mahng went north. He had thought that his spring flight was over, and that he would go no farther, but now the Glimmerglass was

no longer home, and he spread his wings once more and took his way toward the Arctic Circle. Over the hills, crowded with maple and beech and birch; over the Great Tahquamenon Swamp, with its cranberry marshes, its tangles of spruce and cedar, and its thin, scattered ranks of tamarack; over the sandy ridges where the pine trees stand tall and stately, and out on Lake Superior. The water was blue, and the sunshine was bright, the wind was fresh and cool, and the billows rolled and tumbled as if they were alive and were having a good time together. Together – that's the word. They were together, but Mahng was alone; and he wasn't having a good time at all. He wanted a home, and a nest and some young ones, but he didn't find them that year, though he went clear to Hudson Bay, and looked everywhere for a mate. There were loons, plenty of them, but they had already paired and set up housekeeping, and he found no one who was in a position to halve his sorrows and double his joys.

211

THERE WERE LOONS, PLENTY OF THEM, BUT HE FOUND NO ONE WHO WAS IN A POSITION
TO HALVE HIS SORROWS AND DOUBLE HIS JOYS.

Something attracted his attention one afternoon when he was swimming on a little lake far up in the Canadian wilderness — a small red object that kept appearing and disappearing in a very mysterious fashion among the bushes that lined the beach. Mahng's bump of curiosity was large and well developed, and he gave one of his best laughs and paddled slowly in toward the shore. I think he had a faint and utterly unreasonable hope that it might prove to be what he was looking and longing for, though he knew very well that no female loons of his species ever had red feathers — nor a male, either, for that matter. It was a most absurd idea, and his dreams, if he really had them, were cut short by the report of a shotgun. A little cloud of smoke floated up through the bushes, and a charge of heavy shot peppered the water all around him. But if Mahng was curious he was also quick to take a hint. He had heard the click of the gun lock, and before the leaden hail could reach him he was under water. His tail feathers suffered a little, but other-

wise he was uninjured, and he did not come to the surface again till he was far away from that deceitful red handkerchief.

The summer was an entire failure, and after a while Mahng gave it up in despair, and started south much earlier than usual. At the Straits of Mackinac he had another narrow escape, for he came very near killing himself by dashing head first against the lantern of a lighthouse, whose brilliant beams, a thousand times brighter than the light which had lured his first wife to her death, had first distracted and then dazzled and dazed him. Fortunately, he swerved a trifle at the last moment, and, though he brushed against an iron railing, lost his balance, and fell into the water, there were no bones broken and no serious damage done.

The southland, as everybody knows, is the only proper place for a loon courtship. There, I am pleased to say, Mahng found a new wife, and in due time he brought her up to the Glimmerglass. That was only last spring, and there is but one more incident for

me to relate. This summer has been a happy and prosperous one, but there was a time when it seemed likely to end in disaster before it had fairly begun.

Just north-east of the Glimmerglass there lies a long, narrow, shallow pond. I believe I mentioned it when I was telling you about the beaver. One afternoon Mahng had flown across to this pond, and as he was swimming along close to the shore he put his foot into a beaver trap and sprung it. Of course, he did his best to get away, but the only result of his struggling was to work the trap out into deeper and deeper water until he was almost submerged. He made things almost boil with the fierce beating of his wings, but it was no use; he might better have saved his strength. He quieted down at last, and lay very still, with only his head and neck out of water, and there he waited two mortal hours for something to happen.

Meanwhile his wife sat quietly on her eggs — there were three of them this year — and drowsed away the warm spring afternoon. By and by she heard a tramping as of heavy feet approaching, and glancing between the tall grasses she saw, not a bear nor a deer, but something far worse – a man. She waited till he was within a few yards, and then she jumped up, scuttled down to the water as fast as she could go, and dived as if she were made of lead. The trapper glanced after her with a chuckle.

"Seems pretty badly scared," he said to himself, but his voice was not unkindly. His smile faded as he stood a moment beside the nest, looking at the eggs, and thinking of what would some day come forth from them. He was a solitary old fellow, with never a wife nor a child nor a relation of any kind. His life in the woods was just what he had chosen for himself, and he would not have exchanged it for anything else in the world; but sometimes the loneliness of it came over him, and he wished that he had somebody to talk to. And now, looking at those eggs, and thinking of the fledglings that were coming to the loons, he wondered how it would seem if he had some children of his own. Pretty

soon he glanced out on the lake again, and saw Mahng's wife sitting quietly on the water, just out of range.

"Hope she won't stay away till they get cold," he thought, and went on his way across the swamp. The loon watched him till he passed out of sight, and then she swam in to the beach and pushed herself up her narrow runway to her old place. The eggs were still warm.

Half an hour later the trapper stepped out of the bushes beside the pond, and caught sight of Mahng's head sticking out of the water. He was considerably astonished, but he promptly laid hold of the chain and drew bird, trap, and all up on to the bank, and then he sat down on a log and laughed till the echoes went flying back and forth across the pond. Plastered with mud, dripping wet, and with his left leg fast in the big steel killing machine, Mahng was certainly a comical sight. All the fight was soaked out of him, and he lay prone upon the ground, and waited for the trapper to do what he pleased. But the trapper

did nothing – only sat on his log, and presently forgot to laugh. He was thinking of the sitting loon whom he had disturbed a little while before. This was probably her mate, and again there came over him a vague feeling that life had been very good to these birds, and had given them something which he, the man, had missed. He was growing old. A few more seasons, and there would be one trapper less in the Great Tahquamenon Swamp; and he would die without – well, what was the use of talking or thinking about it? But the loons would hatch their young, and care for them and protect them until they were ready to go out into the world, and then they would send them away to the south. A few weeks later they would follow, and next spring, they would come back and do it all over again. That is – they would if he didn't kill them.

He rose from his log, smiling again at the abject look with which Mahng watched him, and, putting one foot on each of the two heavy steel springs, he threw his weight upon them and crushed them down. Mahng felt the jaws relax, and suddenly he knew that he was free. The strength came back with a rush to his weary limbs, and he sprang up, scrambled down the bank and into the water, and he was gone. A few minutes later, he reappeared far down the pond, and rising on the wing he flew away with a laugh toward the Glimmerglass.

Cosy Corner Chats.

XI. – COURTSHIP AND MARRIAGE

By Mrs. Louise Creighton.

MY DEAR R–, – I have been asked to write to you about courtship and marriage. Marriage is the most important step anyone can take in life, and it is not wise to take such an important step rashly, so it is well that the time of courtship should come as a preparation to marriage. A girl should use every opportunity of getting to know a man well, before she makes up her mind to marry him. Unfortunately, girls are often vain enough to wish to have many admirers, many young men with whom they can laugh and joke and talk nonsense. They allow first one young man to court them, and then another, and they like to live in a state of constant flirtation and excitement. Girls ought to remember that this is not only very bad for them, and makes them silly and flighty, and may lead them into grave danger, but that it is very bad indeed for the young men too. It is good for young people to be together, and to take pleasure in one another's companionship, and harmless fun and merriment help to brighten life, and to make it easier to bear the hard times. But true friendship must always rest upon real respect; a girl should never value admiration for its own sake, and ought to feel rather ashamed of being admired by a man whom she cannot respect. Fun is all very well in the right place, but we want to be serious too sometimes with our friends, and to talk to them about our hopes and wishes, and about all that interests us. Life is far from being all play, and you will not find out whether a man will make a good companion for you for your whole life, if you only talk nonsense with him.

Some girls may think that to choose a man to be their husband, the only thing needed is to fall in love with him. I quite believe that a girl ought to be in love with the man she is going to marry, but that is quite another thing from deciding to marry a man only because she has happened to fall in love with him. Very trifling things often make a girl think she is in love with a man. Perhaps she has been reading a very romantic novel all about love-making, and she feels in the mood to fall in love, and so she falls in love with the first man she meets. And then, if he happens to be in the same mood, and to fall in love with her, courtship begins; and if there happens to be no reason why they should not be married quickly, or if they spend all their courtship only in joking and love-making, they may get married without knowing anything about one another's real self, and wake up to find they are not in the least suited to one another. That is one of the ways in which unhappy marriages are made. Or, still worse, a girl may soon see that the man with whom she is in love is not at all steady or likely to

make a good husband, and yet, just because she thinks she is in love with him, she cannot give him up. The only wise thing to do in such a case is to fall out of love again as quickly as possible, and to avoid the man until your fancy for him has passed away.

On the other hand, never say you will marry a man unless you really love him. Reason should tell you if a man has the qualities which will make him a good husband for you, and your heart should tell you whether you can love him enough to be a good wife to him. For married life is not at all a path of roses: you will have to give up a great deal of your own way to your husband, and however good he is, to put up with a great deal in him; and only love can make you do this gladly, and help you through the difficult times in your married life.

Never try to make a man love you when you cannot love him back. A man's love is the most precious thing he has to give. Some girls are very proud of having received many offers of marriage; they ought rather

to be sorry that any man should have come to love them, when they cannot love him in return, and ashamed if they have done anything to draw him on to love them. Never play with the love of an honest man; be kind and true to him even if you are bound to say that you cannot love him.

When you have seriously and prayerfully chosen the man who is to be your companion through life, try from the very first to be a real as well as a loving friend to him. The love of a good girl is the greatest help a man can have to keep him straight. If he really loves you, he will wish to be the kind of man you would like him to be, and you can help him best by being very true, and very loving, and very kind to him. But whilst you are all that, you must remember that you both have something else to do in life, except to live for one another. Your love for one another must not make you selfish. You are to be companions through life. Through courtship and marriage you must be constantly helping one another to grow in wisdom and goodness. A woman must not only be the plaything of a man, and though she should always try to be his comfort, she must be something more. She must help him by her advice and sympathy in all that he has to do, and share his interests as far as she can. Girls and women should not be content to know nothing of what interests their friendships and husbands. Hard-working men find time to take part in the duties of citizenship, to be interested in what is going on in the world, to study and improve themselves. Women can do the same if only they will try. A little better management, a little more industry, and they will be able to save a little time from their domestic duties, or from their daily work, so as to have a chance of learning something, of improving themselves. Then they will be able to be real companions to serious men. Life, after all, is a serious thing.

Athletics for Girls.

LAWN TENNIS . – II.

GENERALLY people are very much what they m a k e themselves. It is sad to see the individual who is content to believe that she is strong enough for all her requirements; one cannot help feeling that this contented person would be a better person in every way by remembering the fact that there is room for improvement in everyone, and that by developing the muscles of the body there would ensue consequent enlargement of the mind. It is a well-known fact that physical development not only endows the individual with health and strength, but improves the character and disposition. A well-known authority says: "It is one of the pleasantest features of to-day to see that so many girls and women realise, and encouraged to participate in, what was once regarded only as man's domain, viz., "the world of sport." Some of the leading physicians now state that bicycling has cured half of the nervous and imaginary ailments due to inactivity of the mind and body. May it be said in future years that sport and honest work have cured the other half.

This training, however, will require patience, for people cannot be made "Samsons" in a week. Regular and consistent practice, night and morning, with dumb-bells &c., even if only for ten minutes, will soon show a good result. A book, entitled "Strength, and How to Obtain It," by Sandow, is most useful in showing the amateur how to go to work.

Fencing and gymnastics of all kinds are very beneficial for all those who have time and inclination to indulge in them. Hockey is also to be recommended for teaching a girl to turn quickly, and run well.

Nerves are a great source of trouble to many. Those suffering from this malady are much to be pitied; but pity without relief is like mustard with-

out beef. Any speedy cure for this evil will be welcomed as a blessing to many.

Drugs and other strong remedies are sometimes resorted to, but as a rule they are to be avoided.

Singles:— The game of singles soon shows a girl the real necessity of training, good lasting powers being of decidedly more value

FIG. 3. – THE FORE-HAND STROKE.

than short-lived brilliancy. The great point of weakness, however, in this game lies in the back-hand stroke, scarcely one girl in six possessing even a moderate back-hand, and consequently adopting the most fatal mistake of running round

all balls placed to her left side, endeavouring to take every ball fore-handed.

The disadvantages of this plan will be seen at a glance, and, moreover, will be forcibly impressed on the memory, when a girl employing these tactics comes against a first-class player, who never hesitates to take full advantage of this weakness.

The correct position to stand for a single is somewhere on an imaginary line drawn straight down the centre of the court (except, of course, when serving or receiving a service). It therefore stands to reason that if a ball is placed to your left side, and you run round and take it fore-handed, you find yourself either tucked up in a corner, or considerably beyond the side-line. This is exactly what your opponent wants, for she has now the whole court vacant to place the ball where she pleases. If the beginner will adopt this suicidal plan, she simply kills herself by madly rushing from side to side of the court, instead of remaining more or less stationary. The best players, when they find

FIG. 4. – OLD STYLE BACK-HAND
STROKE.

themselves out of position,
invariably lob the ball. This
gains time and enables them
to get back into position
before the ball is returned.

Advice. – It is well to
determine, "come what
may," never to run round a
ball. At first, be content
with passing it carefully but
gently back, placing it as
near as possible to your
opponent's back line, as
good length is indispensable
in singles.

When the beginner has
succeeded so far, it will be
time enough to increase the
pace. The player who can
volley has a great advan-
tage, being able to run in

and kill any short balls.

Ladies Doubles:– The
definition of a ladies'
double has been given as
follows: "A court with four
ladies, viz., one at each
corner, all having an
unswerving devotion to the
back line, and who are all
much too tender-hearted to
kill a ball."

This is the unkind criti-
cism of a cynic. It is not to
be disputed, however, that
this event in a tournament is
seldom widely exciting for
the onlookers; neither is it
renowned for great head-
work and punishing strokes.
But, nevertheless, the ladies
enjoy it; this in the meantime is a very good reason
for supporting the ladies'
doubles.

A committee of wicked
men occasionally try to
deprive the ladies of their
doubles, on account of the
great length of time they
take; but every girl should
take up the cudgels against
the perpetrators of such wilful injustice. They cannot
do without the support of
the "fair sex," therefore why
treat them so badly?

Page 57 shows a good
study in positions. Notice
the lady champion in the far

FIG. 5. – CORRECT BACK-HAND
STROKE.

corner has no intention of
losing her balance; the racket is held horizontally, and
she is standing well on her
toes. Note also the exagger-
ated body-swing of the
player administering justice
upon the ball. Apparently
she is a heartless young
woman, trying to prove herself an exception to the rule
by killing a ball!

Mixed Doubles.– The
players who are most suc-
cessful in mixed doubles are
those who can hit hard (not
necessarily always into
court, for the opposing man
will usually try to volley any
ball not going more than a
few feet out). This, combined

with some consistent lobbing, makes an ideal mixed player.

What to do with a bad partner is a question much disputed. A new idea is to ask a really weak girl-player to remain stationary near the side-line and only about three feet from the net, with instructions only to take balls within easy reach. This plan has proved successful on several occasions, but means that the man must do the major part of the work. If the lady is new to this position, it causes much confusion and irritation to the opposite side, as she invariably hits the balls all round the wood of the racket, which consequently fall where least expected.

Others will say a weak partner is best from five to fifty yards outside the court, only coming near the line to serve. Some men even boast of winning in this way, against indifferent opponents, but "weak woman" will not always be downtrodden, and now often asserts her right to a portion of the court. The "lords of creation," however, do not as a rule like their partners to come up to the net and volley. It is a comparatively recent innovation, but time will prove whether it makes a successful combination. At present no doubt it often leads to confusion even among the best players.

"Gallant man" is always most profuse in his praise, often applauding very bad strokes, so long as they go over the net, but at the same time he often complains that his good strokes pass unnoticed.

How to be Strong.

SPECIAL EXERCISES
WITH THE SANDOW GRIP DUMB-BELL.

PART VIII.

IN this last "chat" I should like, by relating an incident which came under my own notice, to point out how necessary it is that you should have the proper material with which to perform the various exercises, and derive from them the greatest and most permanent benefit.

Some while ago I recommended the use of dumb-bells to a young lady of my acquaintance who was complaining of feeling "down," obviously from want of exercise. I pointed out to her that, even if she were unable to perform any of the more exertive outdoor exercises such as tennis, cycling, rowing, &c., by a judicious use of the dumb-bells the whole of the muscles which would be exercised in the outdoor recreations would be brought into play. Notwithstanding the fact that I specially warned her against the use of very heavy bells, I found on visiting her some while after that she had been trying the exercises for some little time with 5lb. dumbbells, as used by her brother, who is a well-known athlete! Consequently, at the end of a fortnight she had had to give up the exercises, as they caused her considerable strain, and I found her unreasonable enough to blame me for recommending such exercises, instead of herself for such a want of discretion in the matter of a proper selection of weight of dumb-bell.

May I, therefore, use this experience to insist that greater weight does not necessarily mean greater power, but more often tends to unduly strain and over-tax the muscles, with disastrous results. I have for some time been using Eugene Sandow's spring-grip dumbbells, in which this famous strong man has brought all his experience to bear for the benefit of others. The Sandow Company are making these bells in a very light form especially for ladies,

EXERCISE 8.

and I can heartily recommend them as being beautifully finished off and remarkably cheap for the amount of work and thought put into their manufacture. These serve a double purpose of ordinary dumbbells, and also a grip machine for strengthening the wrist muscles. They consist of a dumb-bell in two halves, between which are a series of coil springs. The increasing of the number of these springs affects the strength of the gripping power, which I mentioned some while back in an earlier chat. I trust these remarks may be of service in aiding you in the proper selection of dumb-bells and the performance of the exercises.

Without further comment, therefore, I will describe the last of these exercises (No. 8), which is as follows:— The first position of the body should be perfectly upright, with the arms down by the sides and hands firmly gripping the dumb-bells.

The body should then be bent to the right side as far as possible, at the same time bringing the left hand well up under the left armpit, and the right hand stretched down to below the right knee. Return to the upright position, and then proceed to perform the exercise in exactly the reverse manner, bending the body to the left, &c. By this means the muscles of the side are brought into play, and, with the other exercises, tend to assist in the development of a grace of carriage which is one of the chief charms of a well-developed woman.

Cosy Corner Chats.

XII. – THE MANNERS OF THE MODERN GIRL.

MY DEAR MARGARET: A well-known dramatic critic writing recently of Mrs. Curtis, author of a play called "The Spirit of '76," says, "She really predicted in the next sequent generation of young women that union of verile athleticism and sophomoric abandon which makes the manners of the twentieth-century girl so engaging." There is openly spoken the charge that has been whispered for the last fifteen years. It is charged that the manners of the modern girl are lacking in all that they should have, and have all that they should lack. The accusation is supposed to come largely from their elders; but I remember hearing it once in its most scathing form from the mouth of a young girl – and she was a Western girl. She stood, looking out of a window, observing the conduct on the street of a group of New England young women. Her pretty lips curled with scorn as she said, "If I behaved like that on the street in Des Moines, I should never be asked inside a nice house there again in my life."

The unfriendly critic of the liberal education of women is sure to fortify his arguments with the statement that college-bred women are underbred and have none of the graces of life. The pulpit and the newspaper vie with each other in regret or admonition over the decay of social graces. It is high time that we should reason together about this question of the manners of the twentieth-century girl.

First, we must remember that generalisation about

any such matter is sure to be misleading. If we gathered our impressions from the newspapers alone, it would be easy to believe that there were no happy marriages, no honest bank officers, no incorruptible politicians. The discordant makes itself heard above the harmonious. Ugliness pushes beauty aside, and crowds its hateful visage into the foreground. One ill-mannered girl in a railway car full of school-girls off for vacation will obliterate the impression of the gentle and considerate manners of twenty other girls in the same car. I like to bear my testimony to the fact that I know hundreds of girls whose manners are as elegant as those of the seventeenth century, and withal as genuine as the twentieth century could wish them to be.

Still there remains a great mass of rudeness to be accounted for and dealt with. For one reason and another it is here; and, until we acknowledge its presence, we are not prepared to cure it.

Why has it come? Largely as the result of a misconception of the nature of manners and their use in society. Forty years ago there arose a hue and cry for sincerity as against sham. Voice after voice took up the note. Carlyle and Emerson were leaders of the movement. Close on them came John Stuart Mill, and on his heels were all the leaders of the efforts for the so-called emancipation of women. Democracy in the United States had its share in the chorus. Unitarianism was loud in its denunciation of what it characterised as formalism. The new educators, like Horace Mann, and the new theologians, like Horace Bushnell, were allies in their hatred of conventionality of thought and creed.

In the midst of this crusade against forms and conventionalities, it would have been strange, indeed, if the most obvious of all forms and conventionalities had not been attacked — the forms by which for ages civilised men have tacitly agreed to govern the details of their daily life.

The plea that the individual should have full and free development, speedily led to the disuse of authority in respect of the manners of the young, and shortly to their total discredit. A mother once said to me that she did not wish her daughter taught conventional manners, that she thought them as objectionable as borrowed clothes. That same daughter is now one of the most ill-mannered women that I have ever known.

Nothing could be more absurd than this conception of the function and value of manners. They are not a *rôle* assumed for the purpose of deception or a second-hand garment donned to impose upon the spectator with a fraudulent elegance. Gentle manners, in their ultimate analysis, are nothing more nor less than a set of rules adopted by cultivated people to aid in playing their parts in life easily, swiftly, naturally. They are to a woman in society exactly what good training is to a servant. It has long, for example, been the custom — and it is founded on good sense — that a waitress should pass all viands on the left side of a guest, that he may serve himself with his right hand. Suppose some advanced and original waitress organising a rebellion against that excellent rule, and declaring it a slavery to which she and her friends will no longer submit – such a rebellion would be exactly like the reaction against good manners which has afflicted our time.

We may go a step farther in the analysis of manners, and explain that, as the rules governing the waitress are based on convenience and good sense, so those imposing gentle manners are based on good feeling and a warm, sympathetic heart. The egotist, who goes through the world shrieking, "I am as good as you, and better!" can never be possessed either of a clear vision or a ready sympathy. In other words, she is by so much behind her gentler neighbour in the scheme of evolution. That she should pride herself on the very failure is the last touch of absurdity. She vaunts her crudeness as originality, her lawlessness as independence, and her egotism as self-culture. Her audience are fain to smile – since they can do nothing more effectual – and wish her day were over.

There are two human relations, the recognition of which underlies most of the customs required by good manners. These relations are those of the inferior to the superior – whether in age, in learning, or in position – and those of the strong to the weak. The ill-mannered woman continually ignores these, though they are among the most fundamental facts of life. By every act she proclaims her conviction that she has no superior, and so testifies to her own stupidity.

Let me give you a concrete instance of this. A party of young men and women were seated on the verandah of a country house. Every chair was occupied. Presently there walked slowly and feebly up the path an elderly woman, well known to the world of society and of letters. She was a beautiful figure – a woman who had helped to make history and who now wore modestly, but with dignity, the crown of a people's gratitude. Now exactly what should those young people have done on her approach? Various courses were open to them. One

might rise and offer chair and greeting. The boys might rise, and the girls might sit. They might all remain seated – as they did! As a witness to the scene, I received an indelible impression as to the character and breeding of each person in that company. By all the laws of cultivated society the action of each should have been so swift as to be automatic. The Queen! Make way for her! That sense of proportion that is one of the most precious possessions of the educated girl should have grasped in an instant the demand of the situation; and the courteous greeting should have been a tribute not only of age and charm and power, but to the right-mindedness of those who rendered it. I have written at length of this instance because I think the habit of rising when our elders or our superiors enter a room is highly significant of our whole attitude toward the rules of gentle society. The courteous gesture of rising makes a place for itself in the habit of a well-ordered life, and presently becomes as instinctive as it is gracious.

Even more beautiful is the tribute that the strong pay to the weak. When I saw last month a tall, vigorous girl leave a group of laughing friends in a street-car and offer her seat to a working-woman with her arms full of bundles, I knew that I had seen a noble human impulse in its spontaneous expression. So with a voice "soft, gentle, and low" — it is the instinctive recognition of the rights of others and contribution to their comfort. No requirement is made by the code of good manners that judgment and heart will not ratify.

Far down in the scale of being we find the oyster, glued to his rock and oblivious of his neighbour, absorbed in his own absorption. Distant from him, at the other end of the scale of being, is the gently-bred woman, quick to see her relations to one and all and skilful to adapt her own refined and attractive personality to the need of the moment.

One more word, and I have finished. When a woman really has the finest manners, they are not for use on especial occasions or for especial people. They are hers, and wherever she goes, they go with her. The girl who is suave and engaging in public and snappish and inconsiderate at home shows that her breeding is pinchbeck. Years ago I read in some novel a sentence on manners, which clung to my memory, and which puts picturesquely a profound truth. In speaking of the heroine, the author said, "Her manners grow on her like leaves on a tree. They are beautiful, and they are her own." One need not push the analogy too far; but it is easy to see that for a tree to disdain its leaves because they are not its roots would be suicide for the tree. Our twentieth-century girl must not rank gentle manners with mint, anise, and cummin; for they belong to the weightier matters of the law. You and I must try to hasten the day when it shall be a matter of course that a woman that makes claim to be thought an educated woman shall be mistress of a decorous and gracious manner, and shall regard it as a precious heritage to pass on to her daughters.

HELOISE EDWINA HERSEY.